# CHRISTIAN SERVICE

Copyright © 1947 and 2002 by
the Ellen G. White Publications
All rights reserved

Cover design copyright © 2002 by
Review and Herald® Publishing Association
Cover design by Willie Duke
Cover illustration by Lee Christiansen
Type: 12.6/13.5 Bembo

PRINTED IN U.S.A.

ISBN 978-0-8280-1732-9

# CHRISTIAN SERVICE

*A Compilation From the Writings*

*of*
ELLEN G. WHITE

REVIEW AND HERALD® PUBLISHING ASSOCIATION
Since 1861 | www.reviewandherald.com

# The Field of Research

The following-named books, written by Mrs. E. G. White, and articles from her pen appearing in various publications, have furnished the material for this compilation:

*Testimonies for the Church,* volumes 1-10
*The Acts of the Apostles*
*Patriarchs and Prophets*
*The Ministry of Healing*
*The Desire of Ages*
*The Great Controversy Between Christ and Satan*
*Gospel Workers*
*Christ's Object Lessons*
*Steps to Christ*
*Thoughts From the Mount of Blessing*
*Prophets and Kings*
*Early Writings*
*Manual for Canvassers*
*Consecrated Efforts to Reach Unbelievers* (MS.)
*The Colporteur Evangelist*
*Historical Sketches*
*Counsels to Parents, Teachers, and Students*
*Education*
*Life Sketches of Ellen G. White*
*The Spirit of Prophecy*
*Special Testimonies*

Periodicals★ from which extracts have been taken:

*General Conference Bulletin*
*Review and Herald*
*Signs of the Times*
*Signs of the Times* (Australian)
*Bible Echo* (Australian)
*Southern Watchman*
*Youth's Instructor*
*Pacific Union Recorder*

---

★Periodicals dating back to the early days of the message have been accessible in the General Conference files, preserved in the fireproof vault, and from these many rich gems of thought have been collected and placed in convenient form for the use of Christian workers.

# Preface

The writings of Ellen White contain excellent counsel and methodology on the need, importance, methods, and rewards of earnest, consecrated soul winning endeavor. The present volume has been compiled from these inspired writings. Though not exhaustive, it may appropriately be termed an Encyclopedia of Christian Service.

In selecting quotations from the various published sources, great care has been exercised to preserve the proper setting of the thought expressed by the author. We believe that the material which has been brought together will be invaluable to ministers and leaders in all lines of church work, and will be appreciated by every man and woman whose heart has been touched by the Spirit of the Great Soul Winner.

We express sincere gratitude to the secretarial staff of the office that was formerly known as the General Conference Home Missionary Department. They did much of the original work on this volume. Other Christian workers also rendered valuable assistance in reading and marking various books for this compilation. Their suggestions contributed much to the thoroughness and completeness of the task.

We heartily recommend the reading and study of this book as a major source of inspiration and knowledge for the science of soul winning.

GENERAL CONFERENCE SABBATH SCHOOL
AND PERSONAL MINISTRIES DEPARTMENT

# Contents

| | |
|---|---:|
| God's Call to Service | 7 |
| The Call to Young People | 30 |
| Conditions Among God's People | 35 |
| World Conditions Facing the Christian Worker | 50 |
| The Church a Training Center | 58 |
| Students to Do Missionary Work While in Training | 64 |
| Cooperation of Ministers and Laymen | 67 |
| Organizing Christian Forces | 72 |
| The Call to Arouse | 77 |
| Methods | 113 |
| Medical Missionary Work | 132 |
| Bible Evangelism | 141 |
| Ministry of the Printed Page | 145 |
| Religious Liberty | 155 |
| Harvest Ingathering | 167 |
| The Church Expansion Movement | 178 |
| Christian Help Work | 186 |
| The Camp Meeting an Aid in Christian Service | 194 |
| The Home-Foreign Field | 199 |
| Reaching the Wealthy and Influential | 202 |
| The Home a Missionary Training Center | 206 |
| The Prayer and Missionary Meeting | 211 |
| Miscellaneous Lines of Missionary Work | 215 |
| Qualifications for Successful Christian Service | 223 |
| The Holy Spirit | 250 |
| Assurance of Success | 257 |
| Reward of Service | 266 |

# CHAPTER 1

# God's Call to Service

### *Depending on Human Agents*

As His representatives among men, God does not choose angels who have never fallen, but human beings, men of like passions with those they seek to save. Christ took humanity that He might reach humanity. A divine-human Saviour was needed to bring salvation to the world. And to men and women has been committed the sacred trust of making known "the unsearchable riches of Christ." *The Acts of the Apostles,* p. 134.

Look upon the touching scene. Behold the Majesty of heaven surrounded by the twelve whom He has chosen. He is about to set them apart for their work. By these feeble agencies, through His Word and Spirit, He designs to place salvation within the reach of all. *The Acts of the Apostles,* p. 18.

"Send men to Joppa, and call for one Simon." Thus God gave evidence of His regard for the gospel ministry and for His organized church. The angel was not commissioned to tell Cornelius the story of the cross. A man subject, even as the centurion himself, to human frailties and temptations was to be the one to tell him of the crucified and risen Saviour. *The Acts of the Apostles,* p. 134.

The angel sent to Philip could himself have done the work for the Ethiopian, but this is not God's way of working. It is His plan that men are to work for their fellow men. *The Acts of the Apostles,* p. 109.

"We have this treasure," the apostle continued, "in earthen vessels, that the excellency of the power may be of God, and not of us." God could have proclaimed His truth through sinless angels, but this is not His plan. He chooses human beings, men compassed with infirmity, as instruments in the working out of His designs. The priceless treasure is placed in earthen vessels. Through men His blessings are to be conveyed to the world. Through them His glory is to shine forth into the darkness of sin. In loving ministry they are to meet the sinful and the needy, and lead them to the cross. And in all their work, they are to ascribe glory, honor, and praise to Him who is above all and over all. *The Acts of the Apostles,* p. 330.

It was the Saviour's purpose that after He ascended to heaven to become man's intercessor, His followers should carry on the work that He had begun. Shall the human agent show no special interest in giving the light of the gospel message to those who sit in darkness? There are some who are willing to go to the ends of the earth in order to carry the light of truth to men, but God demands that every soul who knows the truth shall seek to win others to the love of the truth. If we are not willing to make special sacrifices in order to save souls that are ready to perish, how can we be counted worthy to enter into the city of God? *Testimonies,* vol. 9, p. 103.

In His wisdom the Lord brings those who are seeking for truth into touch with fellow beings who know the truth. It is the plan of Heaven that those who have received light shall impart it to those in darkness. Humanity, drawing its efficiency from the great Source of wisdom, is made the instrumentality, the working agency, through which the gospel exercises its transforming power on mind and heart. *The Acts of the Apostles,* p. 134.

God could have reached His object in saving sinners without our aid; but in order for us to develop a character like Christ's, we must share in His work. In order to enter into His joy—the joy of seeing souls redeemed by His sacrifice—we must participate in His labors for their redemption. *The Desire of Ages,* p. 142.

As His representatives among men, Christ does not choose angels who have never fallen, but human beings, men of like passions with those they seek to save. Christ took upon Himself humanity, that He might reach humanity. Divinity needed humanity; for it required both the divine and the human to bring salvation to the world. Divinity needed humanity, that humanity might afford a channel of communication between God and man. *The Desire of Ages,* p. 296.

With almost impatient eagerness the angels wait for our cooperation; for man must be the channel to communicate with man. And when we give ourselves to Christ in wholehearted devotion, angels rejoice that they may speak through our voices to reveal God's love. *The Desire of Ages,* p. 297.

We must be laborers together with God; for God will not complete His work without human agencies. *Review and Herald,* Mar. 1, 1887.

## *A Call to the Individual*

A distinct work is assigned to every Christian. *Southern Watchman,* Aug. 2, 1904.

God requires everyone to be a worker in His vineyard. You are to take up the work that has been placed in your charge, and to do it faithfully. *Bible Echo,* June 10, 1901.

Were every one of you a living missionary, the message for this time would speedily be proclaimed in all countries, to every people and nation and tongue. *Testimonies,* vol. 6, p. 438.

Every true disciple is born into the kingdom of God as a missionary. He who drinks of the living water becomes a fountain of life. The receiver becomes a giver. The grace of Christ in the soul is like a spring in the desert, welling up to refresh all, and making those who are ready to perish eager to drink of the water of life. *The Desire of Ages,* p. 195.

God expects personal service from everyone to whom He has intrusted a knowledge of the truth for this time. Not all can go as missionaries to foreign lands, but all can be home missionaries in their families and neighborhoods. *Testimonies,* vol. 9, p. 30.

Christ was standing only a few steps from the heavenly throne when He gave His commission to His disciples. Including as missionaries all who should believe on His name, He said, "Go ye into all the world, and preach the gospel to every creature." God's power was to go with them. *Southern Watchman,* Sept. 20, 1904.

To save souls should be the life work of everyone who professes Christ. We are debtors to the world for the grace given us of God, for the light which has shone upon us, and for the discovered beauty and power of the truth. *Testimonies,* vol. 4, p. 53.

Everywhere there is a tendency to substitute the work of organizations for individual effort. Human wisdom tends to consolidation, to centralization, to the building up of great churches and institutions. Multitudes leave to institutions and organizations the work of benevolence; they excuse themselves from contact with the world, and their hearts grow cold. They become self-absorbed and unimpressible. Love for God and man dies out of the soul. Christ commits to His followers an individual work—a work that cannot be done by proxy. Ministry to the sick and the poor, the giving of the gospel to the lost, is not to be left to committees or organized charities. Individual responsibility, individual effort, personal sacrifice, is the requirement of the gospel. *The Ministry of Healing,* p. 147.

Everyone who has received the divine illumination is to brighten the pathway of those who know not the Light of life. *The Desire of Ages,* p. 152.

To everyone work has been allotted, and no one can be a substitute for another. Each one has a mission of wonderful importance, which he cannot neglect or ignore, as the fulfillment of it involves the weal of some soul, and the neglect of it the woe of one for whom Christ died. *Review and Herald,* Dec. 12, 1893.

We should all be workers together with God. No idlers are acknowledged as His servants. The members of the church should individually feel that the life and prosperity of the church are affected by their course of action. *Review and Herald,* Feb. 15, 1887.

Every soul whom Christ has rescued is called to work in His name for the saving of the lost. This work had been neglected in Israel. It is not neglected today by those who profess to be Christ's followers? *Christ's Object Lessons,* p. 191.

There is something for everyone to do. Every soul that believes the truth is to stand in his lot and place, saying, "Here am I; send me." Isa 6:8. *Testimonies,* vol. 6, p. 49.

It is the privilege of every Christian, not only to look for, but to hasten the coming of our Lord Jesus Christ. *Christ's Object Lessons,* p. 69.

He who becomes a child of God should henceforth look upon himself as a link in the chain let down to save the world, one with Christ in His plan of mercy, going forth with Him to seek and save the lost. *The Ministry of Healing,* p. 105.

All may find something to do. None need feel that there is no place where they can labor for Christ. The Saviour identifies Himself with every child of humanity. *The Ministry of Healing,* p. 104.

Those who have united with the Lord in the covenant of service are under bonds to unite with Him in the great, grand work of soul saving. *Testimonies,* vol. 7, p. 19.

So vast is the field, so comprehensive the design, that every sanctified heart will be pressed into service as an instrument of divine power. *Testimonies,* vol. 9, p. 47.

Men are instruments in the hand of God, employed by Him to accomplish His purposes of grace and mercy. Each has his part to act; to each is granted a measure of light, adapted to the necessities of his time and sufficient to enable him to perform the work which God has given him to do. *The Great Controversy,* p. 343.

Long has God waited for the spirit of service to take possession of the whole church, so that everyone shall be working for Him according to his ability. *The Acts of the Apostles,* p. 111.

When He sent forth the twelve and afterward the seventy, to proclaim the kingdom of God, He was teaching them their duty to impart to others what He had made known to them. In all His work, He was training them for individual labor, to be extended as their numbers increased, and eventually to reach to the uttermost parts of the earth. *The Acts of the Apostles,* p. 32.

Not upon the ordained minister only, rests the responsibility of going forth to fulfill this commission. Everyone who has received Christ is called to work for the salvation of his fellow men. *The Acts of the Apostles,* p. 110.

The real character of the church is measured, not by the high profession she makes, not by the names enrolled upon the church book, but by what she is actually doing for the Master, by the number of her persevering, faithful workers. Personal interest and vigilant, individual effort will accomplish more for the cause of Christ than can be wrought by sermons or creeds. *Review and Herald,* Sept. 6, 1881.

Wherever a church is established, all the members should engage actively in missionary work. They should visit every family in the neighborhood, and know their spiritual condition. *Testimonies,* vol. 6, p. 296.

The members of the church are not all called to labor in foreign lands, but all have a part to act in the great work of giving light to the world. The gospel of Christ is aggressive and diffusive. In the day of God not one will be excused for having been shut up to his own selfish interests. There is work for every mind and for every hand. There is a variety of work, adapted to different minds and varied capabilities. *Historical Sketches,* pp. 290, 291.

He has intrusted you with sacred truth; Christ abiding in the individual members of the church is a well of water springing up into everlasting life. You are guilty before God if you do not make every effort possible to dispense this living water to others. *Historical Sketches,* p. 291.

We are not, as Christians, doing one-twentieth part that we might do in winning souls to Christ. There is a world to be warned, and every sincere Christian will be a guide and an example to others in faithfulness, in crossbearing, in prompt and vigorous action, in unswerving fidelity to the cause of truth, and sacrifices and labors to promote the cause of God. *Review and Herald,* Aug. 23, 1881.

So far as his opportunities extend, everyone who has received the light of truth is under the same responsibility as was the prophet of Israel to whom came the word: "Son of man, I have set thee a watchman unto the house of Israel; therefore thou shalt hear the word at My mouth, and warn them from Me." *Testimonies,* vol. 9, pp. 19, 20.

To everyone who becomes a partaker of His grace, the Lord appoints a work for others. Individually we are to stand in our lot and place, saying, "Here I am; send me." Upon the minister of the word, the missionary nurse, the Christian physician, the individual Christian, whether he be merchant or farmer, professional man or mechanic—the responsibility rests upon all. It is our work to reveal to men the gospel of their salvation. Every enterprise in which we engage should be a means to this end. *The Ministry of Healing,* p. 148.

When the master of the house called his servants, he gave to every man *his* work. The whole family of God are included in the responsibility of using their Lord's goods. Every individual, from the lowest and most obscure to the greatest and most exalted, is a moral agent endowed with abilities for which he is accountable to God. *Bible Echo,* June 10, 1901.

## *Combined Christian Forces*

Brethren and sisters in the faith, does the question arise in your hearts, "Am I my brother's keeper?" If you claim to be children of God, you are your brother's keeper. The Lord holds the church responsible for the souls of those whom they might be the means of saving. *Historical Sketches,* p. 291.

The Saviour has given His precious life in order to establish a church capable of ministering to the suffering, the sorrowful, and the tempted. A company of believers may be poor, uneducated, and unknown; yet in Christ they may do a work in the home, in the community, and even in the "regions beyond," whose results shall be as far-reaching as eternity. *The Ministry of Healing,* p. 106.

Enfeebled and defective as it may appear, the church is the one object upon which God bestows in a special sense His supreme regard. It is the theater of His grace, in which He delights to reveal His power to transform hearts. *The Acts of the Apostles,* p. 12.

Someone must fulfill the commission of Christ; someone must carry on the work which He began to do on earth; and the church has been given this privilege. For this purpose it has been organized. Why, then, have not church members accepted the responsibility? *Testimonies,* vol. 6, p. 295.

He calls upon the church to take up their appointed duty, holding up the standard of true reform in their own territory, leaving the trained and experienced workers to press on into new fields. *Testimonies,* vol. 6, p. 292.

The Thessalonian believers were true missionaries. . . . Hearts were won by the truths presented, and souls were added to the number of believers. *The Acts of the Apostles,* p. 256.

It was at the ordination of the twelve that the first step was taken in the organization of the church that after Christ's departure was to carry on His work on the earth. *The Acts of the Apostles,* p. 18.

God's church is the court of holy life, filled with varied gifts, and endowed with the Holy Spirit. The members are to find their happiness in the happiness of those whom they help and bless. Wonderful is the work which the Lord designs to accomplish through His church, that His name may be glorified. *The Acts of the Apostles,* pp. 12, 13.

Our work is plainly laid down in the Word of God. Christian is to be united to Christian, church to church, the human instrumentality cooperating with the divine, every agency to be subordinated to the Holy Spirit, and all to be combined in giving to the world the good tidings of the grace of God. *General Conference Bulletin,* Feb. 28, 1893, p. 421.

Our churches are to cooperate in the work of spiritual tilling, with the hope of reaping by and by. . . . The soil is stubborn, but the fallow ground must be broken up, the seeds of righteousness must be sown. Pause not, teachers beloved by God, as though doubtful whether to prosecute a labor which will grow as performed. *Testimonies,* vol. 6, p. 420.

The church is God's appointed agency for the salvation of men. It was organized for service, and its mission is to carry the gospel to the world. From the beginning it has been God's plan that through His church shall be reflected to the world His fullness and His sufficiency. The members of the church, those whom He has called out of darkness into His marvelous light, are to show forth His glory. *The Acts of the Apostles,* p. 9.

Let no church think it is too small to exert an influence and do service in the great work for this time.

Go to work, brethren. It is not alone the large camp meetings or conventions and councils that will have the especial favor of God; the humblest effort of unselfish love will be crowned with His blessings, and receive its great reward. Do what you can, and God will increase your ability. *Review and Herald,* Mar. 13, 1888.

## *Witnesses*

We are Christ's witnesses, and we are not to allow worldly interests and plans to absorb our time and attention. *Testimonies,* vol. 9, pp. 53, 54.

"Ye are My witnesses, saith the Lord. . . . I have declared, and have saved, and I have showed, when there was no strange god among you: therefore ye are My witnesses." "I the Lord have called thee in righteousness, and will hold thine hand, and will keep thee, and give thee for a covenant of the people, for a light of the Gentiles; to open the blind eyes, to bring out the prisoners from the prison, and them that sit in darkness out of the prison house." *The Acts of the Apostles,* p. 10.

The people of the world are worshiping false gods. They are to be turned from their false worship, not by hearing denunciation of their idols, but by beholding something better. God's goodness is to be made known. "Ye are My witnesses, saith the Lord, that I am God." *Christ's Object Lessons,* p. 299.

All who would enter the city of God must during their earthly life set forth Christ in their dealings. It is this that constitutes them the messengers of Christ, His witnesses. They are to bear a plain, decided testimony against all evil practices, pointing sinners to the Lamb of God, who taketh away the sin of the world. *Testimonies,* vol. 9, p. 23.

The disciples were to go forth as Christ's witnesses, to declare to the world what they had seen and heard of Him. Their office was the most important to which human beings had ever been called, second only to that of Christ Himself. They were to be workers together with God for the saving of men. *The Acts of the Apostles,* p. 19.

The divine Teacher says: My Spirit alone is competent to teach and to convict of sin. Externals make only a temporary impression upon the mind. I will enforce truth on the conscience, and men shall be My witnesses, throughout the world asserting My claims on man's time, his money, his intellect. *Testimonies,* vol. 7, p. 159.

Our confession of His faithfulness is Heaven's chosen agency for revealing Christ to the world. We are to acknowledge His grace as made known through the holy men of old; but that which will be most effectual is the testimony of our own experience. We are witnesses for God as we reveal in ourselves the working of a power that is divine. Every individual has a life distinct from all others, and an experience differing essentially from theirs. God desires that our praise shall ascend to Him, marked by our own individuality. These precious acknowledgments to the praise of the glory of His grace, when supported by a Christlike life, have an irresistible power, that works for the salvation of souls. *The Desire of Ages,* p. 347.

God cannot display the knowledge of His will and the wonders of His grace among the unbelieving world unless He has witnesses scattered all over the earth. It is His plan that those who are partakers of this great salvation through Jesus Christ should be His missionaries, bodies of light throughout the world, to be as signs to the people, living epistles, known and read of all men, their faith and works testifying to the near approach of the coming Saviour and showing that they have not received the grace of God in vain. The people must be warned to prepare for the coming judgment. *Testimonies,* vol. 2, pp. 631, 632.

## God's Call to Service

As they [the disciples] meditated upon His pure, holy life, they felt that no toil would be too hard, no sacrifice too great, if only they could bear witness in their lives to the loveliness of Christ's character. O, if they could but have the past three years to live over, they thought, how differently they would act! If they could only see the Master again, how earnestly they would strive to show Him how deeply they loved Him, and how sincerely they sorrowed for having ever grieved Him by a word or an act of unbelief! But they were comforted by the thought that they were forgiven. And they determined that, so far as possible, they would atone for their unbelief by bravely confessing Him before the world. *The Acts of the Apostles,* p. 36.

The two restored demoniacs were the first missionaries whom Christ sent to preach the gospel in the region of Decapolis. For a few moments only, these men had been privileged to hear the teachings of Christ. Not one sermon from His lips had ever fallen upon their ears. They could not instruct the people as the disciples who had been daily with Christ were able to do. But they bore in their own persons the evidence that Jesus was the Messiah. They could tell what they knew; what they themselves had seen and heard and felt of the power of Christ. This is what everyone can do whose heart has been touched by the grace of God. John, the beloved disciple, wrote: "That which was from the beginning, which we have heard, which we have seen with our eyes, which we have looked upon, and our hands have handled, of the Word of life; . . . that which we have seen and heard declare we unto you." As witnesses for Christ, we are to tell what we know, what we ourselves have seen and heard and felt. If we have been following Jesus step by step, we shall have something right to the point to tell concerning the way in which He has led us. We can tell how we have tested His promise and found the promise true. We can bear witness to what we have known of the grace of Christ. This is the witness for which our Lord calls, and for want of which the world is perishing. *The Desire of Ages,* p. 340.

## *Channels of Light and Blessing*

We are to be consecrated channels, through which the heavenly life is to flow to others. The Holy Spirit is to animate and pervade the whole church, purifying and cementing hearts. *Testimonies,* vol. 9, p. 20.

Every follower of Jesus has a work to do as a missionary for Christ, in the family, in the neighborhood, in the town or city where he lives. All who are consecrated to God are channels of light. God makes them instruments of righteousness to communicate to others the light of truth. *Testimonies,* 2, p. 632.

The result of the work of Jesus, as He sat, weary and hungry, at the well, was widespread in blessing. The one soul whom He sought to help became a means of reaching others and bringing them to the Saviour. This is ever the way that the work of God has made progress on the earth. Let your light shine, and other lights will be kindled. *Gospel Workers,* p. 195.

Many have an idea that they are responsible to Christ alone for their light and experience, independent of His recognized followers on earth. Jesus is the friend of sinners; and His heart is touched with their woe. He has all power, both in heaven and on earth; but He respects the means that He has ordained for the enlightenment and salvation of men; He directs sinners to the church, which He has made a channel of light to the world. *The Acts of the Apostles,* p. 122.

To the early church had been intrusted a constantly enlarging work—that of establishing centers of light and blessing wherever there were honest souls willing to give themselves to the service of Christ. *The Acts of the Apostles,* p. 90.

As the rays of the sun penetrate to the remotest corners of the globe, so God designs that the light of the gospel shall extend to every soul upon the earth. If the church of Christ were fulfilling the purpose of our Lord, light would be shed upon all that sit in darkness and in the region and shadow of death. *Thoughts From the Mount of Blessing,* p. 42.

It is the privilege of every soul to be a living channel through which God can communicate to the world the treasures of His grace, the unsearchable riches of Christ. There is nothing that Christ desires so much as agents who will represent to the world His Spirit and character. There is nothing that the world needs so much as the manifestation through humanity of the Saviour's love. All heaven is waiting for channels through which can be poured the holy oil to be a joy and blessing to human hearts. *Christ's Object Lessons,* p. 419.

The glory of the church of God is in the piety of its members; for there is the hiding of Christ's power. The influence of the sincere children of God may be esteemed as of little worth, but it will be felt throughout time, and rightly revealed in the day of reward. The light of a true Christian, shining forth in steadfast piety, in unwavering faith, will prove to the world the power of a living Saviour. In His followers Christ will be revealed as a well of water, springing up into everlasting life. Although scarcely known to the world, they are acknowledged as God's peculiar people, His chosen vessels of salvation, His channels whereby light is to come to the world. *Review and Herald,* Mar. 24, 1891.

Church members, let the light shine forth. Let your voices be heard in humble prayer, in witness against intemperance, the folly and the amusements of this world, and in the proclamation of the truth for this time. Your voice, your influence, your time—all these are gifts from God and are to be used in winning souls to Christ. *Testimonies,* vol. 9, p. 38.

I have been shown that the disciples of Christ are His representatives upon the earth; and God designs that they shall be lights in the moral darkness of this world, dotted all over the country, in the towns, villages, and cities, "a spectacle unto the world, to angels, and to man." *Testimonies,* vol. 2, p. 631.

The followers of Christ are to be the light of the world; but God does not bid them make an effort to shine. He does not approve of any self-satisfied endeavor to display superior goodness. He desires that their souls shall be imbued with the principles of heaven; then, as they come in contact with the world, they will reveal the light that is in them. Their steadfast fidelity in every act of life will be a means of illumination. *The Ministry of Healing,* p. 36.

When, in the midst of his blind error and prejudice, Saul was given a revelation of the Christ whom he was persecuting, he was placed in direct communication with the church, which is the light of the world. In this case, Ananias represents Christ, and also represents Christ's ministers upon the earth, who are appointed to act in His stead. In Christ's stead, Ananias touches the eyes of Saul, that they may receive sight. In Christ's stead, he places his hands upon him, and as he prays in Christ's name, Saul receives the Holy Ghost. All is done in the name and by the authority of Christ. Christ is the foundation; the church is the channel of communication. *The Acts of the Apostles,* p. 122.

Error is prevailing everywhere. The great adversary of souls is mustering his forces. He is setting every device in operation in order to confuse the minds of men with specious errors, and thus destroy souls. Those with whom God has intrusted the treasures of His truth are to let the light shine amid the moral darkness. *Historical Sketches,* p. 290.

God requires His people to shine as lights in the world. It is not merely the ministers who are required to do this, but every disciple of Christ. Their conversation should be heavenly. And while they enjoy communion with God they will wish to have intercourse with their fellow men in order to express by their words and acts the love of God which animates their hearts. In this way they will be lights in the world, and the light transmitted through them will not go out or be taken away. *Testimonies,* vol. 2, pp. 122, 123.

Christ's followers should be instruments of righteousness, workmen, living stones, emitting light, that they may encourage the presence of heavenly angels. They are required to be channels, as it were, through which the spirit of truth and righteousness shall flow. *Testimonies,* vol. 2, pp. 126, 127.

The Lord has made His church the repository of divine influence. The heavenly universe is waiting for the members to become channels through which the current of life shall flow to the world, that many may be converted, and in their turn become channels through which the grace of Christ shall flow to the desert portions of the Lord's vineyard. *Bible Echo,* Aug. 12, 1901.

Everyone who is connected with God will impart light to others. If there are any who have no light to give, it is because they have no connection with the Source of light. *Historical Sketches,* p. 291.

God has appointed His children to give light to others, and if they fail to do it, and souls are left in the darkness of error because of their failure to do that which they might have done had they been vitalized by the Holy Spirit, they will be accountable to God. We have been called out of darkness into His marvelous light in order that we may show forth the praises of Christ. *Review and Herald,* Dec. 12, 1893.

All who are consecrated to God will be channels of light. God makes them His agents to communicate to others the riches of His grace. . . . Our influence upon others depends not so much upon what we say, as upon what we are. Men may combat and defy our logic, they may resist our appeals; but a life of disinterested love is an argument they cannot gainsay. A consistent life, characterized by the meekness of Christ, is a power in the world. *The Desire of Ages,* pp. 141, 142.

Those who should have been the light of the world have shed forth but feeble and sickly beams. What is light? It is piety, goodness, truth, mercy, love; it is the revealing of the truth in the character and life. The gospel is dependent on the personal piety of its believers for its aggressive power, and God has made provision through the death of His beloved Son, that every soul may be thoroughly furnished unto every good work. Every soul is to be a bright and shining light, showing forth the praises of Him who has called us out of darkness into His marvelous light. "We are laborers together with God." Yes, laborers; that means doing earnest service in the vineyard of the Lord. There are souls to be saved—souls in our churches, in our Sabbath schools, and in our neighborhoods. *Review and Herald,* Mar. 24, 1891.

It is in working for others that they will keep their own souls alive. If they will become colaborers with Jesus, we shall see the light in our churches steadily burning brighter and brighter, sending forth its rays to penetrate the darkness beyond their own borders. *Historical Sketches,* p. 291.

"Ye are the light of the world." The Jews thought to confine the benefits of salvation to their own nation; but Christ showed them that salvation is like the sunshine. It belongs to the whole world. *The Desire of Ages,* p. 306.

Hearts that respond to the influence of the Holy Spirit are the channels through which God's blessing flows. Were those who served God removed from the earth, and His Spirit withdrawn from among men, this world would be left to desolation and destruction, the fruit of Satan's dominion. Though the wicked know it not, they owe even the blessings of this life to the presence, in the world, of God's people whom they despise and oppress. But if Christians are such in name only, they are like the salt that has lost its savor. They have no influence for good in the world. Through their misrepresentation of God they are worse than unbelievers. *The Desire of Ages,* p. 306.

## *The Divine Commission*

The work which the disciples did, we also are to do. Every Christian is to be a missionary. In sympathy and compassion we are to minister to those in need of help, seeking with unselfish earnestness to lighten the woes of suffering humanity. *The Ministry of Healing,* p. 104.

Before ascending to heaven, Christ gave His disciples their commission. He told them that they were to be the executors of the will in which He bequeathed to the world the treasures of eternal life. *The Acts of the Apostles,* p. 27.

In the trust given to the first disciples, believers in every age have shared. Everyone who has received the gospel has been given sacred truth to impart to the world. God's faithful people have always been aggressive missionaries, consecrating their resources to the honor of His name, and wisely using their talents in His service. *The Acts of the Apostles,* p. 109.

The gospel commission is the great missionary charter of Christ's kingdom. The disciples were to work earnestly for souls, giving to all the invitation of mercy. They were not to wait for the people to come to them; they were to go to the people with their message. *The Acts of the Apostles,* p. 28.

God's messengers are commissioned to take up the very work that Christ did while on this earth. They are to give themselves to every line of ministry that He carried on. With earnestness and sincerity they are to tell men of the unsearchable riches and the immortal treasure of heaven. *Testimonies,* vol. 9, p. 130.

The commission given to the disciples is given also to us. Today, as then, a crucified and risen Saviour is to be uplifted before those who are without God and without hope in the world. The Lord calls for pastors, teachers, and evangelists. From door to door His servants are to proclaim the message of salvation. To every nation, kindred, tongue, and people the tidings of pardon through Christ are to be carried. Not with tame, lifeless utterances is the message to be given, but with clear, decided, stirring utterances. Hundreds are waiting for the warning to escape for their lives. The world needs to see in Christians an evidence of the power of Christianity. Not merely in a few places, but throughout the world, messages of mercy are needed. *Gospel Workers,* p. 29.

When Jesus ascended to heaven, He committed His work on earth to those who had received the light of the gospel. They were to carry the work forward to completion. He has provided no other agency for the promulgation of His truth. "Go ye into all the world, and preach the gospel to every creature." "And, lo, I am with you alway, even unto the end of the world." This solemn commission reaches us in this age. God leaves with His church the responsibility of receiving or rejecting it. *Historical Sketches,* p. 288.

Upon us is laid a sacred charge. The commission has been given us: "Go ye therefore, and make disciples of all nations, baptizing them in the name of the Father, and of the Son, and of the Holy Ghost: teaching them to observe all things whatsoever I have commanded you: and, lo, I am with you alway, even unto the end of the world." Matt. 28:19, 20, margin. You are dedicated to the work of making known the gospel of salvation. Heaven's perfection is to be your power. *Testimonies,* vol. 9, pp. 20, 21.

## *Called From Common Walks of Life*

The common people are to take their place as workers. Sharing the sorrows of their fellowmen as the Saviour shared the sorrows of humanity, they will by faith see Him working with them. *Gospel Workers,* p. 38.

In all fields, nigh and afar off, men will be called from the plow and from the more common commercial business vocations that largely occupy the mind, and will be educated in connection with men of experience. As they learn to labor effectively, they will proclaim the truth with power. Through most wonderful workings of divine providence, mountains of difficulty will be removed and cast into the sea. The message that means so much to the dwellers upon the earth will be heard and understood. Men will know what is truth. Onward and still onward the work will advance, until the whole earth shall have been warned; and then shall the end come. *Testimonies,* vol. 9, p. 96.

God can and will use those who have not had a thorough education in the schools of men. A doubt of His power to do this, is manifest unbelief; it is limiting the omnipotent power of the One with whom nothing is impossible. O for less of this uncalled-for, distrustful caution! It leaves so many forces of the church unused; it closes up the way, so that the Holy Spirit cannot use men; it keeps in idleness those who are willing and anxious to labor in Christ's lines; it discourages from entering the work many who would become efficient laborers together with God if they were given a fair chance. *Gospel Workers,* pp. 488, 489.

It is the privilege of every soul to make advancement. Those who are connected with Christ will grow in grace and in the knowledge of the Son of God, to the full stature of men and women. If all who claim to believe the truth had made the most of their ability and opportunities to learn and to do, they would have become strong in Christ. Whatever their occupation—whether they were farmers, mechanics, teachers, or pastors—if they had wholly consecrated themselves to God, they would have become efficient workers for the heavenly Master. *Testimonies,* vol. 6, p. 423.

Those in the church who have sufficient talent to engage in any of the various vocations of life, such as teaching, building, manufacturing, and farming, generally should be prepared to labor for the upbuilding of the church by serving on committees or as teachers in Sabbath schools, engaging in missionary labor, or filling the different offices connected with the church. *Review and Herald,* Feb. 15, 1887.

For the carrying on of His work, Christ did not choose the learning or eloquence of the Jewish Sanhedrin or the power of Rome. Passing by the self-righteous Jewish teachers, the Master Worker chose humble, unlearned men to proclaim the truths that were to move the world. These men He purposed to train and educate as the leaders of His church. They in turn were to educate others and send them out with the gospel message. That they might have success in their work, they were to be given the power of the Holy Spirit. Not by human might or human wisdom was the gospel to be proclaimed, but by the power of God. *The Acts of the Apostles,* p. 17.

Among those to whom the Saviour had given the commission, "Go ye therefore, and teach all nations," were many from the humbler walks of life—men and women who had learned to love their Lord, and who had determined to follow His example of unselfish service. To these lowly ones, as well as to the disciples who had been with the Saviour during His earthly ministry, had been given a precious trust. They were to carry to the world the glad tidings of salvation through Christ. *The Acts of the Apostles,* pp. 105, 106.

## *The Life That Wins*

It is not only by preaching the truth, not only by distributing literature, that we are to witness for God. Let us remember that a Christlike life is the most powerful argument that can be advanced in favor of Christianity, and that a cheap Christian character works more harm in the world than the character of a worldling. *Testimonies,* vol. 9, p. 21.

Not all the books written can serve the purpose of a holy life. Men will believe, not what the minister preaches, but what the church lives. Too often the influence of the sermon preached from the pulpit is counteracted by the sermon preached in the lives of those who claim to be advocates of truth. *Testimonies,* vol. 9, p. 21.

The life of Christ was an ever-widening, shoreless influence, an influence that bound Him to God and to the whole human family. Through Christ, God has invested man with an influence that makes it impossible for him to live to himself. Individually we are connected with our fellowmen, a part of God's great whole, and we stand under mutual obligations. No man can be independent of his fellowmen; for the well-being of each affects others. It is God's purpose that each shall feel himself necessary to others' welfare, and seek to promote their happiness. *Christ's Object Lessons,* p. 339.

The religion of the Bible is not to be confined between the covers of a book, nor within the walls of a church. It is not to be brought out occasionally for our own benefit, and then to be carefully laid aside again. It is to sanctify the daily life, to manifest itself in every business transaction and in all our social relations. *The Desire of Ages,* pp. 306, 307.

It is the purpose of God to glorify Himself in His people before the world. He expects those who bear the name of Christ to represent Him in thought, word, and deed. Their thoughts are to be pure and their words noble and uplifting, drawing those around them nearer the Saviour. The religion of Christ is to be interwoven with all that they do and say. Their every business transaction is to be fragrant with the presence of God. *Testimonies,* vol. 9, p. 21.

Let the businessman do his business in a way that will glorify his Master because of his fidelity. Let him carry his religion into everything that is done and reveal to men the Spirit of Christ. Let the mechanic be a diligent and faithful representative of Him who toiled in the lowly walks of life in the cities of Judea. Let everyone who names the name of Christ so work that man by seeing his good works may be led to glorify his Creator and Redeemer. *Bible Echo,* June 10, 1901.

## *Women as Missionaries*

Women as well as men can engage in the work of hiding the truth where it can work out and be made manifest. They can take their place in the work at this crisis, and the Lord will work through them. If they are imbued with a sense of their duty, and labor under the influence of the Spirit of God, they will have just the self-possession required for this time. The Saviour will reflect upon these self-sacrificing women the light of His countenance, and this will give them a power that will exceed that of men. They can do in families a work that men cannot do, a work that reaches the inner life. They can come close to the hearts of those whom men cannot reach. Their work is needed. Discreet and humble women can do a good work in explaining the truth to the people in their homes. The Word of God thus explained will do its leavening work, and through its influence whole families will be converted. *Testimonies,* vol. 9, pp. 128, 129.

All who work for God should have the Martha and the Mary attributes blended—a willingness to minister and a sincere love of the truth. Self and selfishness must be put out of sight. God calls for earnest women workers, workers who are prudent, warmhearted, tender, and true to principle. He calls for persevering women who will take their minds from self and their personal convenience, and will center them on Christ, speaking words of truth, praying with the persons to whom they can obtain access, laboring for the conversion of souls. *Testimonies,* vol. 6, p. 118.

The sisters can work efficiently in obtaining subscribers for our periodicals, in this way bringing the light before many minds. *Review and Herald,* June 10, 1880.

There are noble women who have had moral courage to decide in favor of the truth from the weight of evidence. They have conscientiously accepted the truth. They have tact, perception, and good ability, and will make successful workers for their Master. Christian women are called for. *Review and Herald,* Dec. 19, 1878.

Our sisters can serve as vigilant workers in writing, and drawing out the true feelings of friends who have received our papers and tracts. . . . Women of firm principle and decided character are needed, women who believe that we are indeed living in the last days, and that we have the last solemn message of warning to be given to the world. . . . These are the ones whom God can use in the tract and missionary work. . . . These can in many ways do a precious work for God in scattering tracts and judiciously distributing the Signs of the Times. *Review and Herald,* Dec. 19, 1878.

I do not recommend that woman should seek to become a voter or an officeholder; but as a missionary, teaching the truth by epistolary correspondence, distributing tracts and soliciting subscribers for periodicals containing the solemn truth for this time, she may do very much. *Review and Herald,* Dec. 19, 1878.

If there were twenty women where now there is one who would make this holy mission their cherished work, we should see many more converted to the truth. *Review and Herald,* Jan. 2, 1879.

Women who can work are needed now, women who are not self-important, but meek and lowly of heart, who will work with the meekness of Christ wherever they can find work to do for the salvation of souls. *Review and Herald,* Jan. 2, 1879.

Hundreds of our sisters might be at work today if they would. They should dress themselves and their children with simplicity, in neat and durable garments, free from adornment, and devote the time they have spent in needless display to missionary work. Letters may be written to friends at a distance. Our sisters may meet together to consult as to the best manner of labor. Money can be saved to present as an offering to God, to be invested in papers and tracts to send to their friends. Those who are now doing nothing should go to work. Let each sister who claims to be a child of God feel indeed a responsibility to help all within her reach. *Review and Herald,* Dec. 12, 1878.

Our sisters have been too willing to excuse themselves from bearing responsibilities which require thought and close application of the mind; yet this is the very discipline they need to perfect Christian experience. They may be workers in the missionary field, having a personal interest in the distribution of tracts and papers which correctly represent our faith. *Review and Herald,* Dec. 12, 1878.

Sisters, do not become weary of vigilant missionary labor. This is a work that you may all engage in successfully, if you will but connect with God. Before writing letters of inquiry, always lift up your heart to God in prayer, that you may be successful in gathering some wild branches which may be grafted into the true vine, and bear fruit to the glory of God. All who with humble hearts take part in this work will be continually educating themselves as workers in the vineyard of the Lord. *Review and Herald,* June 10, 1880.

CHAPTER 2

# The Call to Young People

### *Divine Appointment*

The Lord has appointed the youth to be His helping hand. *Testimonies,* vol. 7, p. 64.

With such an army of workers as our youth, rightly trained, might furnish, how soon the message of a crucified, risen, and soon-coming Saviour might be carried to the whole world! *Education,* p. 271.

We have an army of youth today who can do much if they are properly directed and encouraged. We want our children to believe the truth. We want them to be blessed of God. We want them to act a part in well-organized plans for helping other youth. Let all be so trained that they may rightly represent the truth, giving the reason of the hope that is within them, and honoring God in any branch of the work where they are qualified to labor. *General Conference Bulletin,* vol. 5, no. 2, p. 24.

### *Youth in Church Work*

Youthful talent, well organized and well trained, is needed in our churches. The youth will do something with their overflowing energies. Unless these energies are directed into right channels, they will be used by the youth in a way that will hurt their own spirituality, and prove an injury to those with whom they associate. *Gospel Workers,* p. 211.

When the youth give their hearts to God, our responsibility for them does not cease. They must be interested in the Lord's work, and led to see that He expects them to do something to advance His cause. It is not enough to show how much needs to be done, and to urge the youth to act a part. They must be taught how to labor for the Master. They must be trained, disciplined, drilled, in the best methods of winning souls to Christ. Teach them to try in a quiet, unpretending way to help their young companions. Let different branches of missionary effort be systematically laid out, in which they may take part, and let them be given instruction and help. Thus they will learn to work for God. *Gospel Workers,* p. 210.

### *In Earliest Years*

Let the kindness and courtesy of the minister be seen in his treatment of children. He should ever bear in mind that they are miniature men and women, younger members of the Lord's family. These may be very near and dear to the Master, and, if properly instructed and disciplined, will do service for Him, even in their youth. *Testimonies,* vol. 4, pp. 397, 398.

Let not the youth be ignored; let them share in the labor and responsibility. Let them feel that they have a part to act in helping and blessing others. Even the children should be taught to do little errands of love and mercy for those less fortunate than themselves. *Testimonies,* vol. 6, p. 435.

Parents should teach their children the value and right use of time. Teach them that to do something which will honor God and bless humanity is worth striving for. Even in their early years they can be missionaries for God. *Christ's Object Lessons,* p. 345.

### *Future Before Youth*

Many a lad of today, growing up as did Daniel in his Judean home, studying God's word and His works, and learning the lessons of faithful service, will yet stand in legislative assemblies, in halls of justice, or in royal courts, as a witness for the King of kings. *Education,* p. 262.

### *Timothy a Mere Youth When Chosen*

Paul saw that Timothy was faithful, steadfast, and true, and he chose him as a companion in labor and travel. Those who had taught Timothy in his childhood were rewarded by seeing the son of their care linked in close fellowship with the great apostle. Timothy was a mere youth when he was chosen by God to be a teacher; but his principles had been so established by his early education that he was fitted to take his place as Paul's helper. And though young, he bore his responsibilities with Christian meekness. *The Acts of the Apostles,* pp. 203, 204.

## *Reserves to Fill Up the Ranks*

The burden-bearers among us are falling in death. Many of those who have been foremost in carrying out the reforms instituted by us as a people, are now past the meridian of life, and are declining in physical and mental strength. With the deepest concern the question may be asked, Who will fill their places? To whom are to be committed the vital interests of the church when the present standard-bearers fall? We cannot but look anxiously upon the youth of today as those who must take these burdens, and upon whom responsibilities must fall. These must take up the work where others leave it, and their course will determine whether morality, religion, and vital godliness shall prevail, or whether immorality and infidelity shall corrupt and blight all that is valuable. *Gospel Workers,* p. 68.

## *Pioneers in Toil and Sacrifice*

We must manifest confidence in our young men. They should be pioneers in every enterprise involving toil and sacrifice, while the overtaxed servants of Christ should be cherished as counselors, to encourage and bless those who strike the heaviest blows for God. *Counsels to Teachers, Parents, and Students,* pp. 516, 517.

Young men are wanted. God calls them to missionary fields. Being comparatively free from care and responsibilities, they are more favorably situated to engage in the work than are those who must provide for the training and support of a large family. Furthermore, young men can more readily adapt themselves to new climates and new society, and can better endure inconveniences and hardships. By tact and perseverance, they can reach the people where they are. *Counsels to Teachers, Parents, and Students,* p. 517.

Many young men who have had the right kind of education at home are to be trained for service and encouraged to lift the standard of truth in new places by well-planned and faithful work. By associating with our ministers and experienced workers in city work, they will gain the best kind of training. Acting under divine guidance and sustained by the prayers of their more experienced fellow workers, they may do a good and blessed work. As they unite their labors with those of the older workers, using their youthful energies to the very best account, they will have the companionship of heavenly angels; and as workers together with God, it is their privilege to sing and pray and believe, and work with courage and freedom. The confidence and trust that the presence of heavenly agencies will bring to them and to their fellow workers will lead to prayer and praise and the simplicity of true faith. *Testimonies,* vol. 9, p. 119.

## Lines of Work

There are many lines in which the youth can find opportunity for helpful effort. Companies should be organized and thoroughly educated to work as nurses, gospel visitors, and Bible readers, as canvassers, ministers, and medical missionary evangelists. *Counsels to Teachers, Parents, and Students,* p. 546.

We should educate the youth to help the youth; and as they seek to do this work they will gain an experience that will qualify them to become consecrated workers in a larger sphere. *Testimonies,* vol. 6, p. 115.

Young men and women should be educated to become workers in their own neighborhoods and in other places. Let all set their hearts and minds to become intelligent in regard to the work for this time, qualifying themselves to do that for which they are best adapted. *Testimonies,* vol. 9, pp. 118, 119.

## Secret of Success

Follow on, young men, to know the Lord, and you will know that "His going forth is prepared as the morning." Seek constantly to improve. Strive earnestly for identity with the Redeemer. Live by faith in Christ. Do the work He did. Live for the saving of the souls for whom He laid down His life. Try in every way to help those with whom you come in contact. . . . Talk with your Elder Brother, who will complete your education, line upon line, precept upon precept, here a little and there a little. A close connection with Him who offered Himself as a sacrifice to save a perishing world will make you acceptable workers. *Testimonies*, vol. 6, p. 416.

## *Organize for Service*

Young men and young women, cannot you form companies and, as soldiers of Christ, enlist in the work, putting all your tact and skill and talent into the Master's service, that you may save souls from ruin? Let there be companies organized in every church to do this work. . . . Will the young men and young women who really love Jesus organize themselves as workers, not only for those who profess to be Sabbathkeepers, but for those who are not of our faith? *Signs of the Times,* May 29, 1893.

Let young men and women and children go to work in the name of Jesus. Let them unite together upon some plan and order of action. Cannot you form a band of workers, and have set times to pray together and ask the Lord to give you His grace, and put forth united action? *Youth's Instructor,* Aug. 9, 1894.

# CHAPTER 3

# Conditions Among God's People

### *Missionary Spirit Lacking*

There has been but little of the missionary spirit among Sabbathkeeping Adventists. If ministers and people were sufficiently aroused, they would not rest thus indifferently while God has honored them by making them the depositaries of His law by printing it in their minds and writing it upon their hearts. *Testimonies,* vol. 3, p. 202.

The true missionary spirit has deserted the churches that make so exalted a profession; their hearts are no longer aglow with love for souls and a desire to lead them into the fold of Christ. We want earnest workers. Are there none to respond to the cry that goes up from every quarter: "Come over and help us"? *Testimonies,* vol. 4, p. 156.

I was shown that as a people we are deficient. Our works are not in accordance with our faith. Our faith testifies that we are living under the proclamation of the most solemn and important message that was ever given to mortals. Yet in full view of this fact, our efforts, our zeal, our spirit of self-sacrifice, do not compare with the character of the work. We should awake from the dead, and Christ will give us life. *Testimonies,* vol. 2, p. 114.

My heart is pained when I think how little our churches sense their solemn accountabilities to God. It is not ministers alone who are soldiers, but every man and woman who has enlisted in Christ's army; and are they willing to receive a soldier's fare, just as Christ has given them an example in His life of self-denial and sacrifice? What self-denial have our churches as a whole manifested? They may have given donations in money, but have withheld themselves. *General Conference Bulletin,* 1893, p. 131.

Many of the professed followers of Christ feel no more burden for souls than do the world. The lusts of the eye, and the pride of life, the love of display, the love of ease, separate the professed Christians from God, and the missionary spirit in reality exists in but few. What can be done to open the eyes of these sinners in Zion, and make hypocrites tremble? *General Conference Bulletin,* 1893, p. 132.

There is a class that are represented by Meroz. The missionary spirit has never taken hold of their souls. The calls of foreign missions have not stirred them to action. What account will those render to God, who are doing nothing in His cause—nothing to win souls to Christ? Such will receive the denunciation, "Thou wicked and slothful servant." *Historical Sketches,* p. 290.

As an illustration of the failure on your part to come up to the work of God, as was your privilege, I was referred to these words: "Curse ye Meroz, said the angel of the Lord, curse ye bitterly the inhabitants thereof; because they came not to the help of the Lord, to the help of the Lord against the mighty." *Testimonies,* vol. 2, p. 247.

## *A Self-complacent Class*

There was presented before me a class who are conscious that they possess generous impulses, devotional feelings, and a love of doing good; yet at the same time they are doing nothing. They possess a self-complacent feeling, flattering themselves that if they had an opportunity, or were circumstanced more favorably, they could and would do a great and good work; but they are waiting the opportunity. They despise the narrow mind of the poor niggard who grudges the small pittance to the needy. They see that he lives for self, that he will not be called from himself to do good to others, to bless them with the talents of influence and of means which have been committed to him to use, not to abuse, nor to permit to rust, or lie buried in the earth. Those who give themselves up to their stinginess and selfishness are accountable for their niggardly acts and are responsible for the talents they abuse. But more responsible are those who have generous impulses and are naturally quick to discern spiritual things, if they remain inactive, waiting an opportunity they suppose has not come, yet contrasting their readiness to do with the unwillingness of the niggard, and reflecting that their condition is more favorable than that of their mean-souled neighbors. Such deceive themselves. The mere possession of qualities which are not used only increases their responsibility; and if they keep their Master's talents unimproved, or hoarded, their condition is no better than that of their neighbors for whom their souls feel such contempt. To them it will be said: Ye knew your Master's will, yet did it not. *Testimonies,* vol. 2, pp. 250, 251.

## *Satanic Death Stupor*

God's people must take warning and discern the signs of the times. The signs of Christ's coming are too plain to be doubted, and in view of these things everyone who professes the truth should be a living preacher. God calls upon all, both preachers and people, to awake. All heaven is astir. The scenes of earth's history are fast closing. We are amid the perils of the last days. Greater perils are before us, and yet we are not awake. This lack of activity and earnestness in the cause of God is dreadful. This death stupor is from Satan. *Testimonies,* vol. 1, pp. 260, 261.

Unbelief, like the pall of death, is surrounding our churches, because they do not exercise the talents God has given them by imparting the light to those who know not the precious truth. The Lord calls for the pardoned souls, those who rejoice in the light, to make known the truth to others. *General Conference Bulletin,* 1893, p. 133.

Satan is now seeking to hold God's people in a state of inactivity, to keep them from acting their part in spreading the truth, that they may at last be weighed in the balance and found wanting. *Testimonies,* vol. 1, p. 260.

Men are in peril. Multitudes are perishing. But how few of the professed followers of Christ are burdened for these souls. The destiny of a world hangs in the balance; but this hardly moves even those who claim to believe the most far-reaching truth ever given to mortals. There is a lack of that love which led Christ to leave His heavenly home and take man's nature, that humanity might touch humanity, and draw humanity to divinity. There is a stupor, a paralysis, upon the people of God, which prevents them from understanding the duty of the hour. *Christ's Object Lessons,* p. 303.

Satan uses the listless, sleepy indolence of professed Christians to strengthen his forces and win souls to his side. Many who think that though they are doing no actual work for Christ, they are yet on His side, are enabling the enemy to preoccupy ground and gain advantages. By their failure to be diligent workers for the Master, by leaving duties undone and words unspoken, they have allowed Satan to gain control of souls who might have been won for Christ. *Christ's Object Lessons,* p. 280.

When I study the Scriptures, I am alarmed for the Israel of God in these last days. They are exhorted to flee from idolatry. I fear that they are asleep and so conformed to the world that it would be difficult to discern between him that serveth God and him that serveth Him not. The distance is widening between Christ and His people, and lessening between them and the world. The marks of distinction between Christ's professed people and the world have almost disappeared. Like ancient Israel, they follow after the abominations of the nations around them. *Testimonies,* vol. 1, p. 277.

## *Spiritual Discernment Dimmed*

And not only in the world do we see the result of the church's neglect to work in Christ's lines. By this neglect a condition of things has been brought into the church that has eclipsed the high and holy interests of the work of God. A spirit of criticism and bitterness has come into the church, and the spiritual discernment of many has been dimmed. Because of this the cause of Christ has suffered great loss. *Testimonies,* vol. 6, p. 297.

I am filled with sadness when I think of our condition as a people. The Lord has not closed heaven to us, but our own course of continual backsliding has separated us from God. Pride, covetousness, and love of the world have lived in the heart without fear of banishment or condemnation. Grievous and presumptuous sins have dwelt among us. And yet the general opinion is that the church is flourishing, and that peace and spiritual prosperity are in all her borders. The church has turned back from following Christ her leader and is steadily retreating toward Egypt. Yet few are alarmed or astonished at their want of spiritual power. Doubt, and even disbelief of the testimonies of the Spirit of God, is leavening our churches everywhere. Satan would have it thus. *Testimonies,* vol. 5, p. 217.

## *A State of Spiritual Weakness*

Accumulated light has shone upon God's people, but many have neglected to follow the light, and for this reason they are in a state of great spiritual weakness. It is not for lack of knowledge that God's people are now perishing. They will not be condemned because they do not know the way, the truth, and the life. The truth that has reached their understanding, the light which has shone on the soul, but which has been neglected or refused, will condemn them. Those who never had the light to reject will not be in condemnation. What more could have been done for God's vineyard than has been done? Light, precious light, shines upon God's people; but it will not save them, unless they consent to be saved by it, fully live up to it, and transmit it to others in darkness. *Testimonies,* vol. 2, p. 123.

## *The Need of Heavenly Eyesalve*

The churches need to have their eyes anointed with the heavenly eyesalve, that they may see the many opportunities all about them to minister for God. Repeatedly God has called upon His people to go out into the highways and hedges, and compel men to come in, that His house may be full; yet even within the shadow of our own doors are families in which we have not shown sufficient interest to lead them to think that we cared for their souls. It is this work lying nearest us that the Lord now calls upon the church to undertake. We are not to stand, saying: "Who is my neighbor?" We are to remember that our neighbor is the one who most needs our sympathy and help. Our neighbor is every soul who is wounded and bruised by the adversary. Our neighbor is everyone who is the property of God. In Christ the distinctions made by the Jews as to who was their neighbor are swept away. There are no territorial lines, no artificial distinctions, no caste, no aristocracy. *Testimonies,* vol. 6, p. 294.

## *Fanaticism and Cold Formalism*

Satan is now working with all his insinuating, deceiving power, to lead men away from the work of the third angel's message, which is to be proclaimed with mighty power. When the enemy sees that the Lord is blessing His people and preparing them to discern his delusions, he will work with his masterly power to bring in fanaticism on one hand and cold formalism on the other, that he may gather in a harvest of souls. Now is the time to watch unceasingly. Watch for the first step of advance that Satan may make among us. *Review and Herald,* Jan. 24, 1893.

There are moral icebergs in our churches. There are plenty of formalists who can make an imposing display, but cannot shine as lights in the world. *Review and Herald,* Mar. 24, 1891.

## *Narrowed by Selfishness*

The reason why God's people are not more spiritual minded, and have not more faith, I have been shown, is because they are narrowed up with selfishness. . . . It is not the abundance of your meetings that God accepts. It is not the numerous prayers, but the rightdoing, doing the right thing and at the right time. *Testimonies,* vol. 2, p. 36.

## *Covetousness*

Yet some refused to be converted. They were not willing to walk in God's way, and when, in order that the work of God might be advanced, calls were made for freewill offerings, some clung selfishly to their earthly possessions. These covetous ones became separated from the company of believers. *Testimonies,* vol. 9, p. 126.

## *Not One in Twenty Prepared*

It is a solemn statement that I make to the church, that not one in twenty whose names are registered upon the church books are prepared to close their earthly history, and would be as verily without God and without hope in the world as the common sinner. They are professedly serving God, but they are more earnestly serving mammon. This half-and-half work is a constant denying of Christ, rather than a confessing of Christ. So many have brought into the church their own unsubdued spirit, unrefined; their spiritual taste is perverted by their own immoral, debasing corruptions, symbolizing the world in spirit, in heart, in purpose, confirming themselves in lustful practices, and are full of deception through and through in their professed Christian life. Living as sinners, claiming to be Christians! Those who claim to be Christians and will confess Christ should come out from among them and touch not the unclean thing, and be separate. . . .

I lay down my pen and lift up my soul in prayer that the Lord would breathe upon His backslidden people, who are as dry bones, that they may live. The end is near, stealing upon us so stealthily, so imperceptibly, so noiselessly, like the muffled tread of the thief in the night, to surprise the sleepers off guard and unready. May the Lord grant to bring His Holy Spirit upon hearts that are now at ease, that they may no longer sleep as do others, but watch and be sober. *General Conference Bulletin,* 1893, pp. 132, 133.

## *Revival and Reformation Needed*

Christians should be preparing for what is soon to break upon the world as an overwhelming surprise, and this preparation they should make by diligently studying the word of God, and striving to conform their lives to its precepts. . . . God calls for a revival and a reformation. *Prophets and Kings,* p. 626.

A revival of true godliness among us is the greatest and most urgent of all our needs. To seek this should be our first work. *Review and Herald,* Mar. 22, 1887.

The time has come for a thorough reformation to take place. When this reformation begins, the spirit of prayer will actuate every believer and will banish from the church the spirit of discord and strife. *Testimonies,* vol. 8, p. 251.

A revival and a reformation must take place under the ministration of the Holy Spirit. Revival and reformation are two different things. Revival signifies a renewal of spiritual life, a quickening of the powers of mind and heart, a resurrection from the spiritual death. Reformation signifies a reorganization, a change in ideas and theories, habits and practices. Reformation will not bring forth the good fruit of righteousness unless it is connected with the revival of the Spirit. Revival and reformation are to do their appointed work, and in doing this work they must blend. *Review and Herald,* Feb. 25, 1902.

Do not the Scriptures call for a more pure and holy work than we have yet seen? . . . God calls upon those who are willing to be controlled by the Holy Spirit to lead out in a work of thorough reformation. I see a crisis before us, and the Lord calls for His laborers to come into line. Every soul should now stand in a position of deeper, truer consecration to God than during the years that have passed. . . . I have been deeply impressed by scenes that have recently passed before me in the night season. There seemed to be a great movement—a work of revival—going forward in many places. Our people were moving into line, responding to God's call. *General Conference Bulletin,* May 29, 1913, p. 34.

In visions of the night representations passed before me of a great reformatory movement among God's people. Many were praising God. The sick were healed, and other miracles were wrought. . . . Hundreds and thousands were seen visiting families and opening before them the Word of God. Hearts were convicted by the power of the Holy Spirit, and a spirit of genuine conversion was manifest. On every side doors were thrown open to the proclamation of the truth. The world seemed to be lightened with the heavenly influence. Great blessings were received by the true and humble people of God. *Testimonies,* vol. 9, p. 126.

There is great necessity for a reformation among the people of God. The present state of the church leads to the inquiry, Is this a correct representation of Him who gave His life for us? *Testimonies,* vol. 3, p. 474.

When the reproach of indolence and slothfulness shall have been wiped away from the church, the Spirit of the Lord will be graciously manifested. Divine power will be revealed. The church will see the providential working of the Lord of hosts. The light of truth will shine forth in clear, strong rays, and as in the time of the apostles, many souls will turn from error to truth. The earth will be lightened with the glory of the Lord. *Testimonies,* vol. 9, p. 46.

## *Delay Is Fatal*

I was shown God's people waiting for some change to take place—a compelling power to take hold of them. But they will be disappointed, for they are wrong. They must act, they must take hold of the work themselves and earnestly cry to God for a true knowledge of themselves. The scenes which are passing before us are of sufficient magnitude to cause us to arouse, and urge the truth home to the hearts of all who will listen. The harvest of the earth is nearly ripe. *Testimonies,* vol. 1, p. 261.

On the other hand, there are some who, instead of wisely improving present opportunities, are idly waiting for some special season of spiritual refreshing by which their ability to enlighten others will be greatly increased. They neglect present duties and privileges and allow their light to burn dim, while they look forward to a time when, without any effort on their part, they will be made the recipients of special blessing, by which they will be transformed and fitted for service. *The Acts of the Apostles,* p. 54

## *Not Producers but Consumers*

The professed followers of Christ are on trial before the heavenly universe; but the coldness of their zeal and the feebleness of their efforts in God's service mark them as unfaithful. If what they are doing were the best they could do, condemnation would not rest upon them; but were their hearts enlisted in the work, they could do much more. They know, and the world knows, that they have to a great degree lost the spirit of self-denial and cross-bearing. Many there are against whose names will be found written in the books of heaven, Not producers, but consumers. By many who bear Christ's name, His glory is obscured, His beauty veiled, His honor withheld. There are many whose names are on the church books, but who are not under Christ's rule. They are not heeding His instruction or doing His work. Therefore they are under the control of the enemy. They are doing no positive good, therefore they are doing incalculable harm. Because their influence is not a savor of life unto life, it is a savor of death unto death. *Christ's Object Lessons,* pp. 303, 304.

## *Commandment Keeping a Cloak for Sin*

The same danger exists today among the people who profess to be the depositaries of God's law. They are too apt to flatter themselves that the regard in which they hold the commandments will preserve them from the power of divine justice. They refuse to be reproved for evil, and charge God's servants with being too zealous in putting sin out of the camp. A sin-hating God calls upon those who profess to keep His law to depart from all iniquity. Neglect to repent and obey His word will bring as serious consequences upon God's people today as did the same sin upon ancient Israel. There is a limit beyond which He will no longer delay His judgments. *Testimonies,* vol. 4, pp. 166, 167.

## *Dead in Trespasses and Sins*

Today a large part of those who compose our congregations are dead in trespasses and sins. They come and go like the door upon its hinges. For years they have complacently listened to the most solemn, soul-stirring truths, but they have not put them in practice. Therefore they are less and less sensible of the preciousness of truth. . . . While making a profession, they deny the power of godliness. If they continue in this state, God will reject them. They are unfitting themselves to be members of His family. *Testimonies,* vol. 6, pp. 426, 427.

## *Human Moralists*

Many who call themselves Christians are mere human moralists. They have refused the gift which alone could enable them to honor Christ by representing Him to the world. The work of the Holy Spirit is to them a strange work. They are not doers of the word. The heavenly principles that distinguish those who are one with Christ from those who are one with the world have become almost indistinguishable. The professed followers of Christ are no longer a separate and peculiar people. The line of demarcation is indistinct. The people are subordinating themselves to the world, to its practices, its customs, its selfishness. The church has gone over to the world in transgression of the law, when the world should have come over to the church in obedience to the law. Daily the church is being converted to the world. *Christ's Object Lessons,* pp. 315, 316.

## *A Spotted Record*

Many have a form of godliness, their names are upon the church records; but they have a spotted record in heaven. The recording angel has faithfully written their deeds. Every selfish act, every wrong word, every unfulfilled duty, and every secret sin, with every artful dissembling, is faithfully chronicled in the book of records kept by the recording angel. *Testimonies,* vol. 2, p. 442.

## *The Burden-Bearers Are Wearing Out*

Because some will not lift the burdens they could lift, or do the work they might do, the work is too great for the few who will engage in it. They see so much to do that they overtax their strength and are fast wearing out. *Testimonies,* vol. 2, p. 645.

## *Unable to Give an Intelligent Reason for Faith*

Many who profess to believe the truth for these last days will be found wanting. They have neglected the weightier matters. Their conversion is superficial, not deep, earnest, and thorough. They do not know why they believe the truth, only because others have believed it, and they take it for granted that it is the truth. They can give no intelligent reason why they believe. . . . Others are not enlightened or edified by their experience or by the knowledge which it was their privilege and duty to obtain. Strength and stability are with truehearted professors. *Testimonies*, vol. 2, p. 634.

## *Some Will Trace Down the Prophetic Roll*

God has a people upon the earth who in faith and holy hope are tracing down the roll of fast-fulfilling prophecy and are seeking to purify their souls by obeying the truth, that they may not be found without the wedding garment when Christ shall appear. *Testimonies*, vol. 4, p. 307.

## *An Impressive Dream*

In a dream given me Sept. 29, 1886, I was walking with a large company who were looking for berries. There were many young men and women in the company who were to help in gathering the fruit. We seemed to be in a city, for there was very little vacant ground; but around the city there were open fields, beautiful groves, and cultivated gardens. A large wagon laden with provisions for our company went before us.

Soon the wagon halted, and the party scattered in every direction to look for fruit. All around the wagon were both high and low bushes, bearing large, beautiful whortleberries, but the company were all looking too far away to see them. I began to gather the fruit nearby, but very carefully, for fear of picking the green berries, which were so mingled with the ripe fruit that I could pick only one or two berries from a cluster.

Some of the nice large berries had fallen to the ground and were half consumed by worms and insects. "Oh," thought I, "if this field had only been entered before, all this precious fruit might have been saved! But it is too late now. I will, however, pick these from the ground and see if there is any good in them. Even if the whole berry is spoiled, I can at least show the brethren what they might have found if they had not been too late."

Just then two or three of the party came sauntering around where I was. They were chatting, and seemed to be much occupied with each other's company. Seeing me, they said, "We have looked everywhere, and can find no fruit." They looked with astonishment at the quantity I had. I said, "There are more to be gathered from these bushes." They began picking, but soon stopped, saying, "It is not fair for us to pick here; you found this spot, and the fruit is yours." But I replied, "That makes no difference. Gather wherever you can find anything. This is God's field, and these are His berries; it is your privilege to pick them."

But soon I seemed to be alone again. Every little while I heard talking and laughing at the wagon. I called out to those who were there, "What are you doing?" They answered, "We could not find any berries, and as we were tired and hungry, we thought we would come to the wagon and take a lunch. After we have rested awhile, we will go out again."

"But," I said, "you have brought in nothing as yet. You are eating up all our supplies, without giving us any more. I cannot eat now; there is too much fruit to be picked. You did not find it because you did not look close enough. It does not hang on the outside of the bushes, you must search for it. True, you cannot pick it by handfuls; but by looking carefully among the green berries, you will find very choice fruit."

My small pail was soon full of berries, and I took them to the wagon. Said I, "This is the nicest fruit that I ever picked, and I gathered it near by, while you have wearied yourselves by searching at a distance without success."

Then all came to see my fruit. They said, "These are high-bush berries, firm and good. We did not think we could find anything on the high bushes, so we hunted for low-bush berries only, and found but few of these."

Then I said, "Will you take care of these berries and then go with me to look for more fruit on the high bushes?" But they had made no preparation to care for the fruit. There were dishes and sacks in abundance but they had been used to hold food. I became tired of waiting, and finally asked, "Did you not come to gather fruit? Then why are you not prepared to take care of it?"

One responded, "Sister White, we did not really expect to find any fruit where there were so many houses, and so much going on; but as you seemed so anxious to gather fruit, we decided to come with you. We thought we would bring enough to eat and would enjoy the recreation, if we did not gather any fruit."

I answered, "I cannot understand this kind of work. I shall go to the bushes again at once. The day is already far spent, soon the night will be here, in which we can gather no fruit." Some went with me, but others remained by the wagon to eat.

In one place a little company had collected, and were busily talking about something in which they seemed much interested. I drew near, and found that a little child in a woman's arms had attracted their attention. I said, "You have but a little time, and might better work while you can."

The attention of many was attracted by a young man and a young woman who were running a race to the wagon. On reaching it, they were so tired that they had to sit down and rest. Others also had thrown themselves down on the grass to rest.

Thus the day wore on, and very little was accomplished. At last I said: "Brethren, you call this an unsuccessful expedition. If this is the way you work, I do not wonder at your lack of success. Your success or failure depends upon the way you take hold of the work. There are berries here; for I have found them. Some of you have been searching the low bushes in vain; others have found a few berries; but the high bushes have been passed by, simply because you did not expect to find fruit on them. You see that the fruit which I have gathered is large and ripe. In a little while other berries will ripen, and we can go over the bushes again. This is the way in which I was taught to gather fruit. If you had searched near the wagon. You might have found fruit as well as I.

"The lesson that you have this day given to those who are just learning how to do this kind of work will be copied by them. The Lord has placed these fruit-bearing bushes right in the midst of these thickly settled places, and He expects you to find them. But you have been altogether too much engaged in eating, and amusing yourselves. You did not come to the field with an earnest determination to find fruit.

"You must hereafter work with more zeal and earnestness, and with an altogether different object in view, or your labors will never be successful. By working in the right way, you will teach the younger workers that such matters as eating and recreation are of minor importance. It has been hard work to bring the wagon of supplies to the ground, but you have thought more of the supplies than of the fruit you ought to carry home as the result of your labors. You should be diligent, first to pick the berries nearest you, and then to search for those farther away; after that you can return and work near by again, and thus you will be successful." *Gospel Workers,* pp. 136-139.

## *The Test to Be Met*

In the last solemn work few great men will be engaged. They are self-sufficient, independent of God, and He cannot use them. The Lord has faithful servants, who in the shaking, testing time will be disclosed to view. There are precious ones now hidden who have not bowed the knee to Baal. They have not had the light which has been shining in a concentrated blaze upon you. But it may be under a rough and uninviting exterior the pure brightness of a genuine Christian character will be revealed. In the daytime we look toward heaven but do not see the stars. They are there, fixed in the firmament, but the eye cannot distinguish them. In the night we behold their genuine luster.

The time is not far distant when the test will come to every soul. . . . In this time the gold will be separated from the dross in the church. True godliness will be clearly distinguished from the appearance and tinsel of it. Many a star that we have admired for its brilliancy will then go out in darkness. Chaff like a cloud will be borne away on the wind, even from places where we see only floors of rich wheat. All who assume the ornaments of the sanctuary, but are not clothed with Christ's righteousness, will appear in the shame of their own nakedness. *Testimonies,* vol. 5, pp. 80, 81.

# CHAPTER 4

# World Conditions Facing the Christian Worker

### *The World Drama*

The world is a theater; the actors, its inhabitants, are preparing to act their part in the last great drama. With the great masses of mankind there is no unity, except as men confederate to accomplish their selfish purposes. God is looking on. His purposes in regard to His rebellious subjects will be fulfilled. The world has not been given into the hands of men, though God is permitting the elements of confusion and disorder to bear sway for a season. A power from beneath is working to bring about the last great scenes in the drama—Satan coming as Christ, and working with all deceivableness of unrighteousness in those who are binding themselves together in secret societies. Those who are yielding to the passion for confederation are working out the plans of the enemy. The cause will be followed by the effect. *Testimonies,* vol. 8, pp. 27, 28.

### *Last Act of the Drama*

Never did this message apply with greater force than it applies today. More and more the world is setting at naught the claims of God. Men have become bold in transgression. The wickedness of the inhabitants of the world has almost filled up the measure of their iniquity. This earth has almost reached the place where God will permit the destroyer to work his will upon it. The substitution of the laws of men for the law of God, the exaltation, by merely human authority, of Sunday in place of the Bible Sabbath, is the last act in the drama. When this substitution becomes universal, God will reveal Himself. He will arise in His majesty to shake terribly the earth. He will come out of His place to punish the inhabitants of the world for their iniquity, and the earth shall disclose her blood and shall no more cover her slain. *Testimonies,* vol. 7, p. 141.

## *The Crisis of the Ages*

We are standing on the threshold of the crisis of the ages. In quick succession the judgments of God will follow one another—fire, and flood, and earthquake, with war and bloodshed. We are not to be surprised at this time by events both great and decisive; for the angel of mercy cannot remain much longer to shelter the impenitent. *Prophets and Kings,* p. 278.

The crisis is stealing gradually upon us. The sun shines in the heavens, passing over its usual round, and the heavens still declare the glory of God. Men are still eating and drinking, planting and building, marrying and giving in marriage. Merchants are still buying and selling. Men are jostling one against another, contending for the highest place. Pleasure lovers are still crowding to theaters, horse races, gambling hells. The highest excitement prevails, yet probation's hour is fast closing, and every case is about to be eternally decided. Satan sees that his time is short. He has set all his agencies at work that men may be deceived, deluded, occupied, and entranced until the day of probation shall be ended, and the door of mercy forever shut. *Southern Watchman,* Oct. 3, 1905.

Transgression has almost reached its limit. Confusion fills the world, and a great terror is soon to come upon human beings. The end is very near. We who know the truth should be preparing for what is soon to break upon the world as an overwhelming surprise. *Testimonies,* vol. 8, p. 28.

In this time of prevailing iniquity we may know that the last great crisis is at hand. When the defiance of God's law is almost universal, when His people are oppressed and afflicted by their fellow men, the Lord will interpose. *Christ's Object Lessons,* p. 178.

We are standing upon the threshold of great and solemn events. Prophecies are fulfilling. Strange, eventful history is being recorded in the books of heaven. Everything in our world is in agitation. There are wars and rumors of wars. The nations are angry, and the time of the dead has come, that they should be judged. Events are changing to bring about the day of God which hasteth greatly. Only a moment of time, as it were, yet remains. But while already nation is rising against nation, and kingdom against kingdom, there is not now a general engagement. As yet the four winds are held until the servants of God shall be sealed in their foreheads. Then the powers of earth will marshal their forces for the last great battle. *Testimonies,* vol. 6, p. 14.

## *Restraining Spirit of God Being Withdrawn*

The restraining Spirit of God is even now being withdrawn from the world. Hurricanes, storms, tempests, fire and flood, disasters by sea and land, follow each other in quick succession. Science seeks to explain all these. The signs thickening around us, telling of the near approach of the Son of God, are attributed to any other than the true cause. Men cannot discern the sentinel angels restraining the four winds that they shall not blow until the servants of God are sealed; but when God shall bid His angels loose the winds, there shall be such a scene of strife as no pen can picture. *Testimonies,* vol. 6, p. 408.

The days in which we live are solemn and important. The Spirit of God is gradually but surely being withdrawn from the earth. Plagues and judgments are already falling upon the despisers of the grace of God. The calamities by land and sea, the unsettled state of society, the alarms of war, are portentous. They forecast approaching events of the greatest magnitude. The agencies of evil are combining their forces, and consolidating. They are strengthening for the last great crisis. Great changes are soon to take place in our world, and the final movements will be rapid ones. *Testimonies,* vol. 9, p. 11.

The time is at hand when there will be sorrow in the world that no human balm can heal. The Spirit of God is being withdrawn. Disasters by sea and by land follow one another in quick succession. How frequently we hear of earthquakes and tornadoes, of destruction by fire and flood, with great loss of life and property! Apparently these calamities are capricious outbreaks of disorganized, unregulated forces of nature, wholly beyond the control of man; but in them all, God's purpose may be read. They are among the agencies by which He seeks to arouse men and women to a sense of their danger. *Prophets and Kings,* p. 277.

## *The World a Pesthouse*

Men in their blindness boast of wonderful progress and enlightenment; but the heavenly watchers see the earth filled with corruption and violence. Because of sin the atmosphere of our world has become as the atmosphere of a pesthouse. *Testimonies,* vol. 6, p. 10.

## *An Epidemic of Crime*

We are living in the midst of an "epidemic of crime," at which thoughtful, God-fearing men everywhere stand aghast. The corruption that prevails, it is beyond the power of the human pen to describe. Every day brings fresh revelations of political strife, bribery, and fraud. Every day brings its heart-sickening record of violence and lawlessness, of indifference to human suffering, of brutal, fiendish destruction of human life. Every day testifies to the increase of insanity, murder, and suicide. Who can doubt that satanic agencies are at work among men with increasing activity to distract and corrupt the mind, and defile and destroy the body? *Ministry of Healing,* pp. 142, 143.

The spirit of anarchy is permeating all nations, and the outbreaks that from time to time excite the horror of the world are but indications of the pent-up fires of passion and lawlessness that, having once escaped control, will fill the earth with woe and desolation. The picture which Inspiration has given of the antediluvian world, represents too truly the condition to which modern society is fast hastening. Even now, in the present century, and in professedly Christian lands, there are crimes daily perpetrated, as black and terrible as those for which the old-world sinners were destroyed. Before the Flood God sent Noah to warn the world, that the people might be led to repentance and thus escape the threatened destruction. As the time of Christ's second appearing draws near, the Lord sends His servants with a warning to the world to prepare for that great event. Multitudes have been living in transgression of God's law, and now He in mercy calls them to obey its sacred precepts. All who will put away their sins by repentance toward God and faith in Christ are offered pardon. *Patriarchs and Prophets,* p. 102.

The condition of things in the world shows that troublous times are right upon us. The daily papers are full of indications of a terrible conflict in the near future. Bold robberies are of frequent occurrence. Strikes are common. Thefts and murders are committed on every hand. Men possessed of demons are taking the lives of men, women, and little children. Men have become infatuated with vice, and every species of evil prevails. *Testimonies,* vol. 9, p. 11.

## *The Archdeceiver at Work*

At the present time, when the end of all things earthly is rapidly approaching, Satan is putting forth desperate efforts to ensnare the world. He is devising many plans to occupy minds and to divert attention from the truths essential to salvation. In every city his agencies are busily organizing into parties those who are opposed to the law of God. The archdeceiver is at work to introduce elements of confusion and rebellion, and men are being fired with a zeal that is not according to knowledge. *The Acts of the Apostles,* p. 219.

Satan is a diligent Bible student. He knows that his time is short, and he seeks at every point to counterwork the work of the Lord upon this earth. *Testimonies,* vol. 9, p. 16.

Satan is now seeking to hold God's people in a state of inactivity, to keep them from acting their part in spreading the truth, that they may at last be weighed in the balance and found wanting. *Testimonies,* vol. 1, p. 260.

## *World Stirred With the Spirit of War*

The world is stirred with the spirit of war. The prophecy of the eleventh chapter of Daniel has nearly reached its complete fulfillment. Soon the scenes of trouble spoken of in the prophecies will take place. *Testimonies,* vol. 9, p. 14.

I was shown the inhabitants of the earth in the utmost confusion. War, bloodshed, privation, want, famine, and pestilence were abroad in the land. . . . My attention was then called from the scene. There seemed to be a little time of peace. Once more the inhabitants of the earth were presented before me; and again everything was in the utmost confusion. Strife, war, and bloodshed, with famine and pestilence, raged everywhere. Other nations were engaged in this war and confusion. War caused famine. Want and bloodshed caused pestilence. And then men's hearts failed them for fear, "and for looking after those things which are coming on the earth." *Testimonies,* vol. 1, p. 268.

## *Spiritual Darkness*

This is a time of spiritual darkness in the churches of the world. Ignorance of divine things has hidden God and the truth from view. The forces of evil are gathering in strength. Satan flatters his coworkers that he will do a work that will captivate the world. While partial inactivity has come upon the church, Satan and his hosts are intensely active. The professed Christian churches are not converting the world; for they are themselves corrupted with selfishness and pride, and need to feel the converting power of God in their midst before they can lead others to a purer or higher standard. *Testimonies,* vol. 9, p. 65.

In our day, as of old, the vital truths of God's word are set aside for human theories and speculations. Many professed ministers of the gospel do not accept the whole Bible as the inspired word. One wise man rejects one portion; another questions another part. They set up their judgment as superior to the Word; and the Scripture which they do teach rests upon their own authority. Its divine authenticity is destroyed. Thus the seeds of infidelity are sown broadcast; for the people become confused, and know not what to believe. There are many beliefs that the mind has no right to entertain. *Christ's Object Lessons,* p. 39.

Wickedness is reaching a height never before attained, and yet many ministers of the gospel are crying, "Peace and safety." But God's faithful messengers are to go steadily forward with their work. Clothed with the panoply of heaven, they are to advance fearlessly and victoriously, never ceasing their warfare until every soul within their reach shall have received the message of truth for this time. *The Acts of the Apostles,* p. 220.

There is a cause for alarm in the condition of the religious world today. God's mercy has been trifled with. The multitude make void the law of Jehovah, "teaching for doctrines the commandments of men." Infidelity prevails in many of the churches in our land; not infidelity in its broadest sense—an open denial of the Bible—but an infidelity that is robed in the garb of Christianity, while it is undermining faith in the Bible as a revelation from God. Fervent devotion and vital piety have given place to hollow formalism. As the result, apostasy and sensualism prevail. Christ declared, "As it was in the days of Lot, . . . even thus shall it be in the day when the Son of man is revealed." The daily record of passing events testifies to the fulfillment of His words. The world is fast becoming ripe for destruction. Soon the judgments of God are to be poured out, and sin and sinners are to be consumed. *Patriarchs and Prophets,* p. 166.

## *Separating the Wheat From the Tares*

The time of God's destructive judgments is the time of mercy for those who have had no opportunity to learn what is truth. Tenderly will the Lord look upon them. His heart of mercy is touched; His hand is still stretched out to save, while the door is closed to those who would not enter. *Testimonies,* vol. 9, p. 97.

Soon the battle will be waged fiercely between those who serve God and those who serve Him not. Soon everything that can be shaken will be shaken, that those things that cannot be shaken may remain. *Testimonies,* vol. 9, pp. 15, 16.

In the time of distress and perplexity of nations there will be many who have not given themselves wholly to the corrupting influences of the world and the service of Satan, who will humble themselves before God and turn to Him with their whole heart and find acceptance and pardon. *Testimonies,* vol. 1, p. 269.

There are many who are reading the Scriptures who cannot understand their true import. All over the world men and women are looking wistfully to heaven. Prayers and tears and inquiries go up from souls longing for light, for grace, for the Holy Spirit. Many are on the verge of the kingdom, waiting only to be gathered in. *The Acts of the Apostles,* p. 109.

## *Lessons From Elijah's Experience*

From Elijah's experience during those days of discouragement and apparent defeat, there are many lessons to be drawn, lessons invaluable to the servants of God in this age, marked as it is by general departure from right. The apostasy prevailing today is similar to that which in the prophet's day overspread Israel. In the exaltation of the human above the divine, in the praise of popular leaders, in the worship of mammon, and in the placing of the teachings of science above the truths of revelation, multitudes today are following after Baal. Doubt and unbelief are exercising their baleful influence over mind and heart, and many are substituting for the oracles of God the theories of men. It is publicly taught that we have reached a time when human reason should be exalted above the teachings of the Word. The law of God, the divine standard of righteousness, is declared to be of no effect. The enemy of all truth is working with deceptive power to cause men and women to place human institutions where God should be, and to forget that which was ordained for the happiness and salvation of mankind. Yet this apostasy, widespread as it has come to be, is not universal. Not all in the world are lawless and sinful; not all have taken sides with the enemy. God has many thousands who have not bowed the knee to Baal, many who long to understand more fully in regard to Christ and the law, many who are hoping against hope that Jesus will come soon to end the reign of sin and death. And there are many who have been worshiping Baal ignorantly, but with whom the Spirit of God is still striving. *Prophets and Kings,* pp. 170, 171.

## CHAPTER 5

# The Church a Training Center

### *The Need of the Hour*
That which is needed now for the upbuilding of our churches is the nice work of wise laborers to discern and develop talent in the church—talent that can be educated for the Master's use. There should be a well-organized plan for the employment of workers to go into all our churches, large and small, to instruct the members how to labor for the upbuilding of the church and also for unbelievers. It is training, education, that is needed. Those who labor in visiting the churches should give the brethren and sisters instruction in practical methods of doing missionary work. *Testimonies,* vol. 9, p. 117.

God expects His church to discipline and fit its members for the work of enlightening the world. An education should be given that would result in furnishing hundreds who would put out to the exchangers valuable talents. By the use of these talents, men would be developed who would be prepared to fill positions of trust and influence, and to maintain pure, uncorrupted principles. Thus great good would be accomplished for the Master. *Testimonies,* vol. 6, pp. 431, 432.

Every worker should be understandingly efficient. Then in a high, broad sense he can present the truth as it is in Jesus. *Testimonies,* vol. 7 p. 70.

There should be no delay in this well-planned effort to educate the church members. *Testimonies,* vol. 9, p. 119.

The greatest help that can be given our people is to teach them to work for God, and to depend on Him, not on the ministers. *Testimonies,* vol. 7, p. 19.

It is evident that all the sermons that have been preached have not developed a large class of self-denying workers. This subject is to be considered as involving the most serious results. Our future for eternity is at stake. The churches are withering up because they have failed to use their talents in diffusing light. Careful instruction should be given which will be as lessons from the Master, that all may put their light to practical use. *Testimonies,* vol. 6, p. 431.

The people have had too much sermonizing; but have they been taught how to labor for those for whom Christ died? Has a line of labor been devised and placed before them in such a way that each has seen the necessity of taking part in the work? *Testimonies,* vol. 6, p. 431.

It is by education and practice that persons are to be qualified to meet any emergency which may arise; and wise planning is needed to place each one in his proper sphere, that he may obtain an experience that will fit him to bear responsibility. *Testimonies,* vol. 9, pp. 221, 222.

## *The Church Missionary Curriculum*

Many would be willing to work if they were taught how to begin. They need to be instructed and encouraged. Every church should be a training school for Christian workers. Its members should be taught how to give Bible readings, how to conduct and teach Sabbath school classes, how best to help the poor and to care for the sick, how to work for the unconverted. There should be schools of health, cooking schools, and classes in various lines of Christian help work. There should not only be teaching, but actual work under experienced instructors. Let the teachers lead the way in working among the people, and others, uniting with them, will learn from their example. One example is worth more than many precepts. *The Ministry of Healing,* p. 149.

## *Special Training*

Greater efforts should be put forth to educate the people in the principles of health reform. Cooking schools should be established, and house-to-house instruction should be given in the art of cooking wholesome food. Old and young should learn how to cook more simply. Wherever the truth is presented, the people are to be taught how to prepare food in a simple, yet appetizing way. They are to be shown that a nourishing diet can be provided without the use of flesh foods. *Testimonies,* vol. 9, p. 161.

In every place where there is a church, instruction should be given in regard to the preparation of simple, wholesome foods, for the use of those who wish to live in accordance with the principles of health. And the church members should impart to the people of their neighborhoods the light they receive on this subject. *Gospel Workers,* p. 362.

## *Adapt the Instruction*

How many useful and honored workers in God's cause have received a training amid the humble duties of the most lowly positions in life! Moses was the prospective ruler of Egypt, but God could not take him from the king's court to do the work appointed him. Only when he had been for forty years a faithful shepherd was he sent to be the deliverer of his people. Gideon was taken from the threshing floor to be the instrument in the hands of God for delivering the armies of Israel. Elisha was called to leave the plow and do the bidding of God. Amos was a husbandman, a tiller of the soil, when God gave him a message to proclaim. All who become coworkers with Christ will have a great deal of hard, uncongenial labor to perform, and their lessons of instruction should be wisely chosen, and adapted to their peculiarities of character, and the work which they are to pursue. *Gospel Workers,* pp. 332, 333.

## *Responsibility for Providing the Training*

When men of promise and ability were converted, as in the case of Timothy, Paul and Barnabas sought earnestly to show them the necessity of laboring in the vineyard. And when the apostles left for another place, the faith of these men did not fail, but rather increased. They had been faithfully instructed in the way of the Lord, and had been taught how to labor unselfishly, earnestly, perseveringly, for the salvation of their fellow men. This careful training of new converts was an important factor in the remarkable success that attended Paul and Barnabas as they preached the gospel in heathen lands. *The Acts of the Apostles,* pp. 186, 187.

As churches are established, it should be set before them that it is even from among them that men must be taken to carry the truth to others and raise new churches; therefore they must all work, and cultivate to the utmost the talents that God has given them, and be training their minds to engage in the service of their Master. *Testimonies,* vol. 3, p. 205.

Missionary operations are constantly embarrassed for want of workers of the right class of mind—workers who have devotion and piety that will correctly represent our faith. There are many who ought to become missionaries, but who never enter the field because those who are united with them in church capacity or in our colleges do not feel the burden to labor with them, to open before them the claims of God upon all their powers, and do not pray with and for them. *Counsels to Teachers, Parents, and Students,* pp. 500, 501.

Those who have the spiritual oversight of the church should devise ways and means by which an opportunity may be given to every member of the church to act some part in God's work. Too often in the past this has not been done. Plans have not been clearly laid and fully carried out whereby the talents of all might be employed in active service. There are but few who realize how much has been lost because of this. *Testimonies,* vol. 9, p. 116.

In every church the members should be so trained that they will devote time to the winning of souls to Christ. How can it be said of the church, "Ye are the light of the world," unless the members of the church are actually imparting light? Let those who have charge of the flock of Christ awake to their duty and set many souls to work. *Testimonies,* vol. 6, p. 436.

## *Select Officers Qualified to Train*

Great care should be exercised in selecting officers for the new churches. Let them be men and women who are thoroughly converted. Let those be chosen who are best qualified to give instruction, those who can minister both in word and in deed. There is a deep-seated necessity for work in every line. *Testimonies,* vol. 6, p. 85.

The elders and those who have leading places in the church should give more thought to their plans for conducting the work. They should arrange matters so that every member of the church shall have a part to act, that none may lead an aimless life, but that all may accomplish what they can according to their several ability. . . . It is very essential that such an education should be given to the members of the church that they will become unselfish, devoted, efficient workers for God; and it is only through such a course that the church can be prevented from becoming fruitless and dead. . . . Let every member of the church become an active worker—a living stone, emitting light in God's temple. *Review and Herald,* Sept. 2, 1890.

## *Church Members to Educate Themselves*

Church members must *work;* they must *educate themselves,* striving to reach the high standard set before them. This the Lord will help them to reach if they will cooperate with Him. *Testimonies,* vol. 9, p. 140.

We should not let slip even one opportunity of qualifying ourselves intellectually to work for God. *Christ's Object Lessons,* p. 334.

## *The Divine Standard*

The Lord desires us to obtain all the education possible, with the object in view of imparting our knowledge to others. None can know where or how they may be called to labor or to speak for God. Our heavenly Father alone sees what He can make of men. There are before us possibilities which our feeble faith does not discern. Our minds should be so trained that if necessary we can present the truths of His word before the highest earthly authorities in such a way as to glorify His name. *Christ's Object Lessons,* pp. 333, 334.

Who have been preparing themselves to go and work in His vineyard? God is not pleased with novices. He wants us to make the very best and highest use that is possible of the talents that He has given us. *Review and Herald,* Apr. 2, 1889.

## *Illustration*

I had dreamed that a person brought to me a web of white cloth, and bade me cut it into garments for persons of all sizes, and all descriptions of character, and circumstances in life. I was told to cut them out and hang them up all ready to be made when called for. I had the impression that many for whom I was required to cut garments were unworthy. I inquired if that was the last piece of cloth I should have to cut, and was told that it was not; that as soon as I had finished this one, there were others for me to take hold of.

I felt discouraged at the amount of work before me, and stated that I had been engaged in cutting garments for others for more than twenty years, and my labors had not been appreciated, neither did I see that my work had accomplished much good. I spoke to the person who brought the cloth to me, of one woman in particular, for whom he had told me to cut a garment. I stated that she would not prize the garment, and that it would be a loss of time and material to present it to her. She was very poor, of inferior intellect, and untidy in her habits, and would soon soil it. The person replied: "Cut out the garments. That is your duty. The loss is not yours, but mine. God sees not as man sees. He lays out the work that He would have done, and you do not know which will prosper, this or that. It will be found that many such poor souls will go into the kingdom, while others, who are favored with all the blessings of life, having good intellects and pleasant surroundings, giving them all the advantages of improvement, will be left out. *Testimonies,* vol. 2, pp. 10, 11.

For hours soldiers are drilled to disencumber themselves of their knapsacks and place them quickly in position again upon the person. They are taught how to stack their arms, and how to seize them quickly. They are drilled in making a charge against the enemy and are trained in all kinds of maneuvers. Thus the drill goes on, preparing men for any emergency. And should those who are fighting the battle for Prince Emmanuel be less earnest and painstaking in their preparation for the spiritual warfare? *Gospel Workers,* p. 75.

## CHAPTER 6

# Students to Do Missionary Work While in Training

### Object of Education

True education is missionary training. Every son and daughter of God is called to be a missionary; we are called to the service of God and our fellow men; and to fit us for this service should be the object of our education. *The Ministry of Healing,* p. 395.

It is to fortify the youth against the temptations of the enemy that we have established schools where they may be qualified for usefulness in this life and for the service of God throughout eternity. *Counsels to Parents, Teachers, and Students,* p. 495.

He who strives to obtain knowledge in order that he may labor for the ignorant and perishing, is acting his part in fulfilling God's great purpose for mankind. In unselfish service for the blessing of others he is meeting the high ideal of Christian education. *Counsels to Parents, Teachers, and Students,* p. 545.

The Lord calls for strong, devoted, self-sacrificing young men and women, who will press to the front, and who, after a short time spent in school, will go forth prepared to give the message to the world. *Counsels to Parents, Teachers, and Students,* p. 549.

### Learning by Doing

It is necessary to their complete education that students be given time to do missionary work—time to become acquainted with the spiritual needs of the families in the community around them. They should not be so loaded down with studies that they have no time to use the knowledge they have acquired. They should be encouraged to make earnest missionary effort for those in error, becoming acquainted with them, and taking to them the truth. By working in humility, seeking wisdom from Christ, praying and watching unto prayer, they may give to others the knowledge that has enriched their lives. *Counsels to Parents, Teachers, and Students,* pp. 545, 546.

Wherever possible, students should, during the school year, engage in city mission work. They should do missionary work in the surrounding towns and villages. They can form themselves into bands to do Christian help work. Students should take a broad view of their present obligations to God. They are not to look forward to a time, after the school term closes, when they will do some large work for God, but should study how, during their student life, to yoke up with Christ in unselfish service for others. *Counsels to Parents, Teachers, and Students,* p. 547.

It is not enough to fill the minds of the youth with lessons of deep importance; they must learn to impart what they have received. *Counsels to Parents, Teachers, and Students,* p. 545.

From our colleges and training schools missionaries are to be sent forth to distant lands. While they are at school, let the students improve every opportunity to prepare for this work. Here they are to be tested and proved, that it may be seen what their adaptability is, and whether they have a right hold from above. *Counsels to Parents, Teachers, and Students,* p. 549.

## *Encourage a Missionary Spirit*

The teachers and students in our schools need the divine touch. God can do much more for them than He has done, because in the past His way has been restricted. If a missionary spirit is encouraged, even if it takes some hours from the program of regular study, much of Heaven's blessing will be given, provided there is more faith and spiritual zeal, more of a realization of what God will do. *Counsels to Parents, Teachers, and Students,* p. 546.

## *When School Closes*

When school closes, there is opportunity for many to go out into the field as evangelistic canvassers. The faithful colporteur finds his way into many homes, where he leaves reading matter containing the truth for this time. Our students should learn how to sell our books. There is need of men of deep Christian experience, men of well-balanced minds, strong, well-educated men, to engage in this branch of the work. Some have the talent, education, and experience that would enable them to educate the youth for canvassing work in such a way that much more would be accomplished than is now being done. Those who have this experience have a special duty to perform in teaching others. *Counsels to Parents, Teachers, and Students,* pp. 546, 547.

## *The Ministry of Song*

Students who have learned to sing sweet gospel songs with melody and distinctness, can do much good as singing evangelists. They will find many opportunities to use the talent that God has given them in carrying melody and sunshine into many lonely places darkened by sorrow and affliction, singing to those who seldom have church privileges.

Students, go out into the highways and hedges. Endeavor to reach the higher as well as the lower classes. Enter the homes of the rich as well as the poor, and as you have opportunity, ask, "Would you be pleased to have us sing some gospel hymns?" Then as hearts are softened, the way may open for you to offer a few words of prayer for the blessing of God. Not many will refuse to listen. Such ministry is genuine missionary work. *Counsels to Parents, Teachers, and Students,* pp. 547, 548.

# CHAPTER 7

# Cooperation of Ministers and Laymen

## *Unitedly Enter the Field of Service*

Let ministers and lay members go forth into the ripening fields. They will find their harvest wherever they proclaim the forgotten truths of the Bible. They will find those who will accept the truth, and who will devote their lives to winning souls to Christ. *Signs of the Times* (Australian), Aug. 3, 1903.

It is not the Lord's purpose that ministers should be left to do the greatest part of the work of sowing the seeds of truth. Men who are not called to the ministry are to be encouraged to labor for the Master according to their several ability. Hundreds of men and women now idle could do acceptable service. By carrying the truth into the homes of their friends and neighbors, they could do a great work for the Master. *Testimonies,* vol. 7, p. 21.

God has given His ministers the message of truth to proclaim. This the churches are to receive, and in every possible way to communicate, catching the first rays of light and diffusing them. *Testimonies,* vol. 6, p. 425.

The people must lift where the minister lifts, thus seconding his efforts and helping him bear his burdens, and then he will not be overworked and become discouraged. There is no influence that can be brought to bear on a church that will be enduring unless the people shall move intelligently, from principle, to do all they can to forward the work. *Review and Herald,* Aug. 23, 1881.

## *A Convincing Combination*

The world will be convinced, not by what the pulpit teaches, but by what the church lives. The minister in the desk announces the theory of the gospel; the practical piety of the church demonstrates its power. *Testimonies,* vol. 7, p. 16.

The work of God in this earth can never be finished until the men and women comprising our church membership rally to the work and unite their efforts with those of ministers and church officers. *Gospel Workers,* p. 352.

Preaching is a small part of the work to be done for the salvation of souls. God's Spirit convicts sinners of the truth, and He places them in the arms of the church. The ministers may do their part, but they can never perform the work that the church should do. *Testimonies,* vol. 4, p. 69.

The dissemination of the truth of God is not confined to a few ordained ministers. The truth is to be scattered by all who claim to be disciples of Christ. It must be sown beside all waters. *Review and Herald,* Aug. 22, 1899.

Ministers may preach pleasing and forcible discourses, and much labor may be put forth to build up and make the church prosperous; but unless its individual members shall act their part as servants of Jesus Christ, the church will ever be in darkness and without strength. Hard and dark as the world is, the influence of a really consistent example will be a power for good. *Testimonies,* vol. 4, pp. 285, 286.

## *A Fatal Mistake*

It is a fatal mistake to suppose that the work of soulsaving depends alone upon the ministry. The humble, consecrated believer upon whom the Master of the vineyard places a burden for souls, is to be given encouragement by the men upon whom the Lord has laid larger responsibilities. Those who stand as leaders in the church of God are to realize that the Saviour's commission is given to all who believe in His name. God will send forth into His vineyard many who have not been dedicated to the ministry by the laying on of hands. *The Acts of the Apostles,* p. 110.

The idea that the minister must carry all the burdens and do all the work is a great mistake. Overworked and broken down, he may go into the grave, when, had the burden been shared as the Lord designed, he might have lived. That the burden may be distributed, an education must be given to the church by those who can teach the workers to follow Christ and to work as He worked. *Testimonies,* vol. 6, p. 435.

The minister should not feel that it is his duty to do all the talking and all the laboring and all the praying; he should educate helpers in every church. Let different ones take turns in leading the meetings, and in giving Bible readings; in so doing they will be calling into use the talents which God has given them, and at the same time be receiving a training as workers. *Gospel Workers,* p. 197.

Ministers should not do the work which belongs to the church, thus wearying themselves, and preventing others from performing their duty. They should teach the members how to labor in the church and in the community. *Historical Sketches,* p. 291.

When an effort is made to present our faith to unbelievers, the members of the church too often stand back, as if they were not an interested party, and let all the burden rest upon the minister. For this reason the labor of our most able ministers has been at times productive of little good. *Gospel Workers,* p. 196.

## *The Minister's Duty*

The best help that ministers can give the members of our churches is not sermonizing, but planning work for them. Give each one something to do for others. Help all to see that as receivers of the grace of Christ they are under obligation to work for Him. And let all be taught how to work. Especially should those who are newly come to the faith be educated to become laborers together with God. *Testimonies,* vol. 9, p. 82.

Ministers, preach the truths that will lead to personal labor for those who are out of Christ. Encourage personal effort in every possible way. *Testimonies,* vol. 9, p. 124.

Let ministers teach church members that in order to grow in spirituality, they must carry the burden that the Lord has laid upon them—the burden of leading souls into the truth. Those who are not fulfilling their responsibility should be visited, prayed with, labored for. Do not lead people to depend upon you as ministers; teach them rather that they are to use their talents in giving the truth to those around them. In thus working they will have the cooperation of heavenly angels, and will obtain an experience that will increase their faith, and give them a strong hold on God. *Gospel Workers,* p. 200.

In laboring where there are already some in the faith, the minister should at first seek not so much to convert unbelievers, as to train the church members for acceptable cooperation. Let him labor for them individually, endeavoring to arouse them to seek for a deeper experience themselves, and to work for others. When they are prepared to sustain the minister by their prayers and labors, greater success will attend his efforts. *Gospel Workers,* p. 196.

In some respects the pastor occupies a position similar to that of the foreman of a gang of laboring men or the captain of a ship's crew. They are expected to see that the men over whom they are set do the work assigned to them correctly and promptly, and only in case of emergency are they to execute in detail. The owner of a large mill once found his superintendent in a wheel-pit, making some simple repairs, while a half-dozen workmen in that line were standing by, idly looking on. The proprietor, after learning the facts, so as to be sure that no injustice was done, called the foreman to his office and handed him his discharge with full pay. In surprise the foreman asked for an explanation. It was given in these words: "I employed you to keep six men at work. I found the six idle, and you doing the work of but one. Your work could have been done just as well by any one of the six. I cannot afford to pay the wages of seven for you to teach the six how to be idle."

This incident may be applicable in some cases, and in others not. But many pastors fail in not knowing how, or in not trying, to get the full membership of the church actively engaged in the various departments of church work. If pastors would give more attention to getting and keeping their flock actively engaged at work, they would accomplish more good, have more time for study and religious visiting, and also avoid many causes of friction. *Gospel Workers,* pp. 197, 198.

## *A Good Example*

The apostle [Paul] felt that he was to a large extent responsible for the spiritual welfare of those converted under his labors. His desire for them was that they might increase in a knowledge of the only true God, and Jesus Christ, whom He had sent. Often in his ministry he would meet with little companies of men and women who loved Jesus, and bow with them in prayer, asking God to teach them how to maintain a living connection with Him. *Often he took counsel with them as to the best methods of giving to others the light of gospel truth.* And often, when separated from those for whom he had thus labored, he pleaded with God to keep them from evil, and help them to be earnest, active missionaries. *The Acts of the Apostles,* p. 262.

# CHAPTER 8

# Organizing Christian Forces

### Organization Essential

Time is short, and our forces must be organized to do a larger work. *Testimonies,* vol. 9, p. 27.

The formation of small companies as a basis of Christian effort has been presented to me by One who cannot err. *Testimonies,* vol. 7, pp. 21, 22.

Let there be in every church, well-organized companies of workers to labor in the vicinity of that church. *Review and Herald,* Sept. 29, 1891.

In every city there should be a corps of organized, well-disciplined workers; not merely one or two, but scores should be set to work. *General Conference Bulletin,* 1893, p. 37.

In our churches let companies be formed for service. Let different ones unite in labor as fishers of men. Let them seek to gather souls from the corruption of the world into the saving purity of Christ's love. *Testimonies,* vol. 7, p. 21.

The church of Christ on earth was organized for missionary purposes, and the Lord desires to see the entire church devising ways and means whereby high and low, rich and poor, may hear the message of truth. *Testimonies,* vol. 6, p. 29.

If there is a large number in the church, let the members be formed into small companies, to work not only for the church members, but for unbelievers. If in one place there are only two or three who know the truth, let them form themselves into a band of workers. *Testimonies,* vol. 7, p. 22.

If discipline and order are necessary for successful action on the battlefield, the same are as much more needful in the warfare in which we are engaged as the object to be gained is of greater value and more elevated in character, than those for which opposing forces contend upon the field of battle. In the conflict in which we are engaged, eternal interests are at stake. *Testimonies,* vol. 1, p. 649.

God is a God of order. Everything connected with heaven is in perfect order; subjection and thorough discipline mark the movements of the angelic host. Success can only attend order and harmonious action. God requires order and system in His work now no less than in the days of Israel. All who are working for Him are to labor intelligently, not in a careless, haphazard manner. He would have His work done with faith and exactness, that He may place the seal of His approval upon it. *Patriarchs and Prophets,* p. 376.

Well-organized work must be done in the church, that its members may understand how to impart the light to others, and thus strengthen their own faith and increase their knowledge. As they impart that which they have received from God they will be confirmed in the faith. A working church is a living church. We are built up as living stones, and every stone is to emit light. Every Christian is compared to a precious stone that catches the glory of God and reflects it. *Testimonies,* vol. 6, p. 435.

## *Lessons in Perfect Organization*

He [God] designs that we should learn lessons of order and organization from the perfect order instituted in the days of Moses, for the benefit of the children of Israel. *Testimonies,* vol. 1, p. 653.

## *First Step in Church Organization*

It was at the ordination of the twelve that the first step was taken in the organization of the church that after Christ's departure was to carry on His work on the earth. *The Acts of the Apostles,* p. 18.

## *Model Church Organization*

The organization of the church at Jerusalem was to serve as a model for the organization of churches in every other place where messengers of truth should win converts to the gospel. . . . Later in the history of the early church, when in various parts of the world many groups of believers had been formed into churches, the organization of the church was further perfected, so that order and harmonious action might be maintained. Every member was exhorted to act well his part. Each was to make a wise use of the talents intrusted to him. *The Acts of the Apostles,* pp. 91, 92.

## *Fitting Each Into His Place*

Every one who is added to the ranks by conversion is to be assigned his post of duty. Every one should be willing to be or to do anything in this warfare. *Testimonies,* vol. 7, p. 30.

It is not numerous institutions, large buildings, or great display that God requires, but the harmonious action of a peculiar people, a people chosen by God and precious. Every man is to stand in his lot and place, thinking, speaking, and acting in harmony with the Spirit of God. Then, and not till then, will the work be a complete, symmetrical whole. *Testimonies,* vol. 6, p. 293.

The strength of an army is measured largely by the efficiency of the men in the ranks. A wise general instructs his officers to train every soldier for active service. He seeks to develop the highest efficiency on the part of all. If he were to depend on his officers alone, he could never expect to conduct a successful campaign. He counts on loyal and untiring service from every man in his army. The responsibility rests largely upon the men in the ranks. *Testimonies,* vol. 9, p. 116.

The Master calls for gospel workers. Who will respond? Not all who enter the army are to be generals, captains, sergeants, or even corporals. Not all have the care and responsibility of leaders. There is hard work of other kinds to be done. Some must dig trenches and build fortifications; some are to stand as sentinels; some to carry messages. While there are but few officers, it requires many soldiers to form the rank and file of the army; yet its success depends upon the fidelity of every soldier. One man's cowardice or treachery may bring disaster upon the entire army. *Gospel Workers,* pp. 84, 85.

## *The Secret of Success*

The secret of our success in the work of God will be found in the harmonious working of our people. There must be concentrated action. Every member of the body of Christ must act his part in the cause of God, according to the ability that God has given him. We must press together against obstructions and difficulties, shoulder to shoulder, heart to heart. *Review and Herald,* Dec. 2, 1890.

If Christians were to act in concert, moving forward as one, under the direction of one Power, for the accomplishment of one purpose, they would move the world. *Testimonies,* vol. 9, p. 221.

Angels work harmoniously. Perfect order characterizes all their movements. The more closely we imitate the harmony and order of the angelic host, the more successful will be the efforts of these heavenly agents in our behalf. If we see no necessity for harmonious action, and are disorderly, undisciplined, and disorganized in our course of action, angels, who are thoroughly organized and move in perfect order, cannot work for us successfully. They turn away in grief, for they are not authorized to bless confusion, distraction, and disorganization. All who desire the cooperation of the heavenly messengers, must work in unison with them. Those who have the unction from on high will in all their efforts encourage order, discipline, and union of action, and then the angels of God can cooperate with them. But never, never will these heavenly messengers place their indorsement upon irregularity, disorganization, and disorder. *Testimonies,* vol. 1, pp. 649, 650.

## *Timely Warning*

There is need of systematic labor; but where some of you are so long in devising, and planning, and getting ready for the work, Satan preoccupies the field with bewitching fables, and the attention of men becomes absorbed in the delusions of the master deceiver. *Review and Herald,* Mar. 13, 1888.

O how Satan would rejoice if he could succeed in his efforts to get in among this people, and disorganize the work at a time when thorough organization is essential, and will be the greatest power to keep out spurious uprisings, and to refute claims not indorsed by the Word of God! We want to hold the lines evenly, that there shall be no breaking down of the system of organization and order that has been built up by wise, careful labor. License must not be given to disorderly elements that desire to control the work at this time. *Gospel Workers,* p. 487.

# CHAPTER 9

# The Call to Arouse

### *The Summons*
Let the gospel message ring through our churches, summoning them to universal action. Let the members of the church have increased faith, gaining zeal from their unseen, heavenly allies, from a knowledge of their exhaustless resources, from the greatness of the enterprise in which they are engaged, and from the power of their Leader. Those who place themselves under God's control, to be led and guided by Him, will catch the steady tread of the events ordained by Him to take place. Inspired with the Spirit of Him who gave His life for the life of the world, they will no longer stand still in impotency, pointing to what they cannot do. Putting on the armor of heaven, they will go forth to the warfare, willing to do and dare for God, knowing that His omnipotence will supply their need. *Testimonies,* vol. 7, p. 14.

Let us arouse! The battle is waging. Truth and error are nearing their final conflict. Let us march under the blood-stained banner of Prince Emmanuel, and fight the good fight of faith, and win eternal honors; for the truth will triumph, and we may be more than conquerors through Him who has loved us. The precious hours of probation are closing. Let us make sure work for eternal life, that we may glorify our heavenly Father, and be the means of saving souls for whom Christ died. *Review and Herald,* Mar. 13, 1888.

### *Marching Orders*
The duke of Wellington was once present where a party of Christian men were discussing the possibility of success in missionary effort among the heathen. They appealed to the duke to say whether in his judgment such efforts were likely to prove a success commensurate to the cost. The old soldier replied: "Gentlemen, what are your marching orders? Success is not the question for you to discuss. If I read your orders aright, they run thus, 'Go ye into all

the world, and preach the gospel to every creature.' Gentlemen, obey your marching orders." *Gospel Workers,* p. 115.

## *No Time for Delay*

"The great day of the Lord is near, it is near, and hasteth greatly." Zeph. 1:14. Let us be shod with the gospel shoes, ready to march at a moment's notice. *Testimonies,* vol. 9, p. 48.

Church members . . . are to be ever ready to spring into action in obedience to the Master's commands. Wherever we see work waiting to be done we are to take it up and do it, constantly looking unto Jesus. . . . If every church member were a living missionary, the gospel would speedily be proclaimed in all countries, to all peoples, nations, and tongues. *Testimonies,* vol. 9, p. 32.

We are nearing the close of this earth's history. We have before us a great work, the closing work of giving the last warning message to a sinful world. There are men who will be taken from the plow, from the vineyard, from various other branches of work, and sent forth by the Lord to give this message to the world. *Testimonies,* vol. 7, pp. 270, 271.

Sound an alarm throughout the length and breadth of the earth. Tell the people that the day of the Lord is near and hasteth greatly. Let none be left unwarned. We might have been in the place of the poor souls that are in error. We might have been placed among barbarians. According to the truth we have received above others, we are debtors to impart the same to them. *Testimonies,* vol. 6, p. 22.

My brethren and sisters, it is too late to devote your time and strength to self-serving. Let not the last day find you destitute of the heavenly treasure. Seek to push the triumphs of the cross, seek to enlighten souls, labor for the salvation of your fellow beings, and your work will abide the trying test of fire. *Testimonies,* vol. 9, p. 56.

We must give this message quickly, line upon line, precept upon precept. Men will soon be forced to great decisions, and it is our duty to see that they are given an opportunity to understand the truth, that they may take their stand intelligently on the right side. The Lord calls upon His people to labor—labor earnestly and wisely—while probation lingers. *Testimonies,* vol. 9, pp. 126, 127.

We have no time to lose. The end is near. The passage from place to place to spread the truth will soon be hedged with dangers on the right hand and on the left. Everything will be placed to obstruct the way of the Lord's messengers, so that they will not be able to do that which it is possible for them to do now. We must look our work fairly in the face and advance as fast as possible in aggressive warfare. From the light given me of God I know that the powers of darkness are working with intense energy from beneath, and with stealthy tread Satan is advancing to take those who are now asleep, as a wolf taking his prey. We have warnings now which we may give, a work now which we may do; but soon it will be more difficult than we can imagine. God help us to keep in the channel of light, to work with our eyes fastened on Jesus our leader, and patiently, perseveringly press on to gain the victory. *Testimonies,* vol. 6, p. 22.

There is danger in delay. That soul whom you might have found, that soul to whom you might have opened the Scriptures, passes beyond your reach. Satan has prepared some net for his feet, and tomorrow he may be working out the plans of the archenemy of God. Why delay one day? Why not go to work at once? *Testimonies,* vol. 6, p. 443.

Vigilance and fidelity have been required of Christ's followers in every age; but now that we are standing upon the very verge of the eternal world, holding the truths we do, having so great light, so important a work, we must double our diligence. Every one is to do to the very utmost of his ability. My brother, you endanger your own salvation if you hold back now. God will call you to account if you fail in the work He has assigned you. *Testimonies,* vol. 5, pp. 460, 461.

## Important Questions

Eternity stretches before us. The curtain is about to be lifted. What are we thinking of, that we cling to our selfish love of ease, while all around us souls are perishing?

Have our hearts become utterly callous?

Can we not see and understand that we have a work to do in behalf of others?

My brethren and sisters, are you among those who, having eyes, see not, and having ears, hear not?

Is it in vain that God has given you a knowledge of His will?

Is it in vain that He has sent you warning after warning of the nearness of the end?

Do you believe the declarations of His word concerning what is coming upon the world?

Do you believe that God's judgments are hanging over the inhabitants of the earth?

How, then, can you sit at ease, careless and indifferent? *Testimonies,* vol. 9, pp. 26, 27.

## The Call to Awake

The work is fast closing up, and on every side wickedness is increasing. We have but a short time in which to work. Let us awake from spiritual slumber, and consecrate all that we have and are to the Lord. His Spirit will abide with true missionaries, furnishing them with power for service. *Southern Watchman,* Apr. 9, 1903.

Wake up, brethren and sisters, wake up. Sleep no longer. "Why stand ye here all the day idle?" Jesus calls you, saying, "Go work today in My vineyard." Whoever has received the Holy Spirit, will make it manifest; for all his powers will be employed in the most active service. All who actually receive Christ by faith, work. They feel the burden of souls. God now calls upon everyone who has a knowledge of the truth, who is a depositary of sacred truth, to arise and impart the light of heaven to others. *Review and Herald,* Dec. 6, 1893.

Wake up, brethren; for your own soul's sake, wake up. Without the grace of Christ you can do nothing. Work while you can. *Southern Watchman,* July 17, 1906.

If our eyes could be opened to discern the fallen angels at work with those who feel at ease and consider themselves safe, we would not feel so secure. Evil angels are upon our track every moment. *Testimonies,* vol. 1, p. 302.

God calls upon all, both preachers and people, to awake. All heaven is astir. The scenes of earth's history are fast closing. We are amid the perils of the last days. Greater perils are before us, and yet we are not awake. This lack of activity and earnestness in the cause of God is dreadful. This death stupor is from Satan. *Testimonies,* vol. 1, pp. 260, 261.

What shall I say to arouse the remnant people of God? I was shown that dreadful scenes are before us; Satan and his angels are bringing all their powers to bear upon God's people. He knows that if they sleep a little longer, he is sure of them, for their destruction is certain. *Testimonies,* vol. 1, p. 263.

In these final hours of probation for the sons of men, when the fate of every soul is so soon to be decided forever, the Lord of heaven and earth expects His church to arouse to action as never before. Those who have been made free in Christ through a knowledge of precious truth, are regarded by the Lord Jesus as His chosen ones, favored above all other people on the face of the earth; and He is counting on them to show forth the praises of Him who hath called them out of darkness into marvelous light. The blessings which are so liberally bestowed, are to be communicated to others. The good news of salvation is to go to every nation, kindred, tongue, and people. *Prophets and Kings,* pp. 716, 717.

Not one in a hundred among us is doing anything beyond engaging in common, worldly enterprises. We are not half awake to the worth of the souls for whom Christ died. *Testimonies,* vol. 8, p. 148.

If the followers of Christ were awake to duty, there would be thousands where there is one today, proclaiming the gospel in heathen lands. And all who could not personally engage in the work would yet sustain it with their means, their sympathy, and their prayers. And there would be far more earnest labor for souls in Christian countries. *Steps to Christ,* p. 81.

Thousands enjoy great light and precious opportunities, but do nothing with their influence or their money to enlighten others. They do not even take the responsibility of keeping their own souls in the love of God, that they may not become a burden to the church. Such ones would be a burden and a clog in heaven. For Christ's sake, for the truth's sake, for their own sakes, such should arouse and make diligent work for eternity. *Review and Herald,* March 1, 1887.

The church of Christ may be fitly compared to an army. The life of every soldier is one of toil, hardship, and danger. On every hand are vigilant foes, led on by the prince of the powers of darkness, who never slumbers and never deserts his post. Whenever a Christian is off his guard, this powerful adversary makes a sudden and violent attack. Unless the members of the church are active and vigilant, they will be overcome by his devices.

What if half the soldiers in an army were idling or asleep when ordered to be on duty; the result would be defeat, captivity, or death. Should any escape from the hands of the enemy, would they be thought worthy of a reward? No; they would speedily receive the sentence of death. And is the church of Christ careless or unfaithful, far more important consequences are involved. A sleeping army of Christian soldiers—what could be more terrible? What advance could be made against the world, who are under the control of the prince of darkness? Those who stand back indifferently in the day of battle, as though they had no interest and felt no responsibility as to the issue of the contest, might better change their course or leave the ranks at once. *Testimonies,* vol. 5, p. 394.

## *There Must Be Action*

I was shown God's people waiting for some change to take place—a compelling power to take hold of them. But they will be disappointed, for they are wrong. They must act; they must take hold of the work themselves, and earnestly cry to God for a true knowledge of themselves. The scenes which are passing before us are of sufficient magnitude to cause us to arouse and urge the truth home to the hearts of all who will listen. The harvest of the earth is nearly ripe. *Testimonies,* vol. 1, p. 261.

Everything in the universe calls upon those who know the truth to consecrate themselves unreservedly to the proclamation of the truth as it has been made known to them in the third angel's message. That which we see and hear calls us to our duty. The working of satanic agencies calls every Christian to stand in his lot. *Testimonies,* vol. 9, pp. 25, 26.

The message of Christ's soon coming is to be given to all the nations of the earth. Vigilant, untiring effort is required to overcome the forces of the enemy. Our part is not to sit still and weep and wring our hands, but to arise and work for time and for eternity. *Southern Watchman,* May 29, 1902.

"Do something, do it soon, with all thy might;
 An angel's wing would droop if long at rest;
 And God Himself, inactive, were no longer blest."

*Testimonies,* vol. 5, p. 308.

Let no one think that he is at liberty to fold his hands and do nothing. That anyone can be saved in indolence and inactivity is an utter impossibility. Think of what Christ accomplished during His earthly ministry. How earnest, how untiring, were His efforts! He allowed nothing to turn Him aside from the work given Him. Are we following in His footsteps? *Colporteur Evangelist,* p. 38.

Divine and human agencies are combined in the work of saving souls. God has done His part, and Christian activity is needed now. God calls for this. He expects His people to bear a part in presenting the light of truth to all nations. Who will enter into this partnership with the Lord Jesus Christ? *Review and Herald,* Mar. 1, 1887.

The church must be a working church if it would be a living church. It should not be content merely to hold its own ground against the opposing forces of sin and error, not be content to advance with dilatory step, but it should bear the yoke of Christ, and keep step with the Leader, gaining new recruits along the way. *Review and Herald,* Aug. 4, 1891.

We have only a little while to urge the warfare; then Christ will come, and this scene of rebellion will close. Then our last efforts will have been made to work with Christ and advance His kingdom. Some who have stood in the forefront of the battle, zealously resisting incoming evil, fall at the post of duty; others gaze sorrowfully at the fallen heroes, but have no time to cease work. They must close up the ranks, seize the banner from the hand palsied by death, and with renewed energy vindicate the truth and the honor of Christ. As never before, resistance must be made against sin—against the powers of darkness. The time demands energetic and determined activity on the part of those who believe present truth. They should teach the truth by both precept and example. *Review and Herald,* Oct. 25, 1881.

The Lord now calls upon Seventh-day Adventists in every locality to consecrate themselves to Him, and to do their very best, according to their circumstances, to assist in His work. *Testimonies,* vol. 9, p. 132.

Idleness and religion do not go hand in hand; and the cause of our great deficiency in the Christian life and experience is inactivity in the work of God. The muscles of your body will become weak and useless if they are not kept in exercise, and it is so with the spiritual nature. If you would be strong, you must exercise your powers. *Review and Herald,* Mar., 13, 1888.

We are to be diligent workers; an idle man is a miserable creature. But what excuse can be offered for idleness in the great work which Christ gave His life to accomplish? The spiritual faculties cease to exist if they are not exercised, and it is Satan's design that they shall perish. All heaven is actively engaged in the work of preparing a people for the second coming of Christ to our world, and "we are laborers together with God." The end of all things is at hand. Now is our opportunity to work. *Review and Herald,* Jan. 24, 1893.

It is heart missionaries that are needed. Spasmodic efforts will do little good. We must arrest the attention. We must be deeply in earnest. *Testimonies,* vol. 9, p. 45.

There are among us those who, if they would take time to consider, would regard their do-nothing position as a sinful neglect of their God-given talents. *Testimonies,* vol. 6, p. 425.

What is our position in the world? We are in the waiting time. But this period is not to be spent in abstract devotion. Waiting, watching, and vigilant working are to be combined. Our life should not be all bustle and drive and planning about the things of the world, to the neglect of personal piety and of the service that God requires. While we should not be slothful in business, we should be fervent in spirit, serving the Lord. The lamp of the soul must be trimmed, and we must have the oil of grace in our vessels with our lamps. Every precaution must be used to prevent spiritual declension, lest the day of the Lord overtake us as a thief. *Testimonies,* vol. 5, p. 276.

We are living in an age when there is to be no spiritual idleness. Every soul is to be charged with the heavenly current of life. *Testimonies,* vol. 8, p. 169.

Crowd all the good works you possibly can into this life. *Testimonies,* vol. 5, p. 488.

Jesus would have all who profess His name become earnest workers. It is necessary that every individual member build upon the rock, Christ Jesus. A storm is arising that will wrench and test the spiritual foundation of everyone to the utmost. Therefore avoid the sand bed; hunt for the rock. Dig deep; lay your foundation sure. Build, oh, build for eternity! Build with tears, with heartfelt prayers. Let every one of you, from henceforth, make your life beautiful by good works. Calebs are the men most needed in these last days. *Testimonies,* vol. 5, pp. 129, 130.

## *The Divine Measurement*

There is a measurement of character constantly going on. The angels of God are estimating your moral value, and ascertaining your needs, and bearing your case to God. *Review and Herald,* Apr. 2, 1889.

We shall individually be held responsible for doing one jot less than we have ability to do. The Lord measures with exactness every possibility for service. The unused capabilities are as much brought into account as are those that are improved. For all that we might become through the right use of our talents God holds us responsible. We shall be judged according to what we ought to have done but did not accomplish because we did not use our powers to glorify God. Even if we do not lose our souls, we shall realize in eternity the result of our unused talents. For all the knowledge and ability that we might have gained and did not, there will be an eternal loss. *Christ's Object Lessons,* p. 363.

## *What Might Have Been*

If every soldier of Christ had done his duty, if every watchman on the walls of Zion had given the trumpet a certain sound, the world might ere this have heard the message of warning. But the work is years behind. While men have slept, Satan has stolen a march upon us. *Testimonies,* vol. 9, p. 29.

Let us now take up the work appointed us, and proclaim the message that is to arouse men and women to a sense of their danger. If every Seventh-day Adventist had done the work laid upon him, the number of believers would now be much larger than it is. In all the cities of America there would be those who had been led to heed the message to obey the law of God. *Testimonies,* vol. 9, p. 25.

Had the purpose of God been carried out by His people in giving to the world the message of mercy, Christ would, ere this, have come to the earth, and the saints would have received their welcome into the city of God. *Testimonies,* vol. 6, p. 450.

## *Heaven's Register*

The world needs missionaries, consecrated home missionaries, and no one will be registered in the books of heaven as a Christian who has not a missionary spirit. *Review and Herald,* Aug. 23, 1892.

If the church members do not individually take hold of this work, then they show that they have no living connection with God. Their names are registered as slothful servants. *Testimonies,* vol. 5, pp. 462, 463.

In every religious movement there are some who, while they cannot deny that the cause is God's, still hold themselves aloof, refusing to make any effort to help. It were well for such ones to remember the record kept on high—that book in which there are no omissions, no mistakes, and out of which they will be judged. There every neglected opportunity to do service for God is recorded; and there, too, every deed of faith and love is held in everlasting remembrance. *Prophets and Kings,* p. 639.

On the morning of Oct. 23, 1879, about two o'clock, the Spirit of the Lord rested upon me, and I beheld scenes in the coming judgment. . . . Ten thousand times ten thousand were assembled before a large throne, upon which was seated a person of majestic appearance. Several books were before Him, and upon the covers of each was written in letters of gold, which seemed like a burning flame of fire: "Ledger of Heaven." One of these books, containing the names of those who claim to believe the truth, was then opened. Immediately I lost sight of the countless millions about the throne, and only those who were professedly children of the light and of the truth engaged my attention. . . .

Another book was opened, wherein were recorded the *sins* of those who profess the truth. Under the general heading of selfishness came every other sin. . . . One class were registered as cumberers of the ground. As the piercing eye of the Judge rested upon these, their sins of neglect were distinctly revealed. With pale, quivering lips they acknowledged that they had been traitors to their holy trust. They had had warnings and privileges but they had not heeded nor improved them. They could now see that they had presumed too much upon the mercy of God. True, they had not such confessions to make as had the vile and basely corrupt; but, like the fig tree, they were cursed because they bore no fruit, because they had not put to use the talents intrusted to them. This class had made *self* supreme, laboring only for selfish interests. They were not rich toward God, not having responded to His claims upon them. Although professing to be servants of Christ, they brought no souls to Him. Had the cause of God been dependent on their efforts, it would have languished; for they not only withheld the means lent them of God, but they withheld themselves. . . . They had allowed others to do the work in the Master's vineyard, and to bear the heaviest responsibilities, while they were selfishly serving their own temporal interests. . . .

Said the Judge: "All will be justified by their faith, and judged by their works." How vividly then appeared their neglect, and how wise the arrangement of God in giving to every man a work to do to promote the cause and save his fellow men. Each was to demonstrate a living faith in his family and in his neighborhood, by showing kindness to the poor, sympathizing with the afflicted, engaging in missionary labor, and by aiding the cause of God with his means. But, like Meroz, the curse of God rested upon them for what they had not done. They had loved that work which would bring the greatest profit in this life; and opposite their names in the ledger devoted to good works there was a mournful blank. *Testimonies,* vol. 4, pp. 384-386.

### *More Required of Us Than of Our Fathers*

Greater light shines upon us than shone upon our fathers. We cannot be accepted or honored of God in rendering the same service, or doing the same works, that our fathers did. In order to be accepted and blessed of God as they were, we must imitate their faithfulness and zeal—improve our light as they improved theirs, and do as they would have done had they lived in our day. We must walk in the light which shines upon us, otherwise that light will become darkness. *Testimonies,* vol. 1, p. 262.

### *An Appeal to the Slothful Church*

It is a mystery that there are not hundreds at work where now there is but one. The heavenly universe is astonished at the apathy, the coldness, the listlessness of those who profess to be sons and daughters of God. In the truth there is a living power. *Testimonies,* vol. 9, p. 42.

We can never be saved in indolence and inactivity. There is no such thing as a truly converted person living a helpless, useless life. It is not possible for us to drift into heaven. No sluggard can enter there. . . . Those who refuse to cooperate with God on earth, would not cooperate with Him in heaven. It would not be safe to take them to heaven. *Christ's Object Lessons,* p. 280.

All heaven is looking with intense interest upon the church, to see what her individual members are doing to enlighten those who are in darkness. *Review and Herald,* Feb. 27, 1894.

You should solemnly consider that you are dealing with the great God, and should ever remember that He is not a child to be trifled with. You cannot engage in His service at will, and let it alone at pleasure. *Testimonies,* vol. 2, p. 221.

Heavenly intelligences have been waiting to cooperate with human agencies, but we have not discerned their presence. *Testimonies,* vol. 6, p. 297.

Heavenly angels have long been waiting for human agents—the members of the church—to cooperate with them in the great work to be done. They are waiting for you. *Testimonies,* vol. 9, pp. 46, 47.

Many, many are approaching the day of God doing nothing, shunning responsibilities, and as the result they are religious dwarfs. So far as work for God is concerned, the pages of their life history present a mournful blank. They are trees in the garden of God, but only cumberers of the ground, darkening with their unproductive boughs the ground which fruit-bearing trees might have occupied. *Review and Herald,* May 22, 1888.

There is danger for those who do little or nothing for Christ. The grace of God will not long abide in the soul of him who, having great privileges and opportunities, remains silent. *Review and Herald,* Aug. 22, 1899.

There is no time to sleep now—no time to indulge in useless regrets. He who ventures to slumber now will miss precious opportunities of doing good. We are granted the blessed privilege of gathering sheaves in the great harvest; and every soul saved will be an additional star in the crown of Jesus, our adorable Redeemer. Who is eager to lay off the armor when by pushing the battle a little longer he will achieve new victories and gather new trophies for eternity? *Review and Herald,* Oct. 25, 1881.

The heavenly messengers are doing their work; but what are we doing? Brethren and sisters, God calls upon you to redeem the time. Draw nigh to God. Stir up the gift that is within you. Let those who have had the opportunity to become familiar with the reasons of our faith, now use this knowledge to some purpose. *Historical Sketches,* p. 288.

How can you who repeat the Lord's prayer, "Thy kingdom come, Thy will be done in earth as it is in heaven," sit at ease in your homes without helping to carry the torch of truth to others? How can you lift up your hands before God and ask His blessing upon yourselves and your families, when you are doing so little to help others? *Historical Sketches,* p. 288.

There are among us those who, if they would take time to consider, would regard their do-nothing position as a sinful neglect of their God-given talents. Brethren and sisters, your Redeemer and all the holy angels are grieved at your hardness of heart. Christ gave His own life to save souls, and yet you who have known His love make so little effort to impart the blessings of His grace to those for whom He died. Such indifference and neglect of duty is an amazement to the angels. In the judgment you must meet the souls you have neglected. In that great day you will be self-convicted and self-condemned. May the Lord lead you now to repentance. May He forgive His people for neglecting the work in His vineyard which He has given them to do. *Testimonies,* vol. 6, pp. 425, 426.

What can we say to the slothful church member to make him realize the necessity of unearthing his talent and putting it out to the exchangers? There will be no idler, no slothful one, found inside the kingdom of heaven. Oh, that God would set this matter in all its importance before the sleeping churches! Oh, that Zion would arise and put on her beautiful garments! Oh, that she would shine! *Testimonies,* vol. 6, p. 434.

There is work to be done for those who know not the truth, just such work as was done for you when you were in darkness. It is too late to sleep, too late to become indolent do-nothings. To everyone the Householder has given a work. Let us go forward, and not backward. We want a new conversion daily. We want the love of Jesus throbbing in our hearts, that we may be instrumental in saving many souls. *Review and Herald,* June 10, 1880.

The Lord Jesus requires that every soul who claims to be a son or daughter of God should not only depart from all iniquity, but be abundant in acts of charity, self-denial, and humility. The Lord has presented the working of a certain law of mind and action that should warn us in regard to our work. He says: "Whosoever hath not, from him shall be taken even that which he seemeth to have." Those who do not improve upon their opportunities, who do not exercise the grace that God gives them, have less inclination to do so, and finally in a sleepy lethargy, lose that which they once possessed. They make no provision for the future time of need in gaining a large experience, in obtaining an increased knowledge of divine things, so that when trial and temptation come upon them, they may be able to stand. When persecution or temptation comes, this class lose their courage and faith, and their foundation is swept away, because they did not see the need of making their foundation sure. They did not rivet their souls to the eternal Rock. *Review and Herald,* Mar. 27, 1894.

How terrible it will be in the last great day to find that those with whom we have been familiarly associated are separated from us forever; to see the members of our families, perhaps our own children, unsaved; to find those who have visited our homes, and eaten at our tables, among the lost. Then we shall ask ourselves the question, Was it because of my impatience, my un-Christlike disposition; was it because self was not under control, that the religion of Christ became distasteful to them?

The world must be warned of the soon coming of the Lord. We have but a little time in which to work. Years have passed into eternity that might have been improved in seeking first the kingdom of God and His righteousness, and in diffusing the light to others. God now calls upon His people who have great light and are established in the truth, having had much labor bestowed upon them, to work for themselves and for others as they have never done before. Make use of every ability; bring into exercise every power, every intrusted talent; use all the light that God has given you to do others good. Do not try to become preachers, but become ministers for God. *Southern Watchman,* June 20, 1905.

## *Forceful Illustrations*

Divine love has been stirred to its unfathomable depths for the sake of men, and angels marvel to behold in the recipients of so great love a mere surface gratitude. Angels marvel at man's shallow appreciation of the love of God. Heaven stands indignant at the neglect shown to the souls of men. Would we know how Christ regards it? How would a father and mother feel, did they know that their child, lost in the cold and the snow, had been passed by and left to perish by those who might have saved it? Would they not be terribly grieved, wildly indignant? Would they not denounce those murderers with wrath hot as their tears, intense as their love? The sufferings of every man are the sufferings of God's child, and those who reach out no helping hand to their perishing fellow beings provoke His righteous anger. *The Desire of Ages,* p. 825.

I have read of a man who, journeying on a winter's day through the deep, drifted snow, became benumbed by the cold, which was almost imperceptibly stealing away his vital powers. And as he was nearly chilled to death by the embrace of the frost king, and about to give up the struggle for life, he heard the moans of a brother traveler, who was perishing with cold as he was about to perish. His humility was aroused to rescue him. He chafed the ice-clad limbs of the unfortunate man, and, after considerable effort, raised him to his feet; and as he could not stand, he bore him in sympathizing arms through the very drifts he had thought he could never succeed in getting through alone. And when he had borne his fellow traveler to a place of safety, the truth flashed home to him that in saving his neighbor he had saved himself also. His earnest efforts to save another quickened the blood which was freezing in his own veins, and created a healthful warmth in the extremities of the body. These lessons must be forced upon young believers continually, not only be precept, but by example, that in their Christian experience they may realize similar results. *Testimonies,* vol. 4, pp. 319, 320.

You are not to shut yourselves up to yourselves, and be content because you have been blessed with a knowledge of the truth. Who brought the truth to you? Who showed the light of the Word of God to you? God has not given you His light to be placed under a bushel. I have read of an expedition that was sent out in search of Sir John Franklin. Brave men left their homes, and wandered about in the North Seas, suffering privation, hunger, cold, and distress. And what was it all for?—Merely for the honor of discovering the dead bodies of the explorers, or, if possible, to rescue some of the party from the terrible death that must surely come upon them, unless help should reach them in time. If they could but save one man from perishing, they would count their suffering well paid for. This was done at the sacrifice of all their comfort and happiness.

Think of this, and then consider how little we are willing to sacrifice for the salvation of the precious souls around us. We are not compelled to go away from home, on a long and tedious journey, to save the life of a perishing mortal. At our very doors, all about us, on every side, there are souls to be saved, souls perishing—men and women dying without hope, without God—and yet we feel unconcerned, virtually saying by our actions, if not by our words, "Am I my brother's keeper?" These men who lost their lives in trying to save others are eulogized by the world as heroes and martyrs. How should we who have the prospect of eternal life before us feel, if we do not make the little sacrifices that God requires of us for the salvation of the souls of men? *Review and Herald,* Aug. 14, 1888.

In a town in New England a well was being dug. When the work was nearly finished, while one man was still at the bottom, the earth caved in and buried him. Instantly the alarm was sent out, and mechanics, farmers, merchants, lawyers, hurried breathlessly to the rescue. Ropes, ladders, spades, and shovels were brought by eager, willing hands. "Save him, O save him!" was the cry.

Men worked with desperate energy, till the sweat stood in beads upon their brows and their arms trembled with the exertion. At length a pipe was thrust down, through which they shouted to the man to answer if he were still alive. The response came, "Alive, but make haste. It is fearful in here." With a shout of joy they renewed their efforts, and at last he was reached and saved, and the cheer that went up seemed to pierce the very heavens. "He is saved!" echoed through every street in the town.

Was this too great zeal and interest, too great enthusiasm, to save one man? It surely was not; but what is the loss of temporal life in comparison with the loss of a soul? If the threatened loss of a life will arouse in human hearts a feeling so intense, should not the loss of a soul arouse even deeper solicitude in men who claim to realize the danger of those apart from Christ? Shall not the servants of God show as great zeal in laboring for the salvation of souls as was shown for the life of that one man buried in a well? *Gospel Workers,* pp. 31, 32.

## *Profession vs. Expression*

Every important truth received into the heart must find expression in the life. It is in proportion to the reception of the love of Christ that men desire to proclaim its power to others; and the very act of proclaiming it, deepens and intensifies its value to their own souls. *Review and Herald,* Feb. 19, 1889.

Our faith should be prolific of good works, for faith without works is dead. *Testimonies,* vol. 4, p. 145.

All who receive the gospel message into the heart will long to proclaim it. The heaven-born love of Christ must find expression. *Christ's Object Lessons,* p. 125.

We are to praise God by tangible service, by doing all in our power to advance the glory of His name. *Christ's Object Lessons,* p. 300.

Our faith at this time must not stop with an assent to, or belief in, the theory of the third angel's message. We must have the oil of the grace of Christ that will feed the lamp and cause the light of life to shine forth, showing the way to those who are in darkness. *Testimonies,* vol. 9, p. 155.

Your spiritual strength and blessing will be proportionate to the labor of love and the good works which you perform. *Testimonies,* vol. 3, p. 526.

Very much more might be done for Christ if all who have the light of truth would practice the truth. *Testimonies,* vol. 9, p. 40.

I was shown that as a people we are deficient. Our works are not in accordance with our faith. Our faith testifies that we are living under the proclamation of the most solemn and important message that was ever given to mortals. Yet in full view of this fact, our efforts, our zeal, our spirit of self-sacrifice, do not compare with the character of the work. We should awake from the dead, and Christ will give us life. *Testimonies,* vol. 2, p. 114.

Go forth in faith, and proclaim the truth as if you believed it. Let those for whom you labor see that to you it is indeed a living reality. *Testimonies,* vol. 9, p. 42.

A Christlike life is the most powerful argument that can be advanced in favor of Christianity. *Testimonies,* vol. 9, p. 21.

There are many who profess the name of Christ whose hearts are not engaged in His service. They have simply arrayed themselves in a profession of godliness, and by this very act they have made greater their condemnation, and have become more deceptive and more successful agents of Satan in the ruin of souls. *Review and Herald,* Mar. 27, 1888.

Those who are watching for the Lord, are purifying their souls by obedience to the truth. With vigilant watching they combine earnest working. Because they know that the Lord is at the door, their zeal is quickened to cooperate with the divine intelligences in working for the salvation of souls. These are the faithful and wise servants who give to the Lord's household "their portion of meat in due season." They are declaring the truth that is now specially applicable. As Enoch, Noah, Abraham, and Moses each declared the truth for his time, so will Christ's servants now give the special warning for their generation. *The Desire of Ages,* p. 634.

Our standing before God depends, not upon the amount of light we have received, but upon the use we make of what we have. Thus even the heathen who choose the right as far as they can distinguish it, are in a more favorable condition than are those who have had great light, and profess to serve God, but who disregard the light, and by their daily life contradict their profession. *The Desire of Ages,* p. 239.

It is the privilege of every Christian, not only to look for, but to hasten the coming of our Lord Jesus Christ. Were all who profess His name bearing fruit to His glory, how quickly the whole world would be sown with the seed of the gospel. Quickly the last great harvest would be ripened, and Christ would come to gather the precious grain. *Christ's Object Lessons,* p. 69.

Christians should arouse themselves and take up their neglected duties, for the salvation of their own souls depends upon their individual efforts. *Review and Herald,* Aug. 23, 1881.

True worship consists in working together with Christ. Prayers, exhortation, and talk are cheap fruits, which are frequently tied on; but fruits that are manifested in good works, in caring for the needy, the fatherless, and widows, are genuine fruits, and grow naturally upon a good tree. *Review and Herald,* Aug. 16, 1881.

Let the individual members of the church take up their appointed work of diffusing as well as receiving light.

Not one is excusable in being an idler in the Lord's vineyard. *Review and Herald,* Feb. 19, 1889.

The *doing principle* is the fruit that Christ requires us to bear; doing deeds of benevolence, speaking kind words, and manifesting tender regard for the poor, the needy, the afflicted. *Review and Herald,* Aug. 16, 1881.

The Samaritan woman who talked with Jesus at Jacob's well had no sooner found the Saviour than she brought others to Him. She proved herself a more effective missionary than His own disciples. The disciples saw nothing in Samaria to indicate that it was an encouraging field. Their thoughts were fixed upon a great work to be done in the future. They did not see that right around them was a harvest to be gathered. But through the woman whom they despised a whole city full were brought to hear Jesus. She carried the light at once to her countrymen. This woman represents the working of a practical faith in Christ. *The Ministry of Healing,* p. 102.

Seventh-day Adventists are making progress, doubling their numbers, establishing missions, and unfurling the banner of truth in the dark places of the earth; and yet the work moves far more slowly than God would have it. [Why?] The members of the church are not individually aroused to put forth the earnest effort they are capable of making, and every branch of the work is crippled by the lack of fervent piety, and devoted, humble, God-fearing laborers. Where are the soldiers of the cross of Christ? Let the God-fearing, the honest, the single-hearted, who look steadfastly to the glory of God, prepare themselves for the battle against error. There are too many faint, cowardly hearts in this hour of spiritual conflict. O that out of weakness they may be made strong, and wax valiant in fight, and put to flight the armies of the aliens! *Historical Sketches,* p. 290.

It is a universal principle that whenever one refuses to use his God-given powers, these powers decay and perish. Truth that is not lived, that is not imparted, loses its life-giving power, its healing virtue. *The Acts of the Apostles,* p. 206.

Nothing will give bone and sinew to your piety like working to advance the cause you profess to love, instead of binding it. *Testimonies,* vol. 4, p. 236.

Those who endeavor to maintain Christian life by passively accepting the blessings that come through the means of grace, and doing nothing for Christ, are simply trying to live by eating without working. And in the spiritual as in the natural world, this always results in degeneration and decay. *Steps to Christ,* pp. 80, 81.

## *Danger Accompanying Missionary Activity*

Let us not forget that as activity increases, and we become successful in doing the work that must be accomplished, there is danger of our trusting in human plans and methods. There will be a tendency to pray less, and to have less faith. We shall be in danger of losing our sense of dependence upon God, who alone can make our work succeed; but although this is the tendency, let no one think that the human instrument is to do less. No, he is not to do less, but to do more by accepting the heavenly gift, the Holy Spirit. *Review and Herald,* July 4, 1893.

There will come times when the church will be stirred by divine power, and earnest activity will be the result; for the life-giving power of the Holy Spirit will inspire its members to go forth and bring souls to Christ. But when this activity is manifested, the most earnest workers will be safe only as they depend upon God through constant, earnest prayer. They will need to make earnest supplication that through the grace of Christ they may be saved from taking pride in their work, or of making a savior of their activity. They must constantly look to Jesus, that they may realize that it is His power which does the work, and thus be able to ascribe all the glory to God. We shall be called upon to make most decided efforts to extend the work of God, and prayer to our heavenly Father will be most essential. It will be necessary to engage in prayer in the closet, in the family, and in the church. *Review and Herald,* July 4, 1893.

In the estimation of the rabbis, it was the sum of religion to be always in a bustle of activity. They depended upon some outward performance to show their superior piety. Thus they separated their souls from God, and built themselves up in self-sufficiency. The same dangers still exist. As activity increases, and men become successful in doing any work for God, there is danger of trusting to human plans and methods. There is a tendency to pray less, and to have less faith. Like the disciples, we are in danger of losing sight of our dependence on God and seeking to make a savior of our activity. We need to look constantly to Jesus, realizing that it is His power which does the work. While we are to labor earnestly for the salvation of the lost, we must also take time for meditation, for prayer, and for the study of the Word of God. Only the work accomplished with much prayer, and sanctified by the merit of Christ, will in the end prove to have been efficient for good. *The Desire of Ages,* p. 362.

## *Encouragement to Beginners in Christian Service*

The most successful toilers are those who cheerfully take up the work of serving God in little things. Every human being is to work with his life-thread, weaving it into the fabric to help complete the pattern. *Testimonies,* vol. 6, p. 115.

We are to make our everyday duties acts of devotion, constantly increasing in usefulness, because we see our work in the light of eternity. *Testimonies,* vol. 9, p. 150.

The Lord has a place for everyone in His great plan. Talents that are not needed are not bestowed. *Testimonies,* vol. 9, p. 37.

Each has his place in the eternal plan of heaven. Each is to work in cooperation with Christ for the salvation of souls. Not more surely is the place prepared for us in the heavenly mansions than is the special place designated on earth where we are to work for God. *Christ's Object Lessons,* pp. 326, 327.

The Lord has His eye upon every one of His people; He has His plans concerning each. *Testimonies,* vol. 6, p. 12.

All can do something in the work. None will be pronounced guiltless before God unless they have worked earnestly and unselfishly for the salvation of souls. *Testimonies,* vol. 5, p. 395.

Your duty cannot be shifted upon another. No one but yourself can do your work. If you withhold your light, someone must be left in darkness through your neglect. *Testimonies,* vol. 5, p. 464.

The humble worker who obediently responds to the call of God may be sure of receiving divine assistance. To accept so great and holy a responsibility is itself elevating to the character. It calls into action the highest mental and spiritual powers, and strengthens and purifies the mind and heart. Through faith in the power of God, it is wonderful how strong a weak man may become, how decided his efforts, how prolific of great results. He who begins with a little knowledge, in a humble way, and tells what he knows, while seeking diligently for further knowledge, will find the whole heavenly treasure awaiting his demand. The more he seeks to impart light, the more light he will receive. The more one tries to explain the Word of God to others, with a love for souls, the plainer it becomes to himself. The more we use our knowledge and exercise our powers, the more knowledge and power we shall have. *Christ's Object Lessons,* p. 354.

Let everyone labor for God and for souls; let each show wisdom, and never be found in idleness, waiting for someone to set him to work. The "someone" who could set you to work is overcrowded with responsibilities, and time is lost in waiting for his directions. God will give you wisdom in reforming at once; for the call is still made, "Son, go work today in My vineyard." "Today if ye will hear His voice, harden not your hearts." Heb. 3:7, 8. The Lord prefaces the requirement with the endearing word "son." How tender, how compassionate, yet withal, how urgent! His invitation is also a command. *Counsels to Parents, Teachers, and Students,* p. 419.

Strength to resist evil is best gained by aggressive service. *The Acts of the Apostles,* p. 105.

Every act, every deed of justice and mercy and benevolence, makes music in heaven. *Review and Herald,* Aug. 16, 1881.

The spirit of Christ is a missionary spirit. The very first impulse of the renewed heart is to bring others also to the Saviour. *The Great Controversy,* p. 70.

The only way to grow in grace is to be interestedly doing the very work Christ has enjoined upon us to do. *Review and Herald,* June 7, 1887.

You are not to wait for great occasions or to expect extraordinary abilities before you go to work for God. *Steps to Christ,* p. 83.

The man who blesses society, and makes a success of life, is the one who, whether educated or uneducated, uses all his powers in the service of God and his fellowmen. *Southern Watchman,* Apr. 2, 1903.

Many whom God has qualified to do excellent work accomplish very little, because they attempt little. *Christ's Object Lessons,* p. 331.

If you fail ninety-nine times in a hundred, but succeed in saving the one soul from ruin, you have done a noble deed for the Master's cause. *Testimonies,* vol. 4, p. 132.

The relations between God and each soul are as distinct and full as though there were not another soul upon the earth to share His watch-care, not another soul for whom He gave His beloved Son. *Steps to Christ,* p. 100.

The Lord sees and understands, and He will use you, despite your weakness, if you offer your talent as a consecrated gift to His service; for in active, disinterested service the weak become strong and enjoy His precious commendation. The joy of the Lord is an element of strength. If you are faithful, the peace that passeth all understanding will be your reward in this life, and in the future life you will enter into the joy of your Lord. *Testimonies,* vol. 8, pp. 33, 34.

Persons of little talent, if faithful in keeping their hearts in the love of God, may win many souls to Christ. Harlan Page was a poor mechanic of ordinary ability and limited education; but he made it his chief business to seek to advance the cause of God, and his efforts were crowned with marked success. He labored for the salvation of his fellowmen in private conversation and in earnest prayer. He established prayer meetings, organized Sunday schools, and distributed tracts and other religious reading. And on his deathbed, with the shadow of eternity resting upon his countenance, he was able to say: "I know that it is all of God's grace, and not through any merit of anything that I have done; but I think I have evidence that more than one hundred souls have been converted to God through my personal instrumentality." *Testimonies,* vol. 5, pp. 307, 308.

This world is not the Christian's heaven, but merely the workshop of God, where we are to be fitted up to unite with sinless angels in a holy heaven. *Testimonies,* vol. 2, p. 187.

The humblest and poorest of the disciples of Jesus can be a blessing to others. They may not realize that they are doing any special good, but by their unconscious influence they may start waves of blessing that will widen and deepen, and the blessed results they may never know until the day of final reward. They do not feel or know that they are doing anything great. They are not required to weary themselves with anxiety about success. They have only to go forward quietly, doing faithfully the work that God's providence assigns, and their life will not be in vain. Their own souls will be growing more and more into the likeness of Christ; they are workers together with God in this life, and are thus fitting for the higher work and the unshadowed joy of the life to come. *Steps to Christ,* p. 83.

There are many who have given themselves to Christ, yet who see no opportunity of doing a large work or making great sacrifices in His service. These may find comfort in the thought that it is not necessarily the martyr's self-surrender which is most acceptable to God; it may not be the missionary who has daily faced danger and death, that stands highest in heaven's records. The Christian who is such in his private life, in the daily surrender of self, in sincerity of purpose and purity of thought, in meekness under provocation, in faith and piety, in fidelity in that which is least, the one who in the home life represents the character of Christ—such a one may in the sight of God be more precious than even the world-renowned missionary or martyr. *Christ's Object Lessons,* p. 403.

Not the amount of labor performed, or its visible results, but the spirit in which the work is done, makes it of value with God. *Christ's Object Lessons,* p. 397.

The approval of the Master is not given because of the greatness of the work performed, because many things have been gained, but because of the fidelity in even a few things. It is not the great results we attain, but the motives from which we act, that weigh with God. He prizes goodness and faithfulness more than the greatness of the work accomplished. *Testimonies,* vol. 2, pp. 510, 511.

Do not pass by the little things, and look for a large work. You might do successfully the small work, but fail utterly in attempting a large work, and fall into discouragement. Take hold wherever you see that there is work to be done. Whether you are rich or poor, great or humble, God calls you into active service for Him. It will be by doing with your might what your hands find to do that you will develop talent and aptitude for the work. And it is by neglecting your daily opportunities that you become fruitless and withered. This is why there are so many fruitless trees in the garden of the Lord. *Testimonies,* vol. 9, p. 129.

The Lord desires us to use every gift we have; and if we do this, we shall have greater gifts to use. He does not supernaturally endow us with the qualifications we lack; but while we use that which we have, He will work with us to increase and strengthen every faculty. By every wholehearted, earnest sacrifice for the Master's service, our powers will increase. *Christ's Object Lessons,* pp. 353, 354.

Christ's heart is cheered by the sight of those who are poor in every sense of the term; cheered by His view of the ill-used ones who are meek; cheered by the seemingly unsatisfied hungering after righteousness, by the inability of many to begin. He welcomes, as it were, the very condition of things that would discourage many ministers. *Gospel Workers,* p. 37.

We need not go to heathen lands, or even leave the narrow circle of the home, if it is there that our duty lies, in order to work for Christ. We can do this in the home circle, in the church, among those with whom we associate, and with whom we do business. *Steps to Christ,* p. 81.

If we are making the life and teachings of Christ our study, every passing event will furnish a text for an impressive discourse. *Testimonies,* vol. 9, p. 63.

The life on earth is the beginning of the life in heaven; education on earth is an initiation into the principles of heaven; the life-work here is a training for the life-work there. What we now are, in character and holy service, is the sure foreshadowing of what we shall be. *Education,* p. 307.

Those who reject the privilege of fellowship with Christ in service, reject the only training that imparts a fitness for participation with Him in His glory. They reject the training that in this life gives strength and nobility of character. *Education,* p. 264.

Let none suppose that they can live a life of selfishness, and then, having served their own interests, enter into the joy of their Lord. In the joy of unselfish love they could not participate. They would not be fitted for the heavenly courts. They could not appreciate the pure atmosphere of love that pervades heaven. The voices of the angels and the music of their harps would not satisfy them. To their minds the science of heaven would be as an enigma. *Christ's Object Lessons,* pp. 364, 365.

Christ calls upon us to labor patiently and perseveringly for the thousands perishing in their sins, scattered in all lands, like wrecks on a desert shore. Those who share in Christ's glory must share also in His ministry, helping the weak, the wretched, and the despondent. *Testimonies,* vol. 9, p. 31.

The common people are to take their place as workers. Sharing the sorrows of their fellowmen as the Saviour shared the sorrows of humanity, they will by faith see Him working with them. *Testimonies,* vol. 7, p. 272.

Christ is sitting for His portrait in every disciple. Everyone God has predestinated to be "conformed to the image of His Son." In everyone Christ's long-suffering love, His holiness, meekness, mercy, and truth, are to be manifested to the world. *The Desire of Ages,* p. 827.

The call to place all on the altar of service comes to each one. We are not all asked to serve as Elisha served, nor are we all bidden to sell everything we have; but God asks us to give His service the first place in our lives, to allow no day to pass without doing something to advance His work in the earth. He does not expect from all the same kind of service. One may be called to ministry in a foreign land; another may be asked to give of his means for the support of gospel work. God accepts the offering of each. It is the consecration of the life and all its interests, that is necessary. Those who make this consecration, will hear and obey the call of Heaven. *Prophets and Kings,* p. 221.

The worldly wise man, who meditates and plans, and whose business is ever in his mind, should seek to become wise in matters of eternal interest. If he would put forth as much energy to secure the heavenly treasure and the life which measures with the life of God as he does to secure worldly gain, what could he not accomplish? *Testimonies,* vol. 6, p. 297.

God will move upon men in humble positions to declare the message of present truth. Many such will be seen hastening hither and thither, constrained by the Spirit of God to give the light to those in darkness. The truth is as a fire in their bones, filling them with a burning desire to enlighten those who sit in darkness. Many, even among the uneducated, will proclaim the word of the Lord. Children will be impelled by the Holy Spirit to go forth to declare the message of heaven. The Spirit will be poured out upon those who yield to His promptings. Casting off man's binding rules and cautious movements, they will join the army of the Lord. *Testimonies,* vol. 7, pp. 26, 27.

## *The Christian Life in Landscape*

The heart that receives the word of God is not as a pool that evaporates, not like a broken cistern that loses its treasure. It is like the mountain stream, fed by unfailing springs, whose cool, sparkling waters leap from rock to rock, refreshing the weary, the thirsty, the heavy-laden. It is like a river constantly flowing, and as it advances, becoming deeper and wider, until its life-giving waters are spread over all the earth. The stream that goes singing on its way, leaves behind its gift of verdure and fruitfulness. The grass on its banks is a fresher green, the trees have a richer verdure, the flowers are more abundant. When the earth lies bare and brown under the summer's scorching heat, a line of verdure marks the river's course.

So it is with the true child of God. The religion of Christ reveals itself as a vitalizing, pervading principle, a living, working, spiritual energy. When the heart is opened to the heavenly influence of truth and love, these principles will flow forth again like streams in the desert, causing fruitfulness to appear where now are barrenness and dearth. *Prophets and Kings,* pp. 233, 234.

## *The Christian's Watchwords*

There are three watchwords in the Christian life, which must be heeded if we would not have Satan steal a march upon us; namely, Watch, Pray, Work. *Testimonies,* vol. 2, p. 283.

Every soul that has made a profession of Christ has pledged himself to be all that it is possible for him to be as a spiritual worker, to be active, zealous, and efficient in his Master's service. Christ expects every man to do his duty; let this be the watchword throughout the ranks of His followers. *Testimonies,* vol. 5, p. 460.

## *A Spiritual Paralytic*

Strength comes by exercise. All who put to use the ability which God has given them, will have increased ability to devote to His service. Those who do nothing in the cause of God will fail to grow in grace and in the knowledge of the truth. A man who would lie down and refuse to exercise his limbs would soon lose all power to use them. Thus the Christian who will not exercise his God-given powers not only fails to grow up into Christ, but he loses the strength which he already has; he becomes a spiritual paralytic. It is those who, with love for God and their fellowmen, are striving to help others, that become established, strengthened, settled, in the truth. The true Christian works for God, not from impulse, but from principle; not for a day or a month, but during the entire period of life. *Testimonies,* vol. 5, p. 393.

## *The Sure Remedy*

For the disheartened there is a sure remedy—faith, prayer, work. Faith and activity will impart assurance and satisfaction that will increase day by day. Are you tempted to give way to feelings of anxious foreboding or utter despondency? In the darkest days, when appearances seem most forbidding, fear not. Have faith in God. He knows your need. He has all power. His infinite love and compassion never weary. Fear not that He will fail of fulfilling His promise. He is eternal truth. Never will He change the covenant He has made with those who love Him. And He will bestow upon His faithful servants the measure of efficiency that their need demands. *Prophets and Kings,* pp. 164, 165.

There is but one genuine cure for spiritual laziness, and that is work—working for souls who need your help. *Testimonies,* vol. 4, p. 236.

This is the recipe that Christ has prescribed for the fainthearted, doubting, trembling soul. Let the sorrowful ones, who walk mournfully before the Lord, arise and help someone who needs help. *Testimonies,* vol. 6, p. 266.

Christians who are constantly growing in earnestness, in zeal, in fervor, in love—such Christians never backslide. *Review and Herald,* June 7, 1887.

It is those who are not engaged in this unselfish labor who have a sickly experience, and become worn out with struggling, doubting, murmuring, sinning, and repenting, until they lose all sense as to what constitutes genuine religion. They feel that they cannot go back to the world, and so they hang on the skirts of Zion, having petty jealousies, envyings, disappointments, and remorse. They are full of fault finding, and feed upon the mistakes and errors of their brethren. They have only a hopeless, faithless, sunless experience in their religious life. *Review and Herald,* Sept. 2, 1890.

## Unwarranted Excuses

When Jesus went away, He left to every man his work, and "nothing to do" is an unwarrantable excuse. "Nothing to do" is the reason of trial among the brethren; for Satan will fill the minds of idlers with his own plans, and set them to work. . . . "Nothing to do" brings evil testimony against the brethren, and dissension into the church of Christ. Jesus says, "He that gathereth not with Me scattereth abroad." *Review and Herald,* March 13, 1888.

Brethren and sisters, many of you excuse yourselves from labor, on the plea of inability to work for others. But did God make you so incapable? Was not this inability produced by your own inactivity, and perpetuated by your own deliberate choice? Did not God give you at least one talent to improve, not for your own convenience and gratification, but for Him? Have you realized your obligation, as His hired servant, to bring a revenue to Him by the wise and skillful use of this intrusted capital? Have you not neglected opportunities to improve your powers to this end? It is too true that few have felt any real sense of their responsibility to God. *Testimonies,* vol. 5, p. 457.

Many have the idea that if their life is a working, business life, they can do nothing for the salvation of souls, nothing to advance the cause of their Redeemer. They say they cannot do things by the halves, and therefore turn from religious duties and religious exercises, and bury themselves up in the world. They make their business primary, and forget God, and He is displeased with them. If any are engaged in business where they cannot advance in the divine life and perfect holiness in the fear of God, they should change to a business in which they can have Jesus with them every hour. *Testimonies,* vol. 2, pp. 233, 234.

## Aim for a Heavy Crown

We must not become weary or faint-hearted. It would be a terrible loss to barter away enduring glory for ease, convenience, and enjoyment, or for carnal indulgences. A gift from the hand of God awaits the overcomer. Not one of us deserves it; it is gratuitous on His part. Wonderful and glorious will be this gift, but let us remember that "one star differeth from another star in glory." But as we are urged to strive for the mastery, let us aim, in the strength of Jesus, for the crown heavy with stars. "They that be wise shall shine as the firmament, and they that win many to righteousness as the stars forever and ever." *Review and Herald,* Oct. 25, 1881.

## *Service Has Been Paid For*

The Lord at His coming will scrutinize every talent; He will demand interest on the capital He has entrusted. By His own humiliation and agony, by His life of toil and His death of shame, Christ has paid for the service of all who have taken His name and profess to be His servants. *Testimonies,* vol. 9, p. 104.

All are under deepest obligation to improve every capability for the work of winning souls to Him. "Ye are not your own," He says; "for ye are bought with a price;" therefore glorify God by a life of service that will win men and women from sin to righteousness. We are bought with the price of Christ's own life, bought that we may return to God His own in faithful service. *Testimonies,* vol. 9, p. 104.

God has given me a message for His people. They must awake, spread their tents, and enlarge their borders. My brethren and sisters, you have been bought with a price, and all that you have and are is to be used to the glory of God and for the good of your fellowmen. Christ died on the cross to save the world from perishing in sin. He asks your cooperation in this work. You are to be His helping hand. With earnest, unwearying effort you are to seek to save the lost. Remember that it was your sins that made the cross necessary. *Testimonies,* vol. 7, p. 9.

Christ's followers have been redeemed for service. Our Lord teaches that the true object of life is ministry. Christ Himself was a worker, and to all His followers He gives the law of service—service to God and to their fellowmen. . . . The law of service becomes the connecting link which binds us to God and to our fellowmen. *Christ's Object Lessons,* p. 326.

## Go Forward

Often the Christian life is beset with dangers, and duty seems hard to perform. The imagination pictures impending ruin before, and bondage and death behind. Yet the voice of God speaks clearly, Go forward. Let us obey the command, even though our sight cannot penetrate the darkness. The obstacles that hinder our progress will never disappear before a halting, doubting spirit. Those who defer obedience till every uncertainty disappears, and there remains no risk of failure or defeat, will never obey. Faith looks beyond the difficulties, and lays hold of the unseen, even Omnipotence, therefore it cannot be baffled. Faith is the clasping of the hand of Christ in every emergency. *Gospel Workers,* p. 262.

Our ideas are altogether too narrow. God calls for continual advancement in the work of diffusing light. We must study improved ways and means of reaching the people. We need to hear with ears of faith the mighty Captain of the Lord's host saying, "Go forward." We must act, and God will not fail us. He will do His part when we in faith do ours. Brethren and sisters who have been long in the truth, you have not done the work God calls upon you to do. Where is your love for souls? *Historical Sketches,* pp. 289, 290.

It was the joy of Christ to save souls. Let this be your work and your joy. Perform all duties and make all sacrifices for Christ's sake, and He will be your constant helper. Go straight forward where the voice of duty calls; let no seeming difficulties hinder you. Take up your God-given responsibilities, and as you bear your sometimes heavy burdens, do not ask, "Why idle stands my brother, no yoke upon him laid?" Do the duty nearest you, and do it thoroughly and well, not coveting praise, but working for the Master because you belong to Him. *Southern Watchman,* Apr. 2, 1903.

The course of God's people should be upward and onward to victory. A greater than Joshua is leading on the armies of Israel. One is in our midst, even the Captain of our salvation, who has said for our encouragement, "Lo, I am with you alway, even unto the end of the world."

"Be of good cheer; I have overcome the world." He will lead us on to certain victory. What God promises, He is able at any time to perform. And the work He gives His people to do, He is able to accomplish by them. *Testimonies,* vol. 2, p. 122.

Why do we not become enthused with the Spirit of Christ? Why are we so little moved by the pitiful cries of a suffering world? Do we consider our exalted privilege of adding a star to Christ's crown—a soul cut loose from the chains with which Satan has bound him, a soul saved in the kingdom of God? The church must realize its obligation to carry the gospel of present truth to every creature. I entreat of you to read the third and fourth chapters of Zechariah. If these chapters are understood, if they are received, a work will be done for those who are hungering and thirsting for righteousness, a work that means to the church: "Go forward and upward." *Testimonies,* vol. 6, p. 296.

The great majority of this earth's inhabitants have given their allegiance to the enemy. But we have not been deceived. Notwithstanding the apparent triumph of Satan, Christ is carrying forward His work in the heavenly sanctuary and on the earth. The Word of God portrays the wickedness and corruption that would exist in the last days. As we see the fulfillment of prophecy, our faith in the final triumph of Christ's kingdom should strengthen; and we should go forth with renewed courage to do our appointed work. *Gospel Workers,* pp. 26, 27.

## *An Impressive Scene*

In the visions of the night a very impressive scene passed before me. I saw an immense ball of fire fall among some beautiful mansions, causing their instant destruction. I heard someone say: "We knew that the judgments of God were coming upon the earth, but we did not know that they would come so soon." Others, with agonized voices, said, "You knew! Why then did you not tell us? We did not know!" On every side I heard similar words of reproach spoken.

In great distress I awoke. I went to sleep again, and I seemed to be in a large gathering. One of authority was addressing the company, before whom was spread out a map of the world. He said that the map pictured God's vineyard, which must be cultivated. As light from heaven shone upon anyone, that one was to reflect the light to others. Lights were to be kindled in many places, and from these lights still other lights were to be kindled.

The words were repeated: "Ye are the salt of the earth: but if the salt have lost his savor, wherewith shall it be salted? it is thenceforth good for nothing, but to be cast out, and to be trodden underfoot of men. Ye are the light of the world. A city that is set on a hill cannot be hid. Neither do men light a candle, and put it under a bushel, but on a candlestick; and it giveth light unto all that are in the house. Let your light so shine before men, that they may see your good works, and glorify your Father which is in heaven." Matt. 5:13-16.

I saw jets of light shining from cities and villages, and from the high places and the low places of the earth. God's word was obeyed, and as a result there were memorials for Him in every city and village. His truth was proclaimed throughout the world. *Testimonies,* vol. 9, pp. 28, 29.

# CHAPTER 10

# Methods

### *House to House*

Of equal importance with special public efforts is house-to-house work in the homes of the people. In large cities there are certain classes that cannot be reached by public meetings. These must be searched out as the shepherd searches for his lost sheep. Diligent, personal effort must be put forth in their behalf. When personal work is neglected, many precious opportunities are lost, which, were they improved, would advance the work decidedly. *Testimonies,* vol. 9, p. 111.

Deeds as well as words of sympathy are needed. Christ prefaced the giving of His message by deeds of love and benevolence. Let these workers go from house to house, helping where help is needed, and, as opportunity offers, telling the story of the cross. Christ is to be their text. They need not dwell upon doctrinal subjects; let them speak of the work and sacrifice of Christ. Let them hold up His righteousness, in their lives revealing His purity. *Testimonies,* vol. 7, p. 228.

God is no respecter of persons. He will use humble, devoted Christians, even if they have not received so thorough an education as some others. Let such ones engage in service for Him by doing house-to-house work. Sitting by the fireside, they can—if humble, discreet, and godly—do more to meet the real needs of families than could an ordained minister. *Testimonies,* vol. 7, p. 21.

Among the members of our churches there should be more house-to-house labor in giving Bible readings and distributing literature. *Testimonies,* vol. 9, p. 127.

Those who engage in house-to-house labor will find opportunities for ministry in many lines. They should pray for the sick and should do all in their power to relieve them from suffering. They should work among the lowly, the poor, and the oppressed. We should pray for and with the helpless ones who have not strength of will to control the appetites that passion has degraded. Earnest, persevering effort must be made for the salvation of those in whose hearts an interest is awakened. Many can be reached only through acts of disinterested kindness. Their physical wants must first be relieved. As they see evidence of our unselfish love, it will be easier for them to believe in the love of Christ. *Testimonies,* vol. 6, pp. 83, 84.

Let the workers go from house to house, opening the Bible to the people, circulating the publications, telling others of the light that has blessed their own souls. *Testimonies,* vol. 9, p. 123.

Our Saviour went from house to house, healing the sick, comforting the mourners, soothing the afflicted, speaking peace to the disconsolate. He took the little children in His arms and blessed them, and spoke words of hope and comfort to the weary mothers. With unfailing tenderness and gentleness, He met every form of human woe and affliction. Not for Himself, but for others did He labor. He was the servant of all. It was His meat and drink to bring hope and strength to all with whom He came in contact. *Gospel Workers,* p. 188.

The presentation of the truth, in love and simplicity, from house to house, is in harmony with the instruction that Christ gave His disciples when He sent them out on their first missionary tour. By songs of praise, by humble, heartfelt prayers, many will be reached. The divine Worker will be present to send conviction to hearts. "I am with you alway," is His promise. With the assurance of the abiding presence of such a helper, we may labor with faith and hope and courage. *Testimonies,* vol. 9, p. 34.

House-to-house laborers are needed. The Lord calls for decided efforts to be put forth in places where the people know nothing of Bible truth. Singing and prayer and Bible readings are needed in the homes of the people. Now, just now, is the time to obey the commission, "Teaching them to observe all things whatsoever I have commanded you." Those who do this work must have a ready knowledge of the Scriptures. "It is written" is to be their weapon of defense. *Counsels to Parents, Teachers, and Students,* p. 540.

My brethren and sisters, visit those who live near you, and by sympathy and kindness seek to reach their hearts. Be sure to work in a way that will remove prejudice instead of creating it. And remember that those who know the truth for this time, and yet confine their efforts to their own churches, refusing to work for their unconverted neighbors, will be called to account for unfulfilled duties. *Testimonies,* vol. 9, p. 34.

On this first tour the disciples were to go only where Jesus had been before them, and had made friends. Their preparation for the journey was to be of the simplest kind. Nothing must be allowed to divert their minds from their great work, or in any way excite opposition and close the door for further labor. They were not to adopt the dress of the religious teachers, nor use any guise in apparel to distinguish them from the humble peasants. They were not to enter into the synagogues and call the people together for public service; their efforts were to be put forth in house-to-house labor. They were not to waste time in needless salutations, or in going from house to house for entertainment. But in every place they were to accept the hospitality of those who were worthy, those who would welcome them heartily as if entertaining Christ Himself. They were to enter the dwelling with the beautiful salutation, "Peace be to this house." That home would be blessed by their prayers, their songs of praise, and the opening of the Scriptures in the family circle. *The Desire of Ages,* pp. 351, 352.

Visit your neighbors in a friendly way, and become acquainted with them. . . . Those who do not take up this work, those who act with the indifference that some have manifested, will soon lose their first love, and will begin to censure, criticize, and condemn their own brethren. *Review and Herald,* May 13, 1902.

The apostle's efforts were not confined to public speaking; there were many who could not have been reached in that way. He spent much time in house-to-house labor, thus availing himself of the familiar intercourse of the home circle. He visited the sick and the sorrowing, comforted the afflicted, and lifted up the oppressed. And in all that he said and did, he magnified the name of Jesus. Thus he labored, "in weakness, and in fear, and in much trembling." He trembled lest his teaching should reveal the impress of the human rather than the divine. *The Acts of the Apostles,* p. 250.

Go to your neighbors one by one, and come close to them till their hearts are warmed by your unselfish interest and love. Sympathize with them, pray with them, watch for opportunities to do them good, and as you can, gather a few together and open the Word of God to their darkened minds. Keep watching, as he who must render an account for the souls of men, and make the most of the privileges that God gives you of laboring with Him in His moral vineyard. Do not neglect speaking to your neighbors, and doing them all the kindness in your power, that you "by all means may save some." We need to seek for the spirit that constrained the apostle Paul to go from house to house pleading with tears, and teaching "repentance toward God, and faith toward our Lord Jesus Christ." *Review and Herald,* Mar. 13, 1888.

The Lord has presented before me the work that is to be done in our cities. The believers in these cities are to work for God in the neighborhood of their homes. They are to labor quietly and in humility, carrying with them wherever they go the atmosphere of heaven. *Testimonies,* vol. 9, p. 128.

## *The One-Soul Audience*

The work of Christ was largely made up of personal interviews. He had a faithful regard for the one-soul audience. From that one soul the intelligence received was carried to thousands. *Testimonies,* vol. 6, p. 115.

He was faint and weary; yet He did not neglect the opportunity of speaking to one woman, though she was a stranger, an alien from Israel, and living in open sin. *The Desire of Ages,* p. 194.

The Saviour did not wait for congregations to assemble. Often He began His lessons with only a few gathered about

Him, but one by one the passers-by paused to listen, until a multitude heard with wonder and awe the words of God through the heaven-sent Teacher. The worker for Christ should not feel that he cannot speak with the same earnestness to a few hearers as to a large company. There may be only one to hear the message; but who can tell how far-reaching will be its influence? It seemed a small matter, even to His disciples, for the Saviour to spend His time upon a woman of Samaria. But He reasoned more earnestly and eloquently with her than with kings, councilors, or high priests. The lessons He gave to that woman have been repeated to the earth's remotest bounds. *The Desire of Ages,* p. 194.

## *Close Personal Touch*

There is need of coming close to the people by personal effort. If less time were given to sermonizing, and more time were spent in personal ministry, greater results would be seen. *The Ministry of Healing,* p. 143.

The Lord desires that His word of grace shall be brought home to every soul. To a great degree this must be accomplished by personal labor. This was Christ's method. *Christ's Object Lessons,* p. 229.

Those who have been most successful in soul-winning were men and women who did not pride themselves on their ability, but who in humility and faith sought to help those about them. Jesus did this very work. He came close to those whom He desired to reach. *Gospel Workers,* p. 194.

In Christlike sympathy we should come close to men individually and seek to awaken their interest in the great things of eternal life. Their hearts may be as hard as the beaten highway, and apparently it may be a useless effort to present the Saviour to them; but while logic may fail to move, and argument be powerless to convince, the love of Christ, revealed in personal ministry, may soften the stony heart, so that the seed of truth can take root. *Christ's Object Lessons,* p. 57.

By personal labor reach those around you. Become acquainted with them. Preaching will not do the work that needs to be done. Angels of God attend you to the dwellings of those you visit. This work cannot be done by proxy. Money lent or given will not accomplish it. Sermons will not do it. By visiting the people, talking, praying, sympathizing with them, you will win hearts. This is the highest missionary work that you can do. To do it, you will need resolute, persevering faith, unwearying patience, and a deep love for souls. *Testimonies,* vol. 9, p. 41.

With the calling of John and Andrew and Simon, of Philip and Nathanael, began the foundation of the Christian church. John directed two of his disciples to Christ. Then one of these, Andrew, found his brother, and called him to the Saviour. Philip was then called, and he went in search of Nathanael. These examples should teach us the importance of personal effort, of making direct appeals to our kindred, friends, and neighbors. There are those who for a lifetime have professed to be acquainted with Christ, yet who have never made a personal effort to bring even one soul to the Saviour. They leave all the work for the minister. He may be well qualified for his calling, but he cannot do that which God has left for the members of the church.

There are many who need the ministration of loving Christian hearts. Many have gone down to ruin who might have been saved, if their neighbors, common men and women, had put forth personal effort for them. Many are waiting to be personally addressed. In the very family, the neighborhood, the town where we live, there is work for us to do as missionaries for Christ. If we are Christians, this work will be our delight. No sooner is one converted than there is born within him a desire to make known to others what a precious friend he has found in Jesus. The saving and sanctifying truth cannot be shut up in his heart. *The Desire of Ages,* p. 141.

One of the most effective ways in which light can be communicated is by private personal effort. In the home circle, at your neighbor's fireside, at the bedside of the sick, in a quiet way you may read the Scriptures and speak a word for Jesus and the truth. Thus you may sow precious seed that will spring up and bring forth fruit. *Testimonies,* vol. 6, pp. 428, 429.

Salt must be mingled with the substance to which it is added; it must penetrate and infuse in order to preserve. So it is through personal contact and association that men are reached by the saving power of the gospel. They are not saved in masses, but as individuals. Personal influence is a power. We must come close to those whom we desire to benefit. *Thoughts from the Mount of Blessing,* p. 36.

Jesus saw in every soul one to whom must be given the call to His kingdom. He reached the hearts of the people by going among them as one who desired their good. He sought them in the public streets, in private houses, on the boats, in the synagogue, by the shores of the lake, and at the marriage feast. He met them at their daily vocations, and manifested an interest in their secular affairs. He carried His instruction into the household, bringing families in their own homes under the influence of His divine presence. His strong personal sympathy helped to win hearts. *The Desire of Ages,* p. 151.

Christ's method alone will give true success in reaching the people. The Saviour mingled with men as one who desired their good. He showed His sympathy for them, ministered to their needs, and won their confidence. Then He bade them, "Follow Me." *The Ministry of Healing,* p. 143.

We should do as Christ did. Wherever He was, in the synagogue, by the wayside, in the boat thrust out a little from the land, at the Pharisee's feast or the table of the publican, He spoke to men of the things pertaining to the higher life. The things of nature, the events of daily life, were bound up by Him with the words of truth. The hearts of His hearers were drawn to Him; for He had healed their sick, had comforted their sorrowing ones, and had taken their children in His arms and blessed them. When He opened His lips to speak, their attention was riveted upon Him, and every word was to some soul a savor of life unto life.

So it should be with us. Wherever we are, we should watch for opportunities of speaking to others of the Saviour. If we follow Christ's example in doing good, hearts will open to us as they did to Him. Not abruptly, but with tact born of divine love, we can tell them of Him who is the "chiefest among ten thousand," and the One "altogether lovely." This is the very highest work in which we can employ the talent of speech. It was given to us that we might present Christ as the sin-pardoning Saviour. *Christ's Object Lessons,* pp. 338, 339.

His presence brought a purer atmosphere into the home, and His life was as leaven working amid the elements of society. Harmless and undefiled, He walked among the thoughtless, the rude, the uncourteous; amid the unjust publicans, the reckless prodigals, the unrighteous Samaritans, the heathen soldiers, the rough peasants, and the mixed multitude. He spoke a word of sympathy here and a word there, as He saw men weary, yet compelled to bear heavy burdens. He shared their burdens, and repeated to them the lessons He had learned from nature, of the love, the kindness, the goodness of God.

He taught all to look upon themselves as endowed with precious talents, which if rightly employed would secure for them eternal riches. He weeded all vanity from life, and by His own example taught that every moment of time is fraught with eternal results; that it is to be cherished as a treasure, and to be employed for holy purposes. He passed by no human being as worthless, but sought to apply the saving remedy to every soul. In whatever company He found Himself, He presented a lesson that was appropriate to the time and the circumstances. He sought to inspire with hope the most rough and unpromising, setting before them the assurance that they might become blameless, and harmless, attaining such a character as would make them manifest as the children of God. Often He met those who had drifted under Satan's control, and who had no power to break from his snare. To such a one, discouraged, sick, tempted, and fallen, Jesus would speak words of tenderest pity, words that were needed and could be understood. Others He met who were fighting a hand-to-hand battle with the adversary of souls. These He encouraged to persevere, assuring them that they would win; for angels of God were on their side, and would give them the victory. *The Desire of Ages,* p. 91.

## *The Combination of Spiritual Revival and Personal Work*

When churches are revived, it is because some individual seeks earnestly for the blessing of God. He hungers and thirsts after God, and asks in faith, and receives accordingly. He goes to work in earnest, feeling his great dependence upon the Lord, and souls are aroused to seek for a like blessing, and a season of refreshing falls on the hearts of men. The extensive work will not be neglected. The larger plans will be laid at the right time; but personal, individual effort and interest for your friends and neighbors will accomplish much more than can be estimated. It is for the want of this kind of labor that souls for whom Christ died are perishing.

One soul is of infinite value; for Calvary speaks its worth. One soul, won to the truth, will be instrumental in winning others, and there will be an ever-increasing result of blessing and salvation. Your work may accomplish more real good than the more extensive meetings, if they lack in personal effort. When both are combined, with the blessing of God, a more perfect and thorough work may be wrought; but if we can have but one part done, let it be the individual labor of opening the Scriptures in households, making personal appeals, and talking familiarly with the members of the family, not about things of little importance, but of the great themes of redemption. Let them see that your heart is burdened for the salvation of souls. *Review and Herald,* Mar. 13, 1888.

## *Go to the People*

We are not to wait for souls to come to us; we must seek them out where they are. When the word has been preached in the pulpit, the work has but just begun. There are multitudes who will never be reached by the gospel unless it is carried to them. *Christ's Object Lessons,* p. 229.

The gospel commission is the great missionary charter of Christ's kingdom. The disciples were to work earnestly for souls, giving to all the invitation of mercy. They were not to wait for the people to come to them; they were to go to the people with their message. *The Acts of the Apostles,* p. 28.

## *Invite to Your Home for Bible Study*

Invite your neighbors to your home, and read with them from the precious Bible and from books that explain its truths. Invite them to unite with you in song and prayer. In these little gatherings, Christ Himself will be present, as He has promised, and hearts will be touched by His grace. *The Ministry of Healing,* pp. 152, 153.

While in Ephesus, Apollos "began to speak boldly in the synagogue." Among his hearers were Aquila and Priscilla, who, perceiving that he had not yet received the full light of the gospel, "took him unto them and expounded unto him the way of God more perfectly." Through their teaching he obtained a clearer understanding of the Scriptures and became one of the ablest advocates of the Christian faith. *The Acts of the Apostles,* p. 270.

## *Be Social*

To all who are working with Christ I would say, Wherever you can gain access to the people by the fireside, improve your opportunity. Take your Bible and open before them its great truths. Your success will not depend so much upon your knowledge and accomplishments, as upon your ability to find your way to the heart. By being social and coming close to the people, you may turn the current of their thoughts more readily than by the most able discourse. The presentation of Christ in the family, by the fireside, and in small gatherings in private houses, is often more successful in winning souls to Jesus than are sermons delivered in the open air, to the moving throng, or even in halls or churches. *Gospel Workers,* p. 193.

The example of Christ in linking Himself with the interests of humanity should be followed by all who preach His word, and by all who have received the gospel of His grace. We are not to renounce social communion. We should not seclude ourselves from others. In order to reach all classes, we must meet them where they are. They will seldom seek us of their own accord. Not alone from the pulpit are the hearts of men touched by divine truth. There is another field of labor, humbler, it may be, but fully as promising. It is found in the home of the lowly, and in the mansion of the great; at the hospitable board, and in gatherings for innocent social enjoyment. *The Desire of Ages,* p. 152.

Christ was not exclusive, and He had given special offense to the Pharisees by departing in this respect from their rigid rules. He found the domain of religion fenced in by high walls of seclusion, as too sacred a matter for everyday life. These walls of partition He overthrew. In His contact with men He did not ask, What is your creed? To what church do you belong? He exercised His helping power in behalf of all who needed help. Instead of secluding Himself in a hermit's cell in order to show His heavenly character, He labored earnestly for humanity. He inculcated the principle that Bible religion does not consist in the mortification of the body. He taught that pure and undefiled religion is not meant only for set times and special occasions. At all times and in all places He manifested a loving interest in men, and shed about Him the light of a cheerful piety. *The Desire of Ages,* p. 86.

In face of their prejudices He accepted the hospitality of this despised people. He slept under their roofs, ate with them at their tables—partaking of the food prepared and served by their hands—taught in their streets, and treated them with the utmost kindness and courtesy. *The Desire of Ages,* p. 193.

## *Manifest Sympathetic Interest*

Those who are fighting the battle of life at great odds may be refreshed and strengthened by little attentions which cost nothing. Kindly words simply spoken, little attentions simply bestowed, will sweep away the clouds of temptation and doubt that gather over the soul. The true heart-expression of Christlike sympathy, given in simplicity, has power to open the door of hearts that need the simple, delicate touch of the Spirit of Christ. *Testimonies,* vol. 9, p. 30.

Thousands of hearts can be reached in the most simple, humble way. The most intellectual, those who are looked upon and praised as the world's most gifted men and women, are often refreshed by the simple words that flow from the heart of one who loves God and who can speak of that love as naturally as the worldling speaks of the things which his mind contemplates and feeds upon. Often the words well prepared and studied have little influence. But the true, honest words of a son or daughter of God, spoken in natural simplicity, will open the door to hearts that have long been locked. *Testimonies,* vol. 6, p. 115.

## *Cite Personal Experience*

Those who have put on Christ will relate their experience, tracing step by step the leadings of the Holy Spirit—their hungering and thirsting for the knowledge of God and of Jesus Christ whom He has sent, the result of their searching of the Scriptures, their prayers, their soul-agony, and the words of Christ to them, "Thy sins be forgiven thee." It is unnatural for any to keep these things secret, and those who are filled with the love of Christ will not do so. In proportion as the Lord has made them the depositaries of sacred truth will be their desire that others shall receive the same blessing. And as they make known the rich treasures of God's grace, more and still more of the grace of Christ will be imparted to them. *Christ's Object Lessons,* p. 125.

Arouse every spiritual energy to action. Tell those whom you visit that the end of all things is at hand. The Lord Jesus Christ will open the door of their hearts, and will make upon their minds lasting impressions. Strive to arouse men and women from their spiritual insensibility. Tell them how you found Jesus, and how blessed you have been since you gained an experience in His service. Tell them what blessing comes to you as you sit at the feet of Jesus and learn precious lessons from His Word. Tell them of the gladness and joy that there is in the Christian life. Your warm, fervent words will convince them that you have found the pearl of great price. Let your cheerful, encouraging words show that you have certainly found the higher way.

This is genuine missionary work, and as it is done, many will awake as from a dream. *Testimonies,* vol. 9, p. 38.

Those whom God employs as His instruments may be regarded by some as inefficient; but if they can pray, if in simplicity they can talk the truth because they love it, they may reach the people through the Holy Spirit's power. As they present the truth in simplicity, reading from the Word, or recalling incidents of experience, the Holy Spirit makes an impression on mind and character. The will becomes subordinate to the will of God; the truth heretofore not understood comes to the heart with living conviction, and becomes a spiritual reality. *Testimonies,* vol. 6, p. 444.

## *Illustrations Effective*

His messages of mercy were varied to suit His audience. He knew "how to speak a word in season to him that is weary;" for grace was poured upon His lips, that He might convey to men in the most attractive way the treasures of truth. He had tact to meet the prejudiced minds and surprise them with illustrations that won their attention. Through the imagination He reached the heart. His illustrations were taken from the things of daily life, and although they were simple, they had in them a wonderful depth of meaning. The birds of the air, the lilies of the field, the seed, the shepherd and the sheep—with these objects Christ illustrated immortal truth; and ever afterward, when His hearers chanced to see these things in nature, they recalled His words. Christ's illustrations constantly repeated His lessons. *The Desire of Ages,* p. 254.

The apostles endeavored to impart to these idolaters a knowledge of God the Creator, and of His Son, the Saviour of the human race. They first directed attention to the wonderful works of God—the sun, the moon, and the stars, the beautiful order of the recurring seasons, the mighty snow-capped mountains, the lofty trees, and other varied wonders of nature, which showed a skill beyond human comprehension. Through these works of the Almighty, the apostles led the minds of the heathen to a contemplation of the great Ruler of the universe. *The Acts of the Apostles,* p. 180.

## Deal With Practical Fundamentals

Paul was an eloquent speaker. Before his conversion he had often sought to impress his hearers by flights of oratory. But now he set all this aside. Instead of indulging in poetic descriptions and fanciful representations, which might please the senses and feed the imagination, but which would not touch the daily experience, Paul sought by the use of simple language to bring home to the heart the truths that are of vital importance. Fanciful representations of truth may cause an ecstasy of feeling; but all too often, truths presented in this way do not supply the food necessary to strengthen and fortify the believer for the battles of life. The immediate needs, the present trials, of struggling souls—these must be met with sound, practical instruction in the fundamental principles of Christianity. *The Acts of the Apostles,* pp. 251, 252.

## Hold to Affirmative Truth

Often, as you seek to present the truth, opposition will be aroused; but if you seek to meet the opposition with argument, you will only multiply it, and that you cannot afford to do. Hold to the affirmative. Angels of God are watching you, and they understand how to impress those whose opposition you refuse to meet with argument. Dwell not on the negative points of questions that arise, but gather to your minds affirmative truths, and fasten them there by much earnest prayer and heart-consecration. *Testimonies,* vol. 9, pp. 147, 148.

## Representatives in the Thoroughfares of Travel

Those who in response to the call of the hour have entered the service of the Master Workman may well study His methods of labor. During His earthly ministry the Saviour took advantage of the opportunities to be found along the great thoroughfares of travel. It was at Capernaum that Jesus dwelt at the intervals of His journeys to and fro, and it came to be known as "His own city." This city was well adapted to be the center of the Saviour's work. Being on the highway from Damascus to Jerusalem and Egypt, and to the Mediterranean Sea, it was a great thoroughfare of travel. People from many lands passed through the city, or tarried for rest on their journeyings to and fro. Here Jesus could meet all nations and all ranks, the rich and great, as well as the poor and lowly; and His lessons would be carried to other countries and into many households. Investigation of the prophecies would thus be excited; attention would be directed to the Saviour, and His mission would be brought before the world. *Testimonies,* vol. 9, p. 121.

In the world-renowned health resorts and centers of tourist traffic, crowded with many thousands of seekers after health and pleasure, there should be stationed ministers and canvassers capable of arresting the attention of the multitudes. Let these workers watch their chance for presenting the message for this time, and hold meetings as they have opportunity. Let them be quick to seize opportunities to speak to the people. Accompanied by the power of the Holy Spirit, let them meet the people with the message borne by John the Baptist: "Repent ye: for the kingdom of heaven is at hand." Matt. 3:2. The word of God is to be presented with clearness and power, that those who have ears to hear may hear the truth. Thus the gospel of present truth will be placed in the way of those who know it not, and it will be accepted by not a few, and carried by them to their own homes in all parts of the world. *Testimonies,* vol. 9, p. 122.

*Ministry of Healing* and *Christ's Object Lessons* are peculiarly adapted for use in tourist centers, and everything possible should be done to place copies of these works in the hands of those who have leisure and inclination to read. *Testimonies,* vol. 9, p. 85.

Health restaurants and treatment rooms should be established. Our efforts in these lines should include the great seaside resorts. As the voice of John the Baptist was heard in the wilderness, "Prepare ye the way of the Lord," so must the voice of the Lord's messengers be heard in the great tourist and seaside resorts. *Testimonies,* vol. 7, pp. 55, 56.

## *Sent Forth Two by Two*

Calling the twelve about Him, Jesus bade them go out two and two through the towns and villages. None were sent forth alone, but brother was associated with brother, friend with friend. Thus they could help and encourage each other, counseling and praying together, each one's strength supplementing the other's weakness. In the same manner He afterward sent forth the seventy. It was the Saviour's purpose that the messengers of the gospel should be associated in this way. In our own time evangelistic work would be far more successful if this example were more closely followed. *The Desire of Ages,* p. 350.

## *Medical Evangelistic Tours*

From the instruction that the Lord has given me from time to time, I know that there should be workers who make medical evangelistic tours among the towns and villages. Those who do this work will gather a rich harvest of souls from both the higher and lower classes. The way for this work is best prepared by the efforts of the faithful canvasser. *Testimonies,* vol. 9, p. 172.

## *Gospel Medical Missionaries*

Workers—gospel medical missionaries—are needed now. You cannot afford to spend years in preparation. Soon doors now open to the truth will be forever closed. Carry the message now. Do not wait, allowing the enemy to take possession of the fields now open before you. Let little companies go forth to do the work to which Christ appointed His disciples. Let them labor as evangelists, scattering our publications, and talking of the truth to those they meet. Let them pray for the sick, ministering to their necessities, not with drugs, but with nature's remedies, and teaching them how to regain health and avoid disease. *Testimonies,* vol. 9, p. 172.

My brethren and sisters, give yourselves to the Lord for service. Allow no opportunity to pass unimproved. Visit the sick and suffering, and show a kindly interest in them. If possible, do something to make them more comfortable. Through this means you can reach their hearts, and speak a word for Christ. Eternity alone will reveal how far-reaching such a line of labor can be. Other lines of usefullness will open before those who are willing to do the duty nearest them. *Testimonies,* vol. 9, p. 36.

## *Industrial Education*

There are multitudes of poor families for whom no better missionary work could be done than to assist them in settling on the land and in learning how to make it yield them a livelihood. The need for such help and instruction is not confined to the cities. Even in the country, with all its possibilities for a better life, multitudes of the poor are in great need. Whole communities are devoid of education in industrial and sanitary lines. Families live in hovels, with scant furniture and clothing, without tools, without books, destitute of both comforts and conveniences, and of means of culture. Imbruted souls, bodies weak and ill-formed, reveal the results of evil heredity and of wrong habits. These people must be educated from the very foundation. They have led shiftless, idle, corrupt lives, and they need to be trained to correct habits. *The Ministry of Healing,* p. 192.

Attention should be given to the establishment of various industries so that poor families can find employment. Carpenters, blacksmiths, and indeed everyone who understands some line of useful labor, should feel a responsibility to teach and help the ignorant and the unemployed. *The Ministry of Healing,* p. 194.

Christian farmers can do real missionary work in helping the poor to find homes on the land, and in teaching them how to till the soil and make it productive. Teach them how to use the implements of agriculture, how to cultivate various crops, how to plant and care for orchards. *The Ministry of Healing,* p. 193.

In ministry to the poor there is a wide field of service for women as well as for men. The efficient cook, the housekeeper, the seamstress, the nurse—the help of all is needed. Let the members of poor households be taught how to cook, how to make and mend their own clothing, how to nurse the sick, how to care properly for the home. Let boys and girls be thoroughly taught some useful trade or occupation. *The Ministry of Healing,* p. 194.

## Invite to Gospel Meetings

There are many things that persons may do if they only have a mind to work. There are many who will not go to church to hear the truth preached. By personal efforts in simplicity and wisdom these might be persuaded to turn their feet to the house of God. Conviction may fasten upon their minds the first time they hear a discourse upon present truth. Should your solicitations be refused, do not be discouraged. Persevere till success crowns your efforts. *Review and Herald,* June 10, 1880.

## Gather Into the Sabbath School

Another work in which all may engage is gathering children and youth into the Sabbath school. The young may in this way labor efficiently for the dear Saviour. They may shape the destinies of souls. They may do a work for the church and the world the extent and greatness of which will never be known until the day of final accounts, when the "Well done" is spoken to the good and faithful. *Review and Herald,* June 10, 1880.

## By Pen and Voice

With pen and voice proclaim that Jesus lives to make intercession for us. Unite with the great Master Worker, follow the self-denying Redeemer through His pilgrimage of love on earth. *Review and Herald,* Jan. 24, 1893.

Some will work in one way and some in another, as the Lord shall call and lead them. But they are all to strive together, seeking to make the work a perfect whole. With pen and voice they are to labor for Him. *Testimonies,* vol. 9, p. 26.

Christ crucified—talk it, pray it, sing it, and it will break and win hearts. *Testimonies,* vol. 6, p. 67.

The pen is a power in the hands of men who feel the truth burning upon the altar of their hearts, and who have an intelligent zeal for God, balanced with sound judgment. The pen, dipped in the fountain of pure truth, can send the beams of light to dark corners of the earth, which will reflect its rays back, adding new power, and giving increased light to be scattered everywhere. *Life Sketches,* p. 214.

Our ministers should not give all their powers to preaching discourses, and let the work end there. They should instruct the members of the church how to take hold of and successfully carry forward this branch of the work [missionary correspondence], which is to our tract and missionary society like a wheel within a wheel. The movement of this inner wheel keeps in healthful, powerful action the outer wheel. Let this inner wheel cease its action, and the result will be seen in diminished life and activity in the tract and missionary society. *Review and Herald,* June 10, 1880.

Do not become weary of vigilant missionary labor. This is a work you may all engage in successfully, if you will but connect with God. Before writing letters of inquiry, always lift up your heart to God in prayer that you may be successful in gathering some wild branches which may be grafted into the true vine and bear fruit to the glory of God. All who with humble hearts take part in this work, will be continually educating themselves as workers in the vineyard of the Lord. *Review and Herald,* June 10, 1880.

## CHAPTER 11

# Medical Missionary Work

### A Work of First Importance

During His ministry, Jesus devoted more time to healing the sick than to preaching. *The Ministry of Healing,* p. 19.

Before the true reformer, the medical missionary work will open many doors. *Testimonies,* vol. 7, p. 62.

Genuine medical missionary work is the gospel practiced. *Testimonies,* vol. 8, p. 168.

Medical missionary work is the pioneer work of the gospel. In the ministry of the word and in the medical missionary work the gospel is to be preached and practiced. *The Ministry of Healing,* p. 144.

The Saviour of the world devoted more time and labor to healing the afflicted of their maladies than to preaching. His last injunction to His apostles, His representatives upon the earth, was to lay hands on the sick that they might recover. When the Master shall come, He will commend those who have visited the sick and relieved the necessities of the afflicted. *Testimonies,* vol. 4, p. 225.

He designs that the medical missionary work shall prepare the way for the presentation of the saving truth for this time, the proclamation of the third angel's message. If this design is met, the message will not be eclipsed nor its progress hindered. *Testimonies,* vol. 6, p. 293.

First meet the temporal necessities of the needy and relieve their physical wants and sufferings, and you will then find an open avenue to the heart, where you may plant the good seeds of virtue and religion. *Testimonies,* vol. 4, p. 227.

Nothing will give greater spiritual strength and a greater increase of earnestness and depth of feeling, than visiting and ministering to the sick and the desponding, helping them to see the light and to fasten their faith upon Jesus. *Testimonies,* vol. 4, pp. 75, 76.

## *The Divine Example*

Christ, the great medical missionary, is our example. . . . He healed the sick and preached the gospel. In His service, healing and teaching were linked closely together. Today they are not to be separated. *Testimonies,* vol. 9, pp. 170, 171.

Christ's servants are to follow His example. As He went from place to place, He comforted the suffering and healed the sick. Then He placed before them the great truths in regard to His kingdom. This is the work of His followers. *Christ's Object Lessons,* pp. 233, 234.

Christ's example must be followed by those who claim to be His children. Relieve the physical necessities of your fellowmen, and their gratitude will break down the barriers and enable you to reach their hearts. Consider this matter earnestly. *Testimonies,* vol. 9, p. 127.

Especially should those who are medical missionaries manifest, in spirit, word, and character, that they are following Christ Jesus, the divine Model of medical missionary effort. *Testimonies,* vol. 7, p. 127.

## *Combine With Gospel Ministry*

The gospel and the medical missionary work are to advance together. The gospel is to be bound up with the principles of true health reform. Christianity is to be brought into the practical life. Earnest, thorough reformatory work is to be done. . . . We are to present the principles of health reform before the people, doing all in our power to lead men and women to see the necessity of these principles, and to practice them. *Testimonies,* vol. 6, p. 379.

It is the divine plan that we shall work as the disciples worked. Physical healing is bound up with the gospel commission. In the work of the gospel, teaching and healing are never to be separated. *The Ministry of Healing,* p. 141.

Medical missionary work and the gospel ministry are the channels through which God seeks to pour a constant supply of His goodness. They are to be as the river of life for the irrigation of His church. *Bible Echo,* Aug. 12, 1901.

Let our ministers, who have gained an experience in preaching the word, learn how to give simple treatments and then labor intelligently as medical missionary evangelists. *Testimonies,* vol. 9, p. 172.

As the canvasser goes from place to place, he will find many who are sick. He should have a practical knowledge of the causes of disease, and should understand how to give simple treatments, that he may relieve the suffering ones. More than this, he should pray in faith and simplicity for the sick, pointing them to the great Physician. As he thus walks and works with God, ministering angels are beside him, giving him access to hearts. What a wide field for missionary effort lies before the faithful, consecrated canvasser; what a blessing he will receive in the diligent performance of his work! *Southern Watchman,* Nov. 20, 1902.

Every gospel worker should feel that the giving of instruction in the principles of healthful living, is a part of his appointed work. Of this work there is great need, and the world is open for it. *The Ministry of Healing,* p. 147.

## *Right Arm of the Message*

Again and again I have been instructed that the medical missionary work is to bear the same relation to the work of the third angel's message that the arm and hand bear to the body. Under the direction of the divine Head they are to work unitedly in preparing the way for the coming of Christ. The right arm of the body of truth is to be constantly active, constantly at work, and God will strengthen it. But it is not to be made the body. At the same time the body is not to say to the arm: "I have no need of thee." The body has need of the arm in order to do active, aggressive work. Both have their appointed work, and each will suffer great loss if worked independently of the other. *Testimonies,* vol. 6, p. 288.

Medical missionary work is to be done. . . . It is to be to the work of God as the hand is to the body. *Testimonies,* vol. 8, p. 160.

## Divine Cooperation

Christ feels the woes of every sufferer. When evil spirits rend a human frame, Christ feels the curse. When fever is burning up the life current, He feels the agony. And He is just as willing to heal the sick now, as when He was personally on earth. Christ's servants are His representatives, the channels for His working. He desires through them to exercise His healing power. *The Desire of Ages,* pp. 823, 824.

Through His servants, God designs that the sick, the unfortunate, and those possessed of evil spirits, shall hear His voice. Through His human agencies He desires to be a comforter, such as the world knows not. *The Ministry of Healing,* p. 106.

Christ cooperates with those who engage in medical missionary work. *Testimonies,* vol. 7, p. 51.

The Lord wrought through them. Wherever they went, the sick were healed, and the poor had the gospel preached unto them. *The Acts of the Apostles,* p. 106.

Christ is no longer in this world in person, to go through our cities and towns and villages, healing the sick; but He has commissioned us to carry forward the medical missionary work that He began. *Testimonies,* vol. 9, p. 168.

## The Work of Every Church

There is a message regarding health reform to be borne in every church. *Testimonies,* vol. 6, p. 370.

The medical missionary work should be a part of the work of every church in our land. *Testimonies,* vol. 6, p. 289.

We have come to a time when every member of the church should take hold of medical missionary work. *Testimonies,* vol. 7, p. 62.

The work of health reform is the Lord's means for lessening suffering in our world and for purifying His church. Teach the people that they can act as God's helping hand by cooperating with the Master Worker in restoring physical and spiritual health. This work bears the signature of heaven and will open doors for the entrance of other precious truths. There is room for all to labor who will take hold of this work intelligently. *Testimonies,* vol. 9, pp. 112, 113.

There are stormy times before us, but let us not utter one word of unbelief or discouragement. Let us remember that we bear a message of healing to a world filled with sin-sick souls. *Special Testimonies,* series B, no. 8, p. 24.

This work, properly conducted, will save many a poor sinner who has been neglected by the churches. Many not of our faith are longing for the very help that Christians are in duty bound to give. If God's people would show a genuine interest in their neighbors, many would be reached by the special truths for this time. Nothing will or ever can give character to the work like helping the people just where they are. Thousands might today be rejoicing in the message if those who claim to love God and keep His commandments would work as Christ worked. When the medical missionary work thus wins men and women to a saving knowledge of Christ and His truth, money and earnest labor may safely be invested in it, for it is a work that will endure. *Testimonies,* vol. 6, p. 280.

Let our people show that they have a living interest in medical missionary work. Let them prepare themselves for usefulness by studying the books that have been written for our instruction in these lines. These books deserve much more attention and appreciation than they have received. Much that is for the benefit of all to understand has been written for the special purpose of instruction in the principles of health. Those who study and practice these principles will be greatly blessed, both physically and spiritually. An understanding of the philosophy of health will be a safeguard against many of the evils that are continually increasing. *Testimonies,* vol. 7, p. 63.

I have been instructed that the medical missionary work will discover, in the very depths of degradation, men who, though they have given themselves up to intemperate, dissolute habits, will respond to the right kind of labor. But they need to be recognized and encouraged. Firm, patient, earnest effort will be required in order to lift them up.

They cannot restore themselves. They may hear Christ's call, but their ears are too dull to take in its meaning; their eyes are too blind to see anything good in store for them. They are dead in trespasses and sins. Yet even these are not to be excluded from the gospel feast. They are to receive the invitation "Come." Though they may feel unworthy, the Lord says, "Compel them to come in." Listen to no excuse. By love and kindness lay right hold of them. *Testimonies,* vol. 6, pp. 279, 280.

Those who take up this line of work [circulating publications] are to go prepared to do medical missionary work. The sick and suffering are to be helped. Many for whom this work of mercy is done will hear and accept the words of life. *Testimonies,* vol. 9, p. 34.

Who is preparing to take hold understandingly of medical missionary work? . . . Every worker should be understandingly efficient. Then in a high, broad sense he can present the truth as it is in Jesus. *Testimonies,* vol. 7, p. 70.

Let the Lord's work go forward. Let the medical missionary and the educational work go forward. I am sure that this is our great lack—earnest, devoted, intelligent, capable workers. *Testimonies,* vol. 9, pp. 168, 169.

Let them take the living principle of health reform into the communities that to a large degree are ignorant of these principles. *Testimonies,* vol. 9, p. 118.

I am instructed to say to health reform educators: Go forward. The world needs every jot of the influence you can exert to press back the tide of moral woe. Let those who teach the third angel's message stand true to their colors. *Testimonies,* vol. 9, p. 113.

## *The Medical Extension Plan*

The Lord will give to our sanitariums whose work is already established an opportunity to cooperate with Him in assisting newly established plants. Every new institution is to be regarded as a sister helper in the great work of proclaiming the third angel's message. God has given our sanitariums an opportunity to set in operation a work that will be as a stone instinct with life, growing as it is rolled by an invisible hand. Let this mystic stone be set in motion. *Testimonies,* vol. 7, p. 59.

## *Institutional Work*

Health restaurants and treatment rooms should be established. Our efforts in these lines should include the great seaside resorts. As the voice of John the Baptist was heard in the wilderness, "Prepare ye the way of the Lord," so must the voice of the Lord's messengers be heard in the great tourist and seaside resorts. *Testimonies,* vol. 7, pp. 55, 56.

I have been given light that in many cities it is advisable for a restaurant to be connected with treatment rooms. The two can cooperate in upholding right principles. In connection with these it is sometimes advisable to have rooms that will serve as lodgings for the sick. These establishments will serve as feeders to the sanitariums located in the country. *Testimonies,* vol. 7, p. 60.

The Lord has a message for our cities, and this message we are to proclaim in our camp meetings and by other public efforts, and also through our publications. In addition to this, hygienic restaurants are to be established in the cities, and by them the message of temperance is to be proclaimed. Arrangements should be made to hold meetings in connection with our restaurants. Whenever possible, let a room be provided where the patrons can be invited to lectures on the science of health and Christian temperance, where they can receive instruction on the preparation of wholesome food, and on other important subjects. *Testimonies,* vol. 7, p. 115.

Those who come to our restaurants should be supplied with reading matter. Their attention should be called to our literature on temperance and dietetic reform, and leaflets treating on the lessons of Christ should also be given them. The burden of supplying this reading matter should be shared by all our people. All who come should be given something to read. It may be that many will leave the tract unread, but some among those in whose hands you place it may be searching for light. They will read and study what you give them, and then pass it on to others. *Testimonies,* vol. 7, p. 116.

I have been instructed that one of the principal reasons why hygienic restaurants and treatment rooms should be established in the centers of large cities is that by this means the attention of leading men will be called to the third angel's message. Noticing that these restaurants are conducted in a way altogether different from the way in which ordinary restaurants are conducted, men of intelligence will begin to inquire into the reasons for the difference in business methods, and will investigate the principles that lead us to serve superior food. Thus they will be led to a knowledge of the message for this time. *Testimonies,* vol. 7, pp. 122, 123.

## *Cooking Schools*

I have been instructed to encourage the conducting of cooking schools in all places where medical missionary work is being done. Every inducement to lead people to reform must be held out before them. Let as much light as possible shine upon them. Teach them to make every improvement that they can in the preparation of food, and encourage them to impart to others that which they learn. *Gospel Workers,* pp. 362, 363

Cooking schools are to be held. The people are to be taught how to prepare wholesome food. They are to be shown the need of discarding unhealthful foods. But we should never advocate a starvation diet. It is possible to have a wholesome, nutritious diet without the use of tea, coffee, and flesh food. The work of teaching the people how to prepare a dietary that is at once wholesome and appetizing is of the utmost importance. *Testimonies,* vol. 9, p. 112.

## *A Timely Message*

I cannot too strongly urge all our church members, all who are true missionaries, all who believe the third angel's message, all who turn away their feet from the Sabbath, to consider the message of the fifty-eighth chapter of Isaiah.

The work of beneficence enjoined in this chapter is the work that God requires His people to do at this time. It is a work of His own appointment. We are not left in doubt as to where the message applies, and the time of its marked fulfillment, for we read: "They that shall be of thee shall build the old waste places; thou shalt raise up the foundations of many generations; and thou shalt be called, The repairer of the breach, The restorer of paths to dwell in."

God's memorial, the seventh-day Sabbath, the sign of His work in creating the world, has been displaced by the man of sin. God's people have a special work to do in repairing the breach that has been made in His law; and the nearer we approach the end, the more urgent this work becomes. All who love God will show that they bear His sign by keeping His commandments. They are the restorers of paths to dwell in. . . . Genuine medical missionary work is bound up inseparably with the keeping of God's commandments, of which the Sabbath is especially mentioned, since it is the great memorial of God's creative work. Its observance is bound up with the work of restoring the moral image of God in man. This is the ministry which God's people are to carry forward at this time. This ministry, rightly performed, will bring rich blessings to the church. *Testimonies,* vol. 6, pp. 265, 266.

# CHAPTER 12

# Bible Evangelism

## *A Heaven-born Idea*

The plan of holding Bible readings was a heaven-born idea. There are many, both men and women, who can engage in this branch of missionary labor. Workers may thus be developed who will become mighty men of God. By this means the Word of God has been given to thousands; and the workers are brought into personal contact with people of all nations and tongues. The Bible is brought into families, and its sacred truths come home to the conscience. Men are entreated to read, examine, and judge for themselves, and they must abide the responsibility of receiving or rejecting the divine enlightenment. God will not permit this precious work for Him to go unrewarded. He will crown with success every humble effort made in His name. *Gospel Workers,* p. 192.

Our work has been marked out for us by our heavenly Father. We are to take our Bibles and go forth to warn the world. We are to be God's helping hands in saving souls—channels through which His love is day by day to flow to the perishing. *Testimonies,* vol. 9, p. 150.

## *The Definite Call*

Many will be called into the field to labor from house to house, giving Bible readings and praying with those who are interested. *Testimonies,* vol. 9, p. 172.

Many workers are to act their part, doing house-to-house work, and giving Bible readings in families. *Testimonies,* vol. 9, p. 141.

Consecrated women should engage in Bible work from house to house. *Testimonies,* vol. 9, pp. 120, 121.

If we follow in Christ's footsteps, we must come close to those who need our ministry. We must open the Bible to the understanding, present the claims of God's law, read the promises to the hesitating, arouse the careless, strengthen the weak. *Gospel Workers,* p. 336.

In the experience of Philip and the Ethiopian is presented the work to which the Lord calls His people. The Ethiopian represents a large class who need missionaries like Philip, missionaries who will hear the voice of God, and go where He sends them. There are those in the world who are reading the Scriptures, but who cannot understand their import. The men and women who have a knowledge of God are needed to explain the word to these souls. *Testimonies,* vol. 8, pp. 58, 59.

Among the members of our churches there should be more house-to-house labor in giving Bible readings. *Testimonies,* vol. 9, p. 127.

Let the workers go from house to house, opening the Bible to the people. *Testimonies,* vol. 9, p. 123.

In many States there are settlements of industrious, well-to-do farmers, who have never had the truth for this time. Such places should be worked. Let our lay members take up this line of service. By lending or selling books, by distributing papers, and by holding Bible readings, our lay members could do much in their own neighborhoods. Filled with love for souls they could proclaim the message with such power that many would be converted. *Testimonies,* vol. 9, p. 35.

### *Impressive Scenes*

Hundreds and thousands were seen visiting families and opening before them the Word of God. Hearts were convicted by the power of the Holy Spirit, and a spirit of genuine conversion was manifest. *Testimonies,* vol. 9, p. 126.

Two Bible workers were seated in a family. With the open Bible before them, they presented the Lord Jesus Christ as the sin-pardoning Saviour. Earnest prayer was offered to God, and hearts were softened and subdued by the influence of the Spirit of God. Their prayers were uttered with freshness and power. As the Word of God was explained, I saw that a soft, radiant light illumined the Scriptures, and I said, softly: "Go out into the highways and hedges, and compel them to come in, that My house may be filled." *Testimonies,* vol. 9, p. 35.

There are many who are reading the Scriptures who cannot understand their true import. All over the world men and women are looking wistfully to heaven. Prayers and tears and inquiries go up from souls longing for light, for grace, for the Holy Spirit. Many are on the verge of the kingdom, waiting only to be gathered in. *The Acts of the Apostles,* p. 109.

## *Preparation for the Work*

The followers of Jesus are not meeting the mind and will of God if they are content to remain in ignorance of His Word. All should become Bible students. Christ commanded His followers: "Search the Scriptures; for in them ye think ye have eternal life: and they are they which testify of Me." Peter exhorts us: "But sanctify the Lord God in your hearts: and be ready always to give an answer to every man that asketh you a reason of the hope that is in you with meekness and fear." *Testimonies,* vol. 2, pp. 633, 634.

Those who are truly converted must become more and more intelligent in their understanding of the Scriptures, that they may be able to speak words of light and salvation to those who are in darkness and perishing in their sins. *Testimonies,* vol. 9, p. 121.

We are to give the last warning of God to men, and what should be our earnestness in studying the Bible, and our zeal in spreading the light! Let every soul who has received the divine illumination seek to impart it. Let the workers go from house to house, opening the Bible to the people, circulating the publications, telling others of the light that has blessed their own souls. *Gospel Workers,* p. 353.

A well-balanced work can be carried on best when a training school for Bible workers is in progress. While the public meetings are being held, connected with this training school or city mission should be experienced laborers of deep spiritual understanding, who can give the Bible workers daily instruction and who can also unite wholeheartedly in the general public effort being put forth. *Testimonies,* vol. 9, p. 111.

## Secret of Success

Bring earnestness and fervency into your prayers, and into your Bible readings, and into your preaching, that you may leave the impression that the sacred truths you are presenting to others are to you a living reality. Whatever you do for Jesus, seek with all your powers to do it with earnestness. Never feel that you have attained to the highest point and can therefore rise no higher. . . . Set your mind to task, that you may present the truth in a manner to interest them. Seize the most interesting portions of Scripture that you can bring before them, come right to the point, and seek to fasten their attention, and instruct them in the ways of the Lord. *Review and Herald,* July 26, 1887.

A great work can be done by presenting to the people the Bible just as it reads. Carry the Word of God to every man's door, urge its plain statements upon every man's conscience, repeat to all the Saviour's command: "Search the Scriptures." Admonish them to take the Bible as it is, to implore divine enlightenment, and then, when the light shines, to gladly accept each precious ray and fearlessly abide the consequences. *Testimonies,* vol. 5, p. 388.

## A Joyous Work

It is a joyous work to open the Scriptures to others. *Testimonies,* vol. 9, p. 118.

Open the Scriptures to someone that is in darkness, and you will not complain of weariness and lack of interest in the cause of truth. Your heart will be awakened to an anxiety for souls, and joy in the evidences of the faith will fill your heart, and you will know that "he that watereth shall be watered also himself." *Review and Herald,* Mar. 13, 1888.

# CHAPTER 13

# Ministry of the Printed Page

### *Work of First Importance*

If there is one work more important than another, it is that of getting our publications before the public, thus leading them to search the Scriptures. Missionary work—introducing our publications into families, conversing, and praying with and for them—is a good work. *The Colporteur Evangelist,* p. 80.

Let every Seventh-day Adventist ask himself, "What can I do to proclaim the third angel's message?" Christ came to this world to give this message to His servant to give to the churches. It is to be proclaimed to every nation, kindred, tongue, and people. How are we to give it? The distribution of our literature is one means by which the message is to be proclaimed. Let every believer scatter broadcast tracts and leaflets and books containing the message for this time. Colporteurs are needed who will go forth to circulate our publications everywhere. *Southern Watchman,* Jan. 5, 1904.

Papers and books are the Lord's means of keeping the message for this time continually before the people. In enlightening and confirming souls in the truth, the publications will do a far greater work than can be accomplished by the ministry of the word alone. The silent messengers that are placed in the homes of the people through the work of the canvasser will strengthen the gospel ministry in every way; for the Holy Spirit will impress minds as they read the books, just as He impresses the minds of those who listen to the preaching of the word. The same ministry of angels attends the books that contain the truth as attends the work of the minister. *Testimonies,* vol. 6, pp. 315, 316.

Let not the canvassing work be left to languish. Let the books containing the light on present truth be placed before as many as possible. The presidents of our conferences and others in responsible positions have a duty to do in this matter. *Southern Watchman,* Apr. 25, 1905.

The world is to receive the light of truth through an evangelizing ministry of the word in our books and periodicals. Our publications are to show that the end of all things is at hand. *The Colporteur Evangelist,* p. 100.

God calls upon His people to act like living men, and not be indolent, sluggish, and indifferent. We must carry the publications to the people and urge them to accept. *Southern Watchman,* Apr. 25, 1905.

Our publications are now sowing the gospel seed, and are instrumental in bringing as many souls to Christ as the preached word. Whole churches have been raised up as the result of their circulation. In this work every disciple of Christ can act a part. *Review and Herald,* June 10, 1880.

A messenger from heaven stood in our midst, and he spoke words of warning and instruction. He made us clearly understand that the gospel of the kingdom is the message for which the world is perishing and that this message, as contained in our publications already in print and those yet to be issued, should be circulated among the people who are nigh and afar off. *Testimonies,* vol. 9, p. 67.

The book work should be the means of quickly giving the sacred light of present truth to the world. *Testimonies,* vol. 9, p. 69.

Satan is busy in this department of his work, scattering literature which is debasing the morals and poisoning the minds of the young. Infidel publications are scattered broadcast throughout the land. Why should not every member of the church be as deeply interested in sending forth publications that will elevate the minds of the people, and bring the truth directly before them? These papers and tracts are for the light of the world, and have often been instrumental in converting souls. *Review and Herald,* June 10, 1880.

We have been asleep, as it were, regarding the work that may be accomplished by the circulation of well-prepared literature. Let us now, by the wise use of periodicals and books, preach the word with determined energy, that the world may understand the message that Christ gave to

John on the isle of Patmos. *The Colporteur Evangelist,* p. 101.

Church members, awake to the importance of the circulation of our literature, and devote more time to this work. Place in the homes of the people papers, tracts, and books that will preach the gospel in its several lines. There is no time to be lost. Let many give themselves willingly and unselfishly to the canvassing work, and thus help to sound a warning that is greatly needed. When the church takes up her appointed work, she will go forth "fair as the moon, clear as the sun, and terrible as an army with banners." *Southern Watchman,* Nov. 20, 1902.

The light of truth is shedding its bright beams upon the world through missionary effort. The press is an instrumentality by which many are reached whom it would be impossible to reach by ministerial effort. *Testimonies,* vol. 5, p. 388.

The night of trial is nearly spent. Satan is bringing in his masterly power because he knoweth that his time is short. The chastisement of God is upon the world, to call all who know the truth to hide in the cleft of the Rock, and view the glory of God. The truth must not be muffled now. Plain statements must be made. Unvarnished truth must be spoken, in leaflets and pamphlets, and these must be scattered like the leaves of autumn. *Testimonies,* vol. 9, pp. 230, 231.

Canvassers are needed to take up the work of carrying these silent messengers of truth to the people—canvassers who feel a burden for souls, and who can speak words in season to those who are seeking for light. Some may say, "I am not a minister; I cannot preach to the people," You may not be able to preach, but you can be an evangelist, ministering to the needs of those with whom you come in contact; you can be God's helping hand, working as the disciples worked; you can ask those you meet if they love the Lord Jesus. *Southern Watchman,* Nov. 20, 1902.

## *Publishing Houses Effective Agencies*

Seventh-day Adventists have been chosen by God as a peculiar people, separate from the world. By the great cleaver of truth He has cut them out from the quarry of the world and brought them into connection with Himself. He has made them His representatives and has called them to be ambassadors for Him in the last work of salvation. The greatest wealth of truth ever intrusted to mortals, the most solemn and fearful warnings ever sent by God to man, have been committed to them to be given to the world; and in the accomplishment of this work our publishing houses are among the most effective agencies. *Testimonies,* vol. 7, p. 138.

Our publishing work was established by the direction of God and under His special supervision. *Testimonies,* vol. 7, p. 138.

In a large degree through our publishing houses is to be accomplished the work of that other angel who comes down from heaven with great power and who lightens the earth with his glory. *Testimonies,* vol. 7, p. 140.

I am bidden to say to our publishing houses: "Lift up the standard; lift it up higher. Proclaim the third angel's message, that it may be heard by all the world. Let it be seen that 'here are they that keep the commandments of God, and the faith of Jesus.' Rev. 14:12. Let our literature give the message as a witness to all the world." *Testimonies,* vol. 9, p. 61.

## *Publishing Extension*

You who believe the truth for this time, wake up. It is your duty now to bring in all the means possible to help those who understand the truth to proclaim it. Part of the money that comes in from the sale of our publications should be used to increase our facilities for the production of more literature that will open blind eyes and break up the fallow ground of the heart. *Testimonies,* vol. 9, p. 62.

Years ago the Lord gave me special directions that buildings should be erected in various places in America, Europe, and other lands, for the publication of literature containing the light of present truth. He gave instruction that every effort should be made to send forth to the world from the press the messages of invitation and warning. Some will be reached by our literature who would not be reached in any other way. From our books and papers bright beams of light are to shine forth to enlighten the world in regard to present truth. *Testimonies,* vol. 8, p. 87.

I have been shown that our publications should be printed in different languages and sent to every civilized country, at any cost. What is the value of money at this time, in comparison with the value of souls? Every dollar of our means should be considered as the Lord's, not ours; and as a precious trust from God to us; not to be wasted for needless indulgences, but carefully used in the cause of God, in the work of saving men and women from ruin. *Life Sketches,* p. 214.

The printed word of truth is to be translated into different languages and carried to the ends of the earth. *Testimonies,* vol. 9, p. 26.

These publications are to be translated into every language, for to all the world the gospel is to be preached. To every worker Christ promises the divine efficiency that will make his labors a success. *Testimonies,* vol. 9, p. 34.

Our publications should go everywhere. Let them be issued in many languages. The third angel's message is to be given through this medium and through the living teacher. You who believe the truth for this time, wake up. *The Colporteur Evangelist,* p. 101.

Many of God's people are to go forth with our publications into places where the third angel's message has never been proclaimed. Our books are to be published in many different languages. With these books, humble, faithful men are to go out as colporteur-evangelists, bearing the truth to those who would otherwise never be enlightened. *Testimonies,* vol. 9, pp. 33, 34.

From city to city, from country to country, they are to carry the publications containing the promises of the Saviour's soon coming. *Testimonies,* vol. 9, p. 34.

I have been shown that the publications already have been doing a work upon some minds in other countries in breaking down the walls of prejudice and superstition. I was shown men and women studying with intense interest papers and few pages of tracts upon present truth. They would read the evidences so wonderful and new to them, and would open their Bibles with a deep and new interest, as subjects of truth that had been dark to them were made plain, especially the light in regard to the Sabbath of the fourth commandment. As they searched the Scriptures to see if these things were so, a new light shone upon their understanding, for angels were hovering over them and impressing their minds with the truths contained in the publications they had been reading.

I saw them holding papers and tracts in one hand and the Bible in the other, while their cheeks were wet with tears; and bowing before God in earnest, humble prayer, to be guided into all truth—the very thing He was doing for them before they called upon Him. And when the truth was received in their hearts, and they saw the harmonious chain of truth, the Bible was to them a new book; they hugged it to their hearts with grateful joy, while their countenances were all aglow with happiness and holy joy.

These were not satisfied with merely enjoying the light themselves, and they began to work for others. Some made great sacrifices for the truth's sake and to help those of the brethren who were in darkness. The way is thus preparing to do a great work in the distribution of tracts and papers in other languages. *Life Sketches,* pp. 214, 215.

## *Opportunities for Free Distribution*

Let literature be distributed judiciously on the trains, in the street, on the great ships that ply the sea, and through the mails. *Gospel Workers,* p. 353.

In these days of travel, the opportunities for coming in contact with men and women of all classes, and of many nationalities, are much greater than in the days of Israel. The thoroughfares of travel have multiplied a thousandfold. God has wonderfully prepared the way. The agency of the printing press, with its manifold facilities, is at our command. Bibles, and publications in many languages setting forth the truth for this time, are at our hand and can be swiftly carried to every part of the world. *Gospel Workers,* p. 352.

Let the leaflets and tracts, the papers and books, go in every direction. Carry with you, wherever you go, a package of select tracts, which you can hand out as you have opportunity. Sell what you can, and lend or give them away as the case may seem to require. Important results will follow. *Review and Herald,* June 10, 1880.

I have been shown that we were not doing our duty in the gratuitous circulation of small publications. There are many honest souls who might be brought to embrace the truth by this means alone. . . . These small tracts of four, eight, or sixteen pages, can be furnished for a trifle, from a fund raised by the donations of those who have the cause at heart. When you write to a friend, you can inclose one or more without increasing postage. When you meet persons in the cars, on the boat, or in the stage who seem to have an ear to hear, you can hand them a tract. *Testimonies,* vol. 1, pp. 551, 552.

## *Secure Subscriptions*

The sisters can work efficiently in obtaining subscribers for our periodicals, in this way bringing the light before many minds. *Review and Herald,* June 10, 1880.

We now have great facilities for spreading the truth; but our people are not coming up to the privileges given them. They do not in every church see and feel the necessity of using their abilities in saving souls. They do not realize their duty to obtain subscribers for our periodicals, including our health journal, and to introduce our books and pamphlets. *Testimonies,* vol. 4, p. 391.

## *Selling Books*

Many are sad and discouraged, weak in faith and trust. Let them do something to help someone more needy than themselves, and they will grow strong in God's strength. Let them engage in the good work of selling our books. Thus they will help others, and the experience gained will give them the assurance that they are God's helping hand. As they plead with the Lord to help them, He will guide them to those who are seeking for the light. Christ will be close beside them, teaching them what to say and do. By comforting others, they themselves will be comforted. *The Colporteur Evangelist,* p. 40.

## *Work in Cities*

We are living in a time when a great work is to be done. There is a famine in the land for the pure gospel, and the bread of life is to be given to hungry souls. There is no better opportunity to do this work than that offered to the consecrated canvasser. Thousands of books containing the precious light of present truth should be placed in the homes of the people in our large cities. *Southern Watchman,* Nov. 20, 1902.

Blessed, soul-saving Bible truths are published in our papers. There are many who can help in the work of selling our periodicals. The Lord calls upon all of us to seek to save perishing souls. Satan is at work to deceive the very elect, and now is our time to work with vigilance. Our books and papers are to be brought before the notice of the people; the gospel of present truth is to be given to our cities without delay. Shall we not arouse to our duties? *Testimonies,* vol. 9, p. 63.

## *Health Literature*

Canvassers should call the attention of those they visit to our health publications, telling them of the valuable instruction these periodicals contain regarding the care of the sick and treatment of diseases. Tell them this instruction, studied and practiced, will bring health to the family. Explain how important it is for every family to understand the science of life. Direct their minds to Him who formed and who keeps in motion the wonderful machinery of the body. Tell them that it is our part to cooperate with God, caring wisely for all our faculties and organs.

The proper care of the body is a great responsibility, and requires an intelligent knowledge of its parts. Tell them that God is dishonored when, for the gratification of appetite and passion, man misuses the machinery of the body, so that it does its work feebly and with difficulty. Tell them that the books you have for sale give much valuable instruction regarding health, and that by practicing this instruction, much suffering and also much of the money spent in paying doctors' bills, will be saved. Tell them that in these books there is advice which they cannot possibly obtain from their physician during the short visits he makes. *Southern Watchman,* Nov. 20, 1902.

When young men take up the canvassing work filled with an intense longing to save their fellowmen, they will see souls converted. From their work a harvest for the Lord will be reaped. Then let them go forth as missionaries to circulate present truth, praying constantly for increased light and knowledge, that they may know how to speak words in season to those that are weary. They should improve every opportunity for doing a deed of kindness, remembering that thus they are doing errands for the Lord. . . . In their work they should always take some health books with them; for health reform is the right hand of the message. *Southern Watchman,* Jan. 15, 1903.

## *Circulate Without Discrimination*

There are many places in which the voice of the minister cannot be heard, places which can be reached only by publications—the books, papers, and tracts that are filled with the Bible truth that the people need. Our literature is to be distributed everywhere. The truth is to be sown beside all waters; for we know not which shall prosper, this or that. In our erring judgment we may think it unwise to give literature to the very ones who would accept the truth most readily. We know not what may be the good results of giving away a leaflet containing present truth. *Southern Watchman,* Jan. 5, 1904.

## *Treasure Every Fragment*

In the miracle of feeding the multitude with a few loaves and fishes, the food was increased as it passed from Christ to those who received it. Thus it will be in the distribution of our literature. God's truth, as it is passed out, will multiply greatly. And as the disciples, by Christ's direction, gathered up the fragments, that nothing might be lost, so we should treasure every fragment of literature containing the truth for this time. None can estimate the influence that even a torn page containing the truths of the third angel's message may have upon the heart of some seeker after truth. *Southern Watchman,* Jan. 5, 1904.

## Establish Depositories

In every important place there should be a depository for publications. And someone who really appreciates the truth should manifest an interest to get these books into the hands of all who will read. *Testimonies,* vol. 1, p. 473.

## Angels Prepare the Way

I saw that the work of present truth should engage the interest of all. The publication of truth is God's ordained plan as a means of warning, comforting, reproving, exhorting, or convicting all to whose notice the silent, voiceless messengers may be brought. Angels of God have a part to act in preparing hearts to be sanctified by the truths published, that they may be prepared for the solemn scenes before them. *Testimonies,* vol. 1, p. 590.

# CHAPTER 14

# Religious Liberty

## An Appropriate Prayer

David prayed, "It is time for Thee, Lord, to work: for they have made void Thy law." This prayer is no less pertinent at the present time. The world has gone astray from God, and its lawless state should strike terror to the heart, and lead all who are loyal to the great King to work for a reformation. The papal power has thought to change the law of God by substituting a spurious Sabbath for that of Jehovah; and all through the religious world the false sabbath is revered, while the true one is trampled beneath unholy feet. . . .

It is on the law of God that the last great struggle of the controversy between Christ and His angels and Satan and his angels will come, and it will be decisive for all the world. . . . Men in responsible positions will not only ignore and despise the Sabbath themselves, but from the sacred desk will urge upon the people the observance of the first day of the week, pleading tradition and custom in behalf of this man-made institution. They will point to calamities on land and sea—to the storms of wind, the floods, the earthquakes, the destruction by fire—as judgments indicating God's displeasure because Sunday is not sacredly observed. These calamities will increase more and more, one disaster will follow close upon the heels of another; and those who make void the law of God will point to the few who are keeping the Sabbath of the fourth commandment as the ones who are bringing wrath upon the world. This falsehood is Satan's device that he may ensnare the unwary. *Southern Watchman,* June 28, 1904.

## Coming Events

Our people have been regarded as too insignificant to be worthy of notice; but a change will come. The Christian world is now making movements which will necessarily bring commandment-keeping people into prominence. There is a constant supplanting of God's truth by the theories and false doctrines of human origin. Movements are being set on foot to enslave the consciences of those who would be loyal to God. The law-making powers will be against God's people. Every soul will be tested. *Testimonies,* vol. 5, p. 546.

Men will exalt and rigidly enforce laws that are in direct opposition to the law of God. Though zealous in enforcing their own commandments, they will turn away from a plain "Thus saith the Lord." Exalting a spurious rest day, they will seek to force men to dishonor the law of Jehovah, the transcript of His character. Though innocent of wrongdoing, the servants of God will be given over to suffer humiliation and abuse at the hands of those who, inspired by Satan, are filled with envy and religious bigotry. *Testimonies,* vol. 9, p. 229.

Religious powers, allied to heaven by profession, and claiming to have the characteristics of a lamb, will show by their acts that they have the heart of a dragon and that they are instigated and controlled by Satan. The time is coming when God's people will feel the hand of persecution because they keep holy the seventh day. . . . But God's people are to stand firm for Him. And the Lord will work in their behalf, showing plainly that He is the God of gods. *Testimonies,* vol. 9, pp. 229, 230.

Every indignity, reproach, and cruelty that Satan could instigate human hearts to devise, has been visited upon the followers of Jesus. And it will be again fulfilled in a marked manner; for the carnal heart is still at enmity with the law of God, and will not be subject to its commands. The world is no more in harmony with the principles of Christ today than it was in the days of the apostles. The same hatred that prompted the cry, "Crucify Him! crucify Him!" the same hatred that led to the persecution of the disciples, still works in the children of disobedience. The same spirit which in the Dark Ages consigned men and women to prison, to exile, and to death, which conceived the exquisite torture of the Inquisition, which planned and executed the massacre of St. Bartholomew, and which kindled the fires of Smithfield, is still at work with malignant energy in unregenerate hearts. The history of truth has ever been the record of a struggle between right and wrong. The proclamation of the gospel has ever been carried forward in this world in the face of opposition, peril, loss, and suffering. *The Acts of the Apostles,* pp. 84, 85.

The remnant church will be brought into great trial and distress. Those who keep the commandments of God and the faith of Jesus will feel the ire of the dragon and his hosts. Satan numbers the world as his subjects, he has gained control of the apostate churches; but here is a little company that are resisting his supremacy. If he could blot them from the earth, his triumph would be complete. As he influenced the heathen nations to destroy Israel, so in the near future he will stir up the wicked powers of earth to destroy the people of God. All will be required to render obedience to human edicts in violation of the divine law. Those who will be true to God and to duty will be . . . betrayed "both by parents, and brethren, and kinsfolks, and friends." *Testimonies,* vol. 9, p. 231.

The time is not far distant when the test will come to every soul. The observance of the false sabbath will be urged upon us. The contest will be between the commandments of God and the commandments of men. Those who have yielded step by step to worldly demands, and conformed to worldly customs, will then yield to the powers that be, rather than subject themselves to derision, insult, threatened imprisonment, and death. At that time the gold will be separated from the dross. . . . Many a star that we have admired for its brilliance will then go out in darkness. Those who have assumed the ornaments of the sanctuary, but are not clothed with Christ's righteousness, will then appear in the shame of their own nakedness. *Prophets and Kings,* p. 188.

There is a prospect before us of a continued struggle, at the risk of imprisonment, loss of property, and even of life itself, to defend the law of God, which is made void by the laws of men. *Testimonies,* vol. 5, p. 712.

The time is hastening on when those who stand in defense of the truth will know by experience what it means to be partakers in Christ's sufferings. The great oppressor sees that he has but a short time in which to work, that soon he will lose his hold upon man and his power be taken from him, and he is working with all deceivableness of unrighteousness in them that perish. Superstition and error are trampling upon truth, justice, and equity. Every power that is antagonistic to truth is strengthening. *Southern Watchman,* Oct. 31, 1905.

The work which the church has failed to do in a time of peace and prosperity she will have to do in a terrible crisis under most discouraging, forbidding circumstances. The warnings that worldly conformity has silenced or withheld must be given under the fiercest opposition from enemies of the faith. And at that time the superficial, conservative class, whose influence has steadily retarded the progress of the work, will renounce the faith and take their stand with its avowed enemies, toward whom their sympathies have long been tending. These apostates will then manifest the most bitter enmity, doing all in their power to oppress and malign their former brethren, and to excite indignation against them. This day is just before us. The members of the church will individually be tested and proved. They will be placed in circumstances where they will be forced to bear witness for the truth. Many will be called to speak before councils and in courts of justice, perhaps separately and alone. The experience which would have helped them in this emergency they have neglected to obtain, and their souls are burdened with remorse for wasted opportunities and neglected privileges. *Testimonies,* vol. 5, p. 463.

The Protestant world today see in the little company keeping the Sabbath a Mordecai in the gate. His character and conduct, expressing reverence for the law of God, are a constant rebuke to those who have cast off the fear of the Lord, and are trampling upon His Sabbath; the unwelcome intruder must by some means be put out of the way. *Testimonies,* vol. 5, p. 450.

Satan will excite indignation against the humble minority who conscientiously refuse to accept popular customs and traditions. Men of position and reputation will join with the lawless and the vile to take counsel against the people of God. Wealth, genius, education, will combine to cover them with contempt. Persecuting rulers, ministers, and church members will conspire against them. With voice and pen, by boasts, threats, and ridicule, they will seek to overthrow their faith. By false representations and angry appeals, they will stir up the passions of the people. Not having a "Thus saith the Scriptures" to bring against the advocates of the Bible Sabbath, they will resort to oppressive enactments to supply the lack. To secure popularity and patronage, legislators will yield to the demand for a Sunday law. . . . On this battlefield comes the last great conflict of the controversy between truth and error. *Testimonies,* vol. 5, pp. 450, 451.

## *Persecution Essential*

When they were scattered by persecution, they went forth filled with missionary zeal. They realized the responsibility of their mission. They knew that they held in their hands the bread of life for a famishing world; and they were constrained by the love of Christ to break this bread to all who were in need. *The Acts of the Apostles,* p. 106.

God means that testing truth shall be brought to the front and become a subject of examination and discussion, even if it is through the contempt placed upon it. The minds of the people must be agitated. Every controversy, every reproach, every slander, will be God's means of provoking inquiry and awakening minds that otherwise would slumber. *Testimonies,* vol. 5, p. 453.

## *Why Persecution Slumbers*

The apostle Paul declares that "all that will live godly in Christ Jesus shall suffer persecution." Why is it, then, that persecution seems in a great degree to slumber? The only reason is that the church has conformed to the world's standard and therefore awakens no opposition. The religion which is current in our day is not of the pure and holy character that marked the Christian faith in the days of Christ and His apostles. It is only because of the spirit of compromise with sin, because the great truths of the Word of God are so indifferently regarded, because there is so little vital godliness in the church, that Christianity is apparently so popular with the world. Let there be a revival of faith and power of the early church, and the spirit of persecution will be revived, and the fires of persecution will be rekindled. *The Great Controversy,* p. 48.

## *Threefold Persecuting Union*

Through the two great errors, the immortality of the soul and Sunday sacredness, Satan will bring the people under his deceptions. While the former lays the foundation of spiritualism, the latter creates a bond of sympathy with Rome. The Protestants of the United States will be foremost in stretching their hands across the gulf to grasp the hand of spiritualism; they will reach over the abyss to clasp hands with the Roman power; and under the influence of this threefold union, this country will follow in the steps of Rome in trampling on the rights of conscience. *The Great Controversy,* p. 588.

## *The Last Act in the Drama*

The substitution of the laws of men for the law of God, the exaltation, by merely human authority, of Sunday in place of the Bible Sabbath, is the last act in the drama. When this substitution becomes universal, God will reveal Himself. He will arise in His majesty to shake terribly the earth. He will come out of His place to punish the inhabitants of the world for their iniquity, and the earth shall disclose her blood, and shall no more cover her slain. *Testimonies,* vol. 7, p. 141.

When our nation shall so abjure the principles of its government as to enact a Sunday law, Protestantism will in this act join hands with popery; it will be nothing else than giving life to the tyranny which has long been eagerly watching its opportunity to spring again into active despotism. *Testimonies,* vol. 5, p. 712.

By the decree of enforcing the institution of the Papacy in violation of the law of God, our nation will disconnect herself fully from righteousness. When Protestantism shall stretch her hand across the gulf to grasp the hand of the Roman power, when she shall reach over the abyss to clasp hands with spiritualism, when, under the influence of this threefold union, our country shall repudiate every principle of its Constitution as a Protestant and republican government, and shall make provision for the propagation of papal falsehoods and delusions, then we may know that the time has come for the marvelous working of Satan and that the end is near. *Testimonies,* vol. 5, p. 451.

The time is not far distant, when, like the early disciples, we shall be forced to seek a refuge in desolate and solitary places. As the siege of Jerusalem by the Roman armies was the signal for flight to the Judean Christians, so the assumption of power on the part of our nation, in the decree enforcing the papal sabbath, will be a warning to us. It will then be time to leave the large cities, preparatory to leaving the smaller ones for retired homes in secluded places among the mountains. *Testimonies,* vol. 5, pp. 464, 465.

## *Many With Blinded Eyes*

There are many, even of those engaged in this movement for Sunday enforcement, who are blinded to the results which will follow this action. They do not see that they are striking directly against religious liberty. There are many who have never understood the claims of the Bible Sabbath, and the false foundation upon which the Sunday institution rests. *Testimonies,* vol. 5, p. 711.

## *Responsibilities and Duties of God's People*

The banner of truth and religious liberty held aloft by the founders of the gospel church and by God's witnesses during the centuries that have passed since then, has, in this last conflict, been committed to our hands. The responsibility for this great gift rests with those whom God has blessed with a knowledge of His Word. We are to receive this Word as a supreme authority. We are to recognize human government as an ordinance of divine appointment, and teach obedience to it as a sacred duty, within its legitimate sphere. But when its claims conflict with the claims of God, we must obey God rather than men. God's word must be recognized as above all human legislation. A "Thus saith the Lord" is not to be set aside for a "Thus saith the church" or a "Thus saith the state." The crown of Christ is to be lifted above the diadems of earthly potentates. *The Acts of the Apostles,* pp. 68, 69.

We as a people have not accomplished the work which God has committed to us. We are not ready for the issue to which the enforcement of the Sunday law will bring us. It is our duty, as we see the signs of approaching peril, to arouse to action. Let none sit in calm expectation of the evil, comforting themselves with the belief that this work must go on because prophecy has foretold it, and that the Lord will shelter his people. We are not doing the will of God if we sit in quietude, doing nothing to preserve liberty of conscience. Fervent, effectual prayer should be ascending to heaven that this calamity may be deferred until we can accomplish the work which has so long been neglected. Let there be more earnest prayer; and then let us work in harmony with our prayers. *Testimonies,* vol. 5, pp. 713, 714.

It is our duty to do all in our power to avert the threatened danger. We should endeavor to disarm prejudice by placing ourselves in a proper light before the people. We should bring before them the real question at issue, thus interposing the most effectual protest against measures to restrict liberty of conscience. *Testimonies,* vol. 5 p. 452.

When God has given us light showing the dangers before us, how can we stand clear in His sight if we neglect to put forth every effort in our power to bring it before the people? Can we be content to leave them to meet this momentous issue unwarned? *Testimonies,* vol. 5, p. 712.

When the National Reformers began to urge measures to restrict religious liberty, our leading men should have been alive to the situation and should have labored earnestly to counteract these efforts. It is not in the order of God that light has been kept from our people—the very present truth which they needed for this time. Not all our ministers who are giving the third angel's message really understand what constitutes that message. The National Reform movement has been regarded by some as of so little importance that they have not thought it necessary to give much attention to it and have even felt that in so doing they would be giving time to questions distinct from the third angel's message. May the Lord forgive our brethren for thus interpreting the very message for this time. *Testimonies,* vol. 5, p. 715.

We have been looking many years for a Sunday law to be enacted in our land; and now that the movement is right upon us, we ask, Will our people do their duty in the matter? Can we not assist in lifting the standard and in calling to the front those who have a regard for their religious rights and privileges? The time is fast approaching when those who choose to obey God rather than man will be made to feel the hand of oppression. Shall we then dishonor God by keeping silent while His holy commandments are trodden under foot? While the Protestant world is by her attitude making concessions to Rome, let us arouse to comprehend the situation and view the contest before us in its true bearings. Let the watchmen now lift up their voice and give the message, which is present truth for this time. Let us show people where we are in prophetic history, and seek to arouse the spirit of true Protestantism, awakening the world to a sense of the value of the privileges of religious liberty so long enjoyed. *Testimonies,* vol. 5, p. 716.

The people of our land need to be aroused to resist the advances of this most dangerous foe to civil and religious liberty. *Spirit of Prophecy,* vol. 4, p. 382.

Shall we sit with folded hands, and do nothing in this crisis? . . . God help us to arouse from the stupor that has hung over us for years. *Review and Herald,* Dec. 18, 1888.

## *A Wise Course to Pursue*

To defy the Sunday laws will but strengthen in their persecution the religious zealots who are seeking to enforce them. Give them no occasion to call you lawbreakers. If they are left to rein up men who fear neither God nor man, the reining up will soon lose its novelty for them, and they will see that it is not consistent nor convenient for them to be strict in regard to the observance of Sunday. Keep right on with your missionary work, with your Bibles in your hands, and the enemy will see that he has worsted his own cause. One does not receive the mark of the beast because he shows that he realizes the wisdom of keeping the peace by refraining from work that gives offense, doing at the same time a work of the highest importance. *Testimonies,* vol. 9, p. 232.

When we devote Sunday to missionary work, the whip will be taken out of the hands of the arbitrary zealots who would be well pleased to humiliate Seventh-day Adventists. When they see that we employ ourselves on Sunday in visiting the people and opening the Scriptures to them, they will know that is useless for them to try to hinder our work by making Sunday laws. *Testimonies,* vol. 9, pp. 232, 233.

Sunday can be used for carrying forward various lines of work that will accomplish much for the Lord. On this day open-air meetings and cottage meetings can be held. House-to-house work can be done. Those who write can devote this day to writing their articles. Whenever it is possible, let religious services be held on Sunday. Make these meetings intensely interesting. Sing genuine revival hymns, and speak with power and assurance of the Saviour's love. Speak on temperance and on true religious experience. *Testimonies,* vol. 9, p. 233.

Let the teachers in our schools devote Sunday to missionary effort. I was instructed that they would thus be able to defeat the purposes of the enemy. Let the teachers take the students with them to hold meetings for those who know not the truth. Thus they will accomplish much more that they could in any other way. *Testimonies,* vol. 9, p. 233.

## *The Triumph of Truth*

Skepticism may treat the claims of God's law with jest, scoffing, and denial. The spirit of worldliness may contaminate the many and control the few; the cause of God may hold its ground only by great exertion and continual sacrifice; yet in the end the truth will triumph gloriously. *Prophets and Kings,* p. 186.

In the closing work of God in the earth, the standard of His law will be again exalted. False religion may prevail, iniquity may abound, the love of many may wax cold, the cross of Calvary may be lost sight of, and darkness, like the pall of death, may spread over the world; the whole force of the popular current may be turned against the truth; plot after plot may be formed to overthrow the people of God; but in the hour of greatest peril, the God of Elijah will raise up human instrumentalities to bear a message that will not be silenced. In the populous cities of the land, and in the places where men have gone to the greatest lengths in speaking against the Most High, the voice of stern rebuke will be heard. Boldly will men of God's appointment denounce the union of the church with the world. Earnestly will they call upon men and women to turn from the observance of a man-made institution to the observance of the true Sabbath. *Prophets and Kings,* pp. 186, 187.

## Light in the Darkness

Among earth's inhabitants, scattered in every land, there are those who have not bowed the knee to Baal. Like the stars of heaven, which appear only at night, these faithful ones will shine forth when darkness covers the earth and gross darkness the people. In heathen Africa, in the Catholic lands of Europe and of South America, in China, in India, in the islands of the sea, and in all the dark corners of the earth, God has in reserve a firmament of chosen ones that will yet shine forth amidst the darkness revealing clearly to an apostate world the transforming power of obedience to His law. Even now they are appearing in every nation, among every tongue and people; and in the hour of deepest apostasy, when Satan's supreme effort is made to cause "all, both small and great, rich and poor, free and bond," to receive, under penalty of death, the sign of allegiance to a false rest day, these faithful ones, "blameless and harmless, the sons of God, without rebuke, " will "shine as lights in the world." The darker the night, the more brilliantly will they shine. *Prophets and Kings,* pp. 188, 189.

When the storm of persecution really breaks upon us, the true sheep will hear the true Shepherd's voice. Self-denying efforts will be put forth to save the lost, and many who have strayed from the fold will come back to follow the great Shepherd. *Signs of the Times* (Australian), Supplement, Jan. 26, 1903.

## *The Divine Protection*

But though the conflict is a ceaseless one, none are left to struggle alone. Angels help and protect those who walk humbly before God. Never will our Lord betray one who trusts in Him. As His children draw near to Him for protection from evil, in pity and love He lifts up for them a standard against the enemy. Touch them not, He says; for they are Mine. I have graven them upon the palms of My hands. *Prophets and Kings,* p. 571.

Heaven is very near those who suffer for righteousness' sake. Christ identifies His interests with the interests of His faithful people; He suffers in the person of His saints; and whoever touches His chosen ones, touches Him. The power that is near to deliver from physical harm or distress, is also near to save from the greater evil, making it possible for the servant of God to maintain his integrity under all circumstances. *Prophets and Kings,* p. 545.

At times the Lord may seem to have forgotten the perils of His church, and the injury done her by her enemies. But God has not forgotten. Nothing in this world is so dear to the heart of God as His church. It is not His will that worldly policy shall corrupt her record. He does not leave His people to be overcome by Satan's temptations. He will punish those who misrepresent Him, but He will be gracious to all who sincerely repent. *Prophets and Kings,* p. 590.

# CHAPTER 15

# Harvest Ingathering

### *The Perplexing Problem*

For years the perplexing question has been before us: How can we raise funds adequate for the support of the missions which the Lord has gone before us to open? We read the plain commands of the gospel; and the missions, in both home and foreign fields, present their necessities. The indications, yea, the positive revelations of Providence unite in urging us to do quickly the work that is waiting to be done. *Testimonies,* vol. 9, p. 114.

### *A Successful Plan*

One of the new plans for reaching unbelievers is the Harvest Ingathering campaign for missions. In many places during the past few years, this has proved a success, bringing blessing to many, and increasing the flow of means into the mission treasury. As those not of our faith have been made acquainted with the progress of the third angel's message in heathen lands, their sympathies have been aroused, and some have sought to learn more of the truth that has such power to transform hearts and lives. Men and women of all classes have been reached, and the name of God has been glorified. MS, "Consecrated Efforts to Reach Unbelievers," June 5, 1914.

Some may question the propriety of receiving gifts from unbelievers. Let such ask themselves: "Who is the real owner of our world? To whom belong its houses and lands, and its treasures of gold and silver?" God has an abundance in our world, and He has placed His goods in the hands of all, both the obedient and the disobedient. He is ready to move upon the hearts of worldly men, even idolaters, to give of their abundance for the support of His work; and He will do this as soon as His people learn to approach these men wisely and to call their attention to that which it is their privilege to do. If the needs of the Lord's work were set forth in a proper light before those who have means and influence, these men might do much to advance the cause of present truth. God's people have lost many privileges of which they could have taken advantage, had they not chosen to stand independent of the world. *Southern Watchman,* Mar. 15, 1904.

The Lord still moves upon the hearts of kings and rulers in behalf of His people. Those who are laboring for Him are to avail themselves of the help that He prompts men to give for the advancement of His cause. The agents through whom these gifts come, may open ways by which the light of truth shall be given to many benighted lands. These men may have no sympathy with God's work, no faith in Christ, no acquaintance with His word; but their gifts are not on this account to be refused. *Southern Watchman,* Mar. 15, 1904.

The Lord has placed His goods in the hands of unbelievers as well as believers; all may return to Him His own for the doing of the work that must be done for a fallen world. As long as we are in this world, as long as the Spirit of God strives with the children of men, so long are we to receive favors as well as to impart them. We are to give to the world the light of truth, as revealed in the Scriptures; and we are to receive from the world that which God moves upon them to give in behalf of His cause. *Southern Watchman,* Mar. 15, 1904.

Although now almost wholly in the possession of wicked men, all the world, with its riches and treasures, belongs to God. "The earth is the Lord's, and the fulness thereof." "The silver is Mine, and the gold is Mine, saith the Lord of hosts." "Every beast of the forest is Mine, and the cattle upon a thousand hills. I know all the birds of the mountains; and the wild beasts of the field are Mine. If I were hungry, I would not tell thee; for the world is Mine, and the fulness thereof." O that Christians might realize more and still more fully that it is their privilege and their duty, while cherishing right principles, to take advantage of every heaven-sent opportunity for advancing God's kingdom in this world. *Southern Watchman,* Mar. 15, 1904.

## *Admonition to Workers*

To all who are about to take up special missionary work with the paper prepared for use in the Harvest Ingathering campaign, I would say: Be diligent in your efforts; live under the guidance of the Holy Spirit. Add daily to your Christian experience. Let those who have special aptitude work for unbelievers in the high places as well as in the low places of life. Search diligently for perishing souls. Oh, think of the yearning desire Christ has to bring to His fold again those who have gone astray! Watch for souls as they that must give an account. In your church and neighborhood missionary work, let your light shine forth in such clear, steady rays that no man can stand up in the judgment, and say, "Why did you not tell me about this truth? Why did you not care for my soul?" Then let us be diligent in the distribution of literature that has been carefully prepared for use among those not of our faith. Let us make the most of every opportunity to arrest the attention of unbelievers. Let us put literature into every hand that will receive it. Let us consecrate ourselves to the proclamation of the message, "Prepare ye the way of the Lord, make straight in the desert a highway for our God." MS, "Consecrated Efforts to Reach Unbelievers," June 5, 1914.

## *Essentials to Success*

In following any plan that may be set in operation for carrying to others a knowledge of present truth, and of the marvelous providences connected with the advancing cause, let us first consecrate ourselves fully to Him whose name we wish to exalt. Let us also pray earnestly in behalf of those whom we expect to visit, by living faith bringing them, one by one, into the presence of God. The Lord knows the thought and purposes of man, and how easily He can melt us! How His Spirit, like a fire, can subdue the flinty heart! How He can fill the soul with love and tenderness! How He can give us the graces of His Holy Spirit, and fit us to go in and out, in laboring for souls! MS, "Consecrated Efforts to Reach Unbelievers," June 5, 1914.

The Lord's work might receive far greater favors than it is now receiving, if we would approach men in wisdom, acquainting them with the work, and giving them an opportunity of doing that which it is our privilege to induce them to do for its advancement. If we, as God's servants, would take a wise and prudent course, His good hand would prosper us in our efforts. *Southern Watchman,* Mar. 15, 1904.

If all who are engaged in the Lord's work would realize how much depends upon their fidelity and wise forethought, far greater prosperity would attend their efforts. Through diffidence and backwardness we often fail of securing that which is attainable as a right, from the powers that be. God will work for us, when we are ready to do what we can and should do on our part. *Southern Watchman,* Mar. 15, 1904.

## *Home Missions vs. Foreign Missions*

The home missionary work will be farther advanced in every way when a more liberal, self-denying, self-sacrificing spirit is manifested for the prosperity of foreign missions; for the prosperity of the home work depends largely, under God, upon the reflex influence of the evangelical work done in countries afar off. It is in working actively to supply the necessities of the cause of God that we bring our souls in touch with the Source of all power. *Testimonies,* vol. 6, p. 27.

An American businessman who was an earnest Christian, in conversation with a fellow worker, remarked that he himself worked for Christ twenty-four hours of the day. "In all my business relations," he said, "I try to represent my Master. As I have opportunity, I try to win others to Him. All day I am working for Christ. And at night, while I sleep, I have a man working for Him in China." In explanation, He added: "In my youth I determined to go as a missionary to the heathen. But on the death of my father I had to take up his business in order to provide for the family. Now, instead of going myself, I support a missionary. In such a town of such a province of China, my worker is stationed. And so, even while I sleep, I am, through my representative, still working for Christ."

Are there not Seventh-day Adventists who will do likewise? Instead of keeping the ministers at work for the churches that already know the truth, let the members of the churches say to these laborers: "Go work for souls that are perishing in darkness. We ourselves will carry forward the services of the church. We will keep up the meetings, and, by abiding in Christ, will maintain spiritual life. We will work for souls that are about us, and we will send our prayers and our gifts to sustain the laborers in more needy and destitute fields." *Testimonies,* vol. 6, pp. 29, 30.

## *A Worthy Example*

The poor widow who cast her two mites into the Lord's treasury little knew what she was doing. Her example of self-sacrifice has acted and reacted upon thousands of hearts in every land and in every age. It has brought to the treasury of God gifts from the high and the low, the rich and the poor. It has helped to sustain missions, to establish hospitals, to feed the hungry, clothe the naked, heal the sick, and preach the gospel to the poor. Multitudes have been blessed through her unselfish deed. *Testimonies,* vol. 6, p. 310.

## *Lessons From the Life of Nehemiah*

In years past I have spoken in favor of the plan of presenting our mission work and its progress before our friends and neighbors, and have referred to the example of Nehemiah. And now I desire to urge our brethren and sisters to study anew the experience of this man of prayer and faith and sound judgment, who made bold to ask his friend, King Artaxerxes, for help with which to advance the interests of God's cause. MS, "Consecrated Efforts to Reach Unbelievers," June 5, 1914.

*Solicited Means From Those Able to Bestow.*—Men of prayer should be men of action. Those who are ready and willing will find ways and means of working. Nehemiah did not depend upon uncertainties. The means which he lacked he solicited from those who were able to bestow. *Southern Watchman,* Mar. 15, 1904.

*Courage for the Task Came Through Power.*—Nehemiah and Artaxerxes stood face to face—the one a servant of a downtrodden race, the other the monarch of the world's great empire. But infinitely greater than the disparity of rank was the moral distance which separated them. Nehemiah had complied with the invitation of the King of kings, "Let him take hold of My strength, that he may make peace with Me, and he shall make peace with Me." The silent petition that he sent up to heaven was the same that he had offered for many weeks, that God would prosper his request. And now, taking courage at the thought that he had a Friend, omniscient and omnipotent, to work in his behalf, the man of God made known to the king his desire for release for a time from his office at the court, and for authority to build up the waste places of Jerusalem, and make it once more a strong and defended city. Momentous results to the Jewish city and nation hung upon this request. "And," says Nehemiah, "the king granted me according to the good hand of my God upon me." *Southern Watchman,* Mar. 8, 1904.

*Secured Official Indorsement.*—As his [Nehemiah's] request to the king had been so favorably received, he was encouraged to ask for such assistance as was needed for the carrying out of his plans. To give dignity and authority to his mission, as well as to provide for protection on the journey, he secured a military escort. He obtained royal letters to the governors of the provinces beyond the Euphrates, the territory through which he must pass on his way to Judea; and he obtained, also, a letter to the keeper of the king's forest in the mountains of Lebanon, directing him to furnish such timber as would be needed for the wall of Jerusalem and the buildings that Nehemiah proposed to erect. In order that there might be no occasion for complaint that he had exceeded his commission, Nehemiah was careful to have the authority and privileges accorded him clearly defined. *Southern Watchman,* Mar. 15, 1904.

The royal letters to the governors of the provinces along his route secured to Nehemiah an honorable reception and prompt assistance. And no enemy dared molest the official who was guarded by the power of the Persian king and treated with marked consideration by the provincial rulers. Nehemiah's journey was safe and prosperous. *Southern Watchman,* Mar. 22, 1904.

*Encountering Obstacles.*—His arrival at Jerusalem, however, with the attendance of a military guard, showing that he had come on some important mission, excited the jealousy and hatred of the enemies of Israel. The heathen tribes settled near Jerusalem had previously indulged their enmity against the Jews by heaping upon them every insult and injury which they dared inflict. Foremost in this evil work were certain chiefs of these tribes, Sanballat the Horonite, Tobiah the Ammonite, and Geshem the Arabian; and from this time these leaders watched with jealous eye the movements of Nehemiah and endeavored by every means in their power to thwart his plans and hinder his work. *Southern Watchman,* Mar. 22, 1904.

They attempted to cause division among the workmen by suggesting doubts and arousing unbelief as to their success. They also ridiculed the efforts of the builders, declared the enterprise an impossibility, and predicted a disgraceful failure. . . . The builders on the wall were soon beset by more active opposition. They were compelled to guard continually against the plots of their sleepless adversaries. The emissaries of the enemy endeavored to destroy their courage by the circulation of false reports; conspiracies were formed on various pretexts to draw Nehemiah into their toils; and false-hearted Jews were found ready to aid the treacherous undertaking. . . . Emissaries of the enemy, professing friendliness, mingled with the builders, suggesting changes in the plan, seeking in various ways to divert the attention of the workers, to cause confusion and perplexity, and to arouse distrust and suspicion. *Southern Watchman,* Apr. 12, 1904.

*Same Obstacles Confront Leaders Today.*—The experience of Nehemiah is repeated in the history of God's people in this time. Those who labor in the cause of truth will find that they cannot do this without exciting the anger of its enemies. Though they have been called of God to the work in which they are engaged, and their course is approved of Him, they cannot escape reproach and derision. They will be denounced as visionary, unreliable, scheming, hypocritical—anything, in short, that will suit the purpose of their enemies. The most sacred things will be represented in a ridiculous light to amuse the ungodly. A very small amount of sarcasm and low wit, united with envy, jealousy, impiety, and hatred, is sufficient to excite the mirth of the profane scoffer. And these presumptuous jesters sharpen one another's ingenuity, and embolden each other in their blasphemous work. Contempt and derision are indeed painful to human nature; but they must be endured by all who are true to God. It is the policy of Satan thus to turn souls from doing the work which the Lord has laid upon them. *Southern Watchman,* Apr. 12, 1904.

*Rallying the Dispirited Forces.*—In secrecy and silence, Nehemiah completed his circuit of the walls. He declares, "The rulers knew not whither I went, or what I did; neither had I as yet told it to the Jews, nor to the priests, nor to the nobles, nor to the rulers, nor to the rest that did the work." In this painful survey he did not wish to attract the attention of either friends or foes, lest an excitement should be created, and reports be put in circulation that might defeat, or at least hinder, his work. Nehemiah devoted the remainder of the night to prayer; in the morning there must be earnest effort to arouse and unite his dispirited and divided countrymen. *Southern Watchman,* Mar. 22, 1904.

Although Nehemiah bore a royal commission requiring the inhabitants to cooperate with him in rebuilding the walls of the city, he chose not to depend upon the mere exercise of authority. He sought rather to gain the confidence and sympathy of the people, well knowing that a union of hearts as well as hands was essential to success in the great work which he had undertaken.

When he called the people together on the morrow, he presented such arguments as were calculated to arouse their dormant energies and to unite their scattered numbers. . . . And having laid the matter fully before them, showing that he was sustained by the combined authority of the Persian king and the God of Israel, Nehemiah put to the people directly the question whether they would take advantage of this favorable occasion, and arise with him and build the wall. This appeal went straight to their hearts; the manifestation of the favor of Heaven toward them put their fears to shame. With new courage they cried out with one voice, "Let us rise up and build." *Southern Watchman,* Mar. 29, 1904.

The holy energy and high hope of Nehemiah were communicated to the people. As they caught the spirit, they rose for a time to the moral level of their leader. Each, in his own sphere, was a sort of Nehemiah; and each strengthened and upheld his brother in the work. *Southern Watchman,* Mar. 29, 1904.

*The Priests of Israel Among the First to Respond.*—Among the first to catch Nehemiah's spirit of zeal and earnestness were the priests of Israel. From the position of influence which they occupied, these men could do much to hinder or advance the work. Their ready cooperation at the very outset contributed not a little to its success. Thus should it be in every holy enterprise. Those who occupy positions of influence and responsibility in the church, should be foremost in the work of God. If they move reluctantly, others will not move at all. But "their zeal will provoke very many." When their light burns brightly, a thousand torches will be kindled at the flame. *Southern Watchman,* Apr. 5, 1904.

*Nehemiah as an Organizer.*—The people in general were animated with one heart and one soul of patriotism and cheerful activity. Men of ability and influence organized the various classes of citizens into companies, each leader making himself responsible for the erection of a certain portion of the wall. It was a sight well pleasing to God and angels to see the busy companies working harmoniously upon the broken-down walls of Jerusalem, and it was a joyous sound to hear the noise of instruments of labor from the earliest dawn "till the stars appeared." *Southern Watchman,* Apr. 5, 1904.

*The Demonstration of True Leadership.*—Nehemiah's zeal and energy did not abate, now that the work was actually begun. He did not fold his hands, feeling that he might let fall the burden. With tireless vigilance he constantly superintended the work, directing the workmen, noting every hindrance, and providing for every emergency. His influence was constantly felt along the whole extent of those three miles of wall. With timely words he encouraged the fearful, approved the diligent, or aroused the laggard. And again he watched with eagle eye the movements of their enemies, who at times collected at a distance and engaged in earnest conversation, as if plotting mischief, and then drawing near the workmen, attempted to divert their attention and hinder the work.

While the eye of every worker is often directed to Nehemiah, ready to heed the slightest signal, his eye and heart are uplifted to God, the great Overseer of the whole work, the one who put it into the heart of His servant to build. And as faith and courage strengthen in his own heart, Nehemiah exclaims, and his words, repeated and re-echoed, thrill the hearts of the workers all along the line, "The God of heaven, He will prosper us!" *Southern Watchman,* Apr. 5, 1904.

Nehemiah and his companions did not shrink from hardships or excuse themselves from trying service. Neither by night nor by day, not even during the brief time given to slumber, did they put off their clothing or even lay aside their armor. "So neither I, nor my brethren, nor my servants, nor the men of the guard which followed me, none of us put off our clothes, saving that every one put them off for washing." *Southern Watchman,* Apr. 26, 1904.

*Counteracting Influence in Every Religious Movement.*—A majority of the nobles and rulers of Israel also came nobly up to their duty; but there were a few, the Tekoite nobles, who "put not their necks to the work of their Lord." While the faithful builders have honorable mention in the book of God, the memory of these slothful servants is branded with shame, and handed down as a warning to all future generations.

In every religious movement there are some who, while they cannot deny that it is the work of God, will keep themselves aloof, refusing to make any effort to advance it. But in enterprises to promote their selfish interests, these men are often the most active and energetic workers. It were well to remember that record kept on high, the book of God, in which all our motives and our works are written—that book in which there are no omissions, no mistakes, and out of which we are to be judged. There every neglected opportunity to do service for God will be faithfully reported, and every deed of faith and love, however humble, will be held in everlasting remembrance. *Southern Watchman,* April 5, 1904.

## *The Call for Modern Nehemiahs*

There is need of Nehemiahs in the church today—not men who can pray and preach only, but men whose prayers and sermons are braced with firm and eager purpose. The course pursued by this Hebrew patriot in the accomplishment of his plans is one that should still be adopted by ministers and leading men. When they have laid their plans, they should present them to the church in such a manner as to win their interest and cooperation. Let the people understand the plans and share in the work, and they will have a personal interest in its prosperity. The success attending Nehemiah's efforts shows what prayer, faith, and wise, energetic action will accomplish. Living faith will prompt to energetic action. The spirit manifested by the leader will be, to a great extent, reflected by the people. If the leaders professing to believe the solemn, important truths that are to test the world at this time manifest no ardent zeal to prepare a people to stand in the day of God, we must expect the church to be careless, indolent, and pleasure-loving. *Southern Watchman,* Mar. 29, 1904.

# CHAPTER 16

# The Church Expansion Movement

### The Divine Plan

It is not the purpose of God that His people should colonize, or settle together in large communities. The disciples of Christ are His representatives upon the earth, and God designs that they shall be scattered all over the country, in the towns, cities, and villages, as lights amidst the darkness of the world. *Testimonies,* vol. 8, p. 244.

The plan of colonizing, or moving from different localities where there is but little strength or influence, and concentrating the influence of many in one locality, is removing the light from places where God would have it shine. *Testimonies,* vol. 2, p. 633.

If the church of Christ were fulfilling the purpose of our Lord, light would be shed upon all that sit in darkness and in the region and shadow of death. Instead of congregating together and shunning responsibility and cross-bearing, the members of the church would scatter into all lands, letting the light of Christ shine out from them, working as He did for the salvation of souls, and this "gospel of the kingdom" would speedily be carried to all the world. *Thoughts From the Mount of Blessing,* pp. 42, 43.

Brethren and sisters, why hover about the churches? Study the parable of the lost sheep, and go forth as true shepherds, seeking the lost one who is in the wilderness of sin. Rescue the perishing. *Review and Herald,* Dec. 12, 1893.

The lay members of our churches can accomplish a work which, as yet, they have scarcely begun. None should move into new places merely for the sake of worldly advantage; but where there is an opening to obtain a livelihood, let families that are well grounded in the truth enter, one or two families in a place, to work as missionaries. They should feel a love for souls, a burden of labor for them, and should make it a study how to bring them into the truth. They can distribute our publications, hold meetings in their homes, become acquainted with their neighbors, and invite them to come to these meetings. Thus they can let their light shine in good works. *Testimonies,* vol. 8, p. 245.

Brethren who wish to change their location, who have the glory of God in view, and feel that individual responsibility rests upon them to do others good, to benefit and save souls for whom Christ withheld not His precious life, should move into towns and villages where there is but little or no light and where they can be of real service and bless others with their labor and experience. Missionaries are wanted to go into towns and villages and raise the standard of truth, that God may have His witnesses scattered all over the land, that the light of truth may penetrate where it has not yet reached, and the standard of truth be raised where it is not yet known. *Testimonies,* vol. 2, p. 115.

Nothing will so arouse a self-sacrificing zeal and broaden and strengthen the character as to engage in work for others. Many professed Christians, in seeking church relationship, think only of themselves. They wish to enjoy church fellowship and pastoral care. They become members of large and prosperous churches, and are content to do little for others. In this way they are robbing themselves of the most precious blessings. Many would be greatly benefited by sacrificing their pleasant, ease-conducing associations. They need to go where their energies will be called out in Christian work, and they can learn to bear responsibilities. *The Ministry of Healing,* p. 151.

There are thousands of places to be entered where the standard of truth has never been raised, where the proclamation of the truth has never been heard in America. And there are thousands who might enter the harvest field who are now religiously idle, and as a result, go crippling their way to heaven, expressing their doubt whether they are Christians. Their need is a vital union with Jesus Christ. Then it can be said of them, "Ye are laborers together with God." I want to say to many, You are waiting for someone to carry you to the vineyard and set you to work, or to bring the vineyard to you, that you may experience no inconvenience in labor. You will wait in vain. If you will lift up your eyes, you will see the harvest ripe, ready for the sickle, whichever way you may look; you will find work close by and far off. But of how many will Christ say in the judgment, "Good and faithful servants"? I think how the angels must feel seeing the end approaching, and those who claim to have a knowledge of God and Jesus Christ whom He hath sent, huddle together, colonize, and attend the meetings, and feel dissatisfied if there is not much preaching to benefit their souls and strengthen the church, while they are doing literally nothing. . . . If their temporal, financial prospects are not as prosperous by moving to localities where the truth has not been proclaimed, or where there has been but a glimmering of light, will they not be doing just the work that Jesus has done to save them? *General Conference Bulletin,* 1893, p. 131.

We see the great need of missionary work to carry the truth not only to foreign countries, but to those who are near us. Close around us are cities and towns in which no efforts are made to save souls. Why should not families who know the present truth settle in these cities and villages, to set up there the standard of Christ, working in humility, not in their own way, but in God's way, to bring the light before those who have no knowledge of it?

When the church shall truly have the spirit of the message, they will throw all their energies into the work of saving the souls for whom Christ has died. They will enter new fields. Some who are not ordained ministers will be laborers together with God in visiting the churches, and trying to strengthen the things that remain, that are ready to die. There will be laymen who will move into towns and cities, and into apparently out-of-the-way places, that they may let the light which God has given them, shine forth to others. Some whom they meet will not appear to be the most promising subjects, but the only question should be, Will they come into harmony with Christ? Will they become partakers of His spirit, so that their influence, in precept and example, will present the attractions of the Author of truth and righteousness?

In places where the truth is not known, brethren who are adapted to the work might hire a hall, or some other suitable place to assemble, and gather together all who will come. Then let them instruct the people in the truth. They need not sermonize, but take the Bible, and let God speak directly out of His Word. If there is only a small number present, they can read a "Thus saith the Lord," without a great parade or excitement; just read and explain the simple gospel truth, and sing and pray with them. *Review and Herald,* Sept. 29, 1891.

## *Abraham a Worthy Example*

It was no light test that was thus brought upon Abraham, no small sacrifice that was required of him. There were strong ties to bind him to his country, his kindred, and his home. But he did not hesitate to obey the call. He had no question to ask concerning the Land of Promise—whether the soil was fertile, and the climate healthful; whether the country offered agreeable surroundings, and would afford opportunities for amassing wealth. God had spoken, and His servant must obey; the happiest place on earth for him was the place where God would have him to be.

Many are still tested as was Abraham. They do not hear the voice of God speaking directly from the heavens, but He calls them by the teachings of His Word and the events of this providence. They may be required to abandon a career that promises wealth and honor, to leave congenial and profitable associations, and separate from kindred, to enter upon what appears to be only a path of self-denial, hardship, and sacrifice. God has a work for them to do; but a life of ease and the influence of friends and kindred would hinder the development of the very traits essential for its accomplishment. He calls them away from human influences and aid, and leads them to feel the need of His help, and to depend upon Him alone, that He may reveal Himself to them.

Who is ready at the call of Providence to renounce cherished plans and familiar associations? Who will accept new duties and enter untried fields, doing God's work with firm and willing hearts, for Christ's sake counting His losses again? He who will do this has the faith of Abraham, and will share with him that "far more exceeding and eternal weight of glory," with which "the sufferings of this present time are not worthy to be compared." *Patriarchs and Prophets,* pp. 126, 127.

## *What Doest Thou Here?*

Much depends on the unceasing activity of those who are true and loyal; and for this reason Satan puts forth every possible effort to thwart the divine purpose to be wrought out through the obedient. He causes some to lose sight of their high and holy mission, and to become satisfied with the pleasures of this life. He leads them to settle down at ease, or, for the sake of greater worldly advantages, to remove from places where they might be a power for good. Others he causes to flee in discouragement from duty, because of opposition or persecution. But all such are regarded by Heaven with tenderest pity. To every child of God whose voice the enemy of souls had succeeded in silencing, the question is addressed, "What doest thou here?" I commissioned you to go into all the world and preach the gospel, to prepare a people for the day of God. Why are you here? Who sent you? *Prophets and Kings,* pp. 171, 172.

Of families, as of individuals, the question is asked, "What doest thou here?" In many churches there are families well instructed in the truths of God's Word, who might widen the sphere of their influence by moving to places in need of the ministry they are capable of giving. *Prophets and Kings,* p. 172.

## *The Call to Christian Families*

Missionary families are needed to settle in the waste places. Let farmers, financiers, builders, and those who are skilled in various arts and crafts, go to neglected fields, to improve the land, to establish industries, to prepare humble homes for themselves, and to help their neighbors. *The Ministry of Healing,* p. 194.

God calls for Christian families to go into communities that are in darkness and error, and work wisely and perseveringly for the Master. To answer this call requires self-sacrifice. While many are waiting to have every obstacle removed, souls are dying without hope and without God in the world. Many, very many, for the sake of worldly advantage, for the sake of acquiring scientific knowledge, will venture into pestilential regions, and endure hardship and privation. Where are those who are willing to do this for the sake of telling others of the Saviour? Where are the men and women who will move into regions that are in need of the gospel, that they may point those in darkness to the Redeemer? *Testimonies,* vol. 9, p. 33.

There are whole families who might be missionaries, engaging in personal labor, toiling for the Master with busy hands and active brains, devising new methods for the success of His work. *Testimonies,* vol. 9, p. 40.

If families would locate in the dark places of the earth, places where the people are enshrouded in spiritual gloom, and let the light of Christ's life shine out through them, a great work might be accomplished. Let them begin their work in a quiet, unobtrusive way, not drawing on the funds of the conference until the interest becomes so extensive that they cannot manage it without ministerial help. *Testimonies,* vol. 6, p. 442.

## *Transplanting Requires Wise Nurserymen*

Prepare workers to go out into the highways and hedges. We need wise nurserymen who will transplant trees to different localities and give them advantages, that they may grow. It is the positive duty of God's people to go into the regions beyond. Let forces be set at work to clear new ground, to establish new centers of influence wherever an opening can be found. Rally workers who possess true missionary zeal, and let them go forth to diffuse light and knowledge far and near. *Testimonies,* vol. 9, p. 118.

Many of the members of our large churches are doing comparatively nothing. They might accomplish a good work if, instead of crowding together, they would scatter into places that have not yet been entered by the truth. Trees that are planted too thickly do not flourish. They are transplanted by the gardener, that they may have room to grow, and not become dwarfed and sickly. The same rule would work well for our large churches. Many of the members are dying spiritually for want of this very work. They are becoming sickly and inefficient. Transplanted, they would have room to grow strong and vigorous. *Testimonies,* vol. 8 p. 244.

## Assurance of Results

If the lay members of the church will arouse to do the work that they can do, going on a warfare at their own charges, each seeing how much he can accomplish in winning souls to Jesus, we shall see many leaving the ranks of Satan to stand under the banner of Christ. If our people will act upon the light that is given in these few words of instruction, we shall surely see of the salvation of God. Wonderful revivals will follow. Sinners will be converted, and many souls will be added to the church. *Testimonies,* vol. 8, p. 246.

Our church members should feel a deep interest in home and foreign missions. Great blessings will come to them as they make self-sacrificing efforts to plant the standard of truth in new territory. The money invested in this work will bring rich returns. New converts, rejoicing in the light received from the Word, will in their turn give of their means to carry the light of truth to others. *Testimonies,* vol. 9, p. 49.

In fields where the conditions are so objectionable and disheartening that many workers refuse to go to them, most remarkable changes for the better may be brought about by the efforts of self-sacrificing lay members. These humble workers will accomplish much because they put forth patient, persevering effort, not relying upon human power, but upon God, who gives them His favor. The amount of good that these workers accomplish will never be known in this world. *Testimonies,* vol. 7 pp. 22, 23.

## A Lesson From the Failure of Ancient Israel

When the Israelites entered Canaan, they did not fulfill God's purpose by taking possession of the whole land. After making a partial conquest, they settled down to enjoy the fruit of their victories. In their unbelief and love of ease they congregated in the portions already conquered, instead of pushing forward to occupy new territory. Thus they began to depart from God. By their failure to carry out His purpose they made it impossible for Him to fulfill to them His promise of blessing. Is not the church of today doing the same thing? With the whole world before them in need of the gospel, professed Christians congregate where they themselves can enjoy gospel privileges. They do not feel the necessity of occupying new territory, carrying the message of salvation into regions beyond. They refuse to fulfill Christ's commission, "Go ye into all the world, and preach the gospel to every creature." Are they less guilty than was the Jewish church? *Testimonies,* vol. 8, p. 119.

# CHAPTER 17

# Christian Help Work

### Tracing the Divine Footprints

Many feel that it would be a great privilege to visit the scenes of Christ's life on earth, to walk where He trod, to look upon the lake beside which He loved to teach, and the hills and valleys on which His eyes so often rested. But we need not go to Nazareth, to Capernaum, or to Bethany, in order to walk in the steps of Jesus. We shall find His footprints beside the sick-bed, in the hovels of poverty, in the crowded alleys of the great city, and in every place where there are human hearts in need of consolation. In doing as Jesus did when on earth, we shall walk in His steps. *The Desire of Ages,* p. 640.

Jesus worked to relieve every case of suffering that He saw. He had little money to give, but He often denied Himself of food in order to relieve those who appeared more needy than He. His brothers felt that His influence went far to counteract theirs. He possessed a tact which none of them had, or desired to have. When they spoke harshly to poor, degraded beings, Jesus sought out these very ones, and spoke to them words of encouragement. To those who were in need He would give a cup of cold water, and would quietly place His own meal in their hands. As He relieved their sufferings, the truths He taught were associated with His acts of mercy and were thus riveted in the memory. *The Desire of Ages,* pp. 86, 87.

### The Indorsement

The followers of Christ are to labor as He did. We are to feed the hungry, clothe the naked, and comfort the suffering and afflicted. We are to minister to the despairing and inspire hope in the hopeless. And to us also the promise will be fulfilled, "Thy righteousness shall go before thee; the glory of the Lord shall be thy rearward." *The Desire of Ages,* p. 350.

Those who have been engaged in this Christian help work have been doing what the Lord desires to have done, and He has accepted their labors. That which has been done in this line is a work which every Seventh-day Adventist should heartily sympathize with and indorse, and take hold of earnestly. In neglecting this work which is within their own borders, in refusing to bear these burdens, the church is meeting with great loss. Had the church taken up this work as they should have done, they would have been the means of saving many souls.—*Testimonies,* vol. 6, p. 295.

All His gifts are to be used in blessing humanity, in relieving the suffering and the needy. We are to feed the hungry, to clothe the naked, to care for the widow and the fatherless, to minister to the distressed and downtrodden. God never meant that the widespread misery in the world should exist. He never meant that one man should have an abundance of the luxuries of life, while the children of others should cry for bread. The means over and above the actual necessities of life are intrusted to man to do good, to bless humanity. The Lord says, "Sell that ye have, and give alms." Be "ready to distribute, willing to communicate." "When thou makest a feast, call the poor, the maimed, the lame, the blind." "Loose the bands of wickedness," "undo the heavy burdens," "let the oppressed go free," "break every yoke." "Deal thy bread to the hungry," "bring the poor that are cast out to thy house." "When thou seest the naked, . . . cover him." "Satisfy the afflicted soul." "Go ye into all the world, and preach the gospel to every creature." These are the Lord's commands. Are the great body of professed Christians doing this work? *Christ's Object Lessons,* pp. 370, 371.

Good deeds are the fruit that Christ requires us to bear: kind words, deeds of benevolence, of tender regard for the poor, the needy, the afflicted. When hearts sympathize with hearts burdened with discouragement and grief, when the hand dispenses to the needy, when the naked are clothed, the stranger made welcome to a seat in your parlor and a place in your heart, angels are coming very near, and an answering strain is responded to in heaven. Every act of justice, mercy, and benevolence, makes melody in heaven. The Father from His throne beholds those who do these acts of mercy, and numbers them with His most precious treasures. "And they shall be Mine, saith the Lord of hosts, in that day when I make up My jewels." Every merciful act to the needy, the suffering, is regarded as though done to Jesus. When you succor the poor, sympathize with the afflicted and oppressed, and befriend the orphan, you bring yourselves into a closer relationship to Jesus. *Testimonies,* vol. 2, p. 25.

The work of gathering in the needy, the oppressed, the suffering, the destitute, is the very work which every church that believes the truth for this time should long since have been doing. We are to show the tender sympathy of the Samaritan in supplying physical necessities, feeding the hungry, bringing the poor that are cast out to our homes, gathering from God every day grace and strength that will enable us to reach to the very depths of human misery and help those who cannot possibly help themselves. In doing this work we have a favorable opportunity to set forth Christ the crucified One. *Testimonies,* vol. 6, p. 276.

Many wonder why their prayers are so lifeless, their faith so feeble and wavering, their Christian experience so dark and uncertain. Have we not fasted, they say, "and walked mournfully before the Lord of hosts?" In the fifty-eighth chapter of Isaiah Christ has shown how this condition of things may be changed. . . . Verses 6, 7. This is the recipe that Christ has prescribed for the faint-hearted, doubting, trembling soul. Let the sorrowful ones, who walk mournfully before the Lord, arise and help someone who needs help. *Testimonies,* vol 6, p. 266.

The glory of heaven is in lifting up the fallen, comforting the distressed. And wherever Christ abides in human hearts, He will be revealed in the same way. Wherever it acts, the religion of Christ will bless. Wherever it works, there is brightness. *Christ's Object Lessons,* p. 386.

The widow of Zarephath shared her morsel with Elijah; and in return, her life and that of her son were preserved. And to all who, in time of trial and want, give sympathy and assistance to others more needy, God has promised great blessing. He has not changed. His power is no less now than in the days of Elijah. *Prophets and Kings,* pp. 131, 132.

The love of Christ, manifested in unselfish ministry, will be more effective in reforming the evil-doer than will the sword or the court of justice. These are necessary to strike terror to the lawbreaker, but the loving missionary can do more than this. Often the heart that hardens under reproof will melt under the love of Christ. *The Ministry of Healing,* p. 106.

## *To Be Remembered*

In all our associations it should be remembered that in the experience of others there are chapters sealed from mortal sight. On the pages of memory are sad histories that are sacredly guarded from curious eyes. There stand registered long, hard battles with trying circumstances, perhaps troubles in the home life, that day by day weaken courage, confidence, and faith. Those who are fighting the battle of life at great odds may be strengthened and encouraged by little attentions that cost only a loving effort. To such the strong, helpful grasp of the hand by a true friend is worth more than gold or silver. Words of kindness are as welcome as the smile of angels.

There are multitudes struggling with poverty, compelled to labor hard for small wages, and able to secure but the barest necessities of life. Toil and deprivation, with no hope of better things, make their burden very heavy. When pain and sickness are added, the burden is almost insupportable. Careworn and oppressed, they know not where to turn for relief. Sympathize with them in their trials, their heartaches, and disappointments. This will open the way for you to help them. Speak to them of God's promises, pray with and for them, inspire them with hope. *The Ministry of Healing,* p. 158.

There are many to whom life is a painful struggle; they feel their deficiencies, and are miserable and unbelieving; they think they have nothing for which to be grateful. Kind words, looks of sympathy, expressions of appreciation, would be to many a struggling and lonely one as the cup of cold water to a thirsty soul. A word of sympathy, an act of kindness, would lift burdens that rest heavily upon weary shoulders. And every word or deed of unselfish kindness is an expression of the love of Christ for lost humanity. *Thoughts From the Mount of Blessing,* p. 23.

## *Extend a Helping Hand*

Sin is the greatest of all evils, and it is ours to pity and help the sinner. But not all can be reached in the same way. There are many who hide their soul-hunger. These would be greatly helped by a tender word or a kind remembrance. There are others who are in the greatest need, yet they know it not. They do not realize the terrible destitution of the soul. Multitudes are so sunken in sin that they have lost the sense of eternal realities, lost the similitude of God, and they hardly know whether they have souls to be saved or not. They have neither faith in God nor confidence in man. Many of these can be reached only through acts of disinterested kindness. Their physical wants must first be cared for. They must be fed, cleansed, and decently clothed. As they see the evidence of your unselfish love, it will be easier for them to believe in the love of Christ.

There are many who err, and who feel their shame and their folly. They look upon their mistakes and errors until they are driven almost to desperation. These souls we are not to neglect. When one has to swim against the stream, there is all the force of the current driving him back. Let a helping hand then be held out to him as was the elder Brother's hand to the sinking Peter. Speak to him hopeful words that will establish confidence and awaken love. *Christ's Object Lessons,* p. 387.

To the soul weary of a life of sin but knowing not where to find relief, present the compassionate Saviour. Take him by the hand, lift him up, speak to him words of courage and hope. Help him to grasp the hand of the Saviour. *The Ministry of Healing,* p. 168.

## *Hospitality a Christian Duty*

Our work in this world is to live for others' good, to bless others, to be hospitable; and frequently it may be only at some inconvenience that we can entertain those who really need our care and the benefit of our society and our homes. Some avoid these necessary burdens. But some one must bear them; and because the brethren in general are not lovers of hospitality, and do not share equally in these Christian duties, a few who have willing hearts, and who cheerfully make the cases of those who need help their own, are burdened. *Testimonies,* vol. 2, p. 645.

"Be not forgetful to entertain strangers: for thereby some have entertained angels unawares." These words have lost none of their force through the lapse of time. Our heavenly Father still continues to place in the pathway of His children opportunities that are blessings in disguise; and those who improve these opportunities find great joy. *Prophets and Kings,* p. 132.

## *The Testing Process*

God tests and proves us by the common occurrences of life. It is the little things which reveal the chapters of the heart. It is the little attentions, the numerous small incidents and simple courtesies of life, that make up the sum of life's happiness; and it is the neglect of kindly, encouraging, affectionate words, and the little courtesies of life, which helps compose the sum of life's wretchedness. It will be found at last that the denial of self for the good and happiness of those around us, constitutes a large share of the life record in heaven. *Testimonies,* vol. 2, p. 133.

I saw that it is in the providence of God that widows and orphans, the blind, the deaf, the lame, and persons afflicted in a variety of ways, have been placed in close Christian relationship to His church; it is to prove His people and develop their true character. Angels of God are watching to see how we treat these persons who need our sympathy, love, and disinterested benevolence. This is God's test of our character. If we have the true religion of the Bible, we shall feel that a debt of love, kindness, and interest is due to Christ in behalf of His brethren; and we can do no less than to show our gratitude for His immeasurable love to us while we were sinners unworthy of His grace, by having a deep interest and unselfish love for those who are our brethren, and who are less fortunate than ourselves. *Testimonies,* vol. 3, p. 511.

## *A Parable Applied*

The two great principles of the law of God are supreme love to God and unselfish love to our neighbor. The first four commandments and the last six hang upon, or grow out of, these two principles. Christ explained to the lawyer who his neighbor was in the illustration of the man who was traveling from Jerusalem to Jericho, and who fell among thieves, and was robbed and beaten and left half dead. The priest and the Levite saw this man suffering, but their hearts did not respond to his wants. They avoided him by passing by on the other side. The Samaritan came that way, and when he saw the stranger's need of help, he did not question whether he was a relative or was of his country or creed; but he went to work to help the sufferer because there was work which needed to be done. He relieved him as best he could, put him upon his own beast, and carried him to an inn and made provision for his wants at his own expense.

This Samaritan, said Christ, was neighbor to him who fell among thieves. The Levite and the priest represent a class in the church who manifest an indifference to the very ones who need their sympathy and help. This class, notwithstanding their position in the church, are commandment breakers. The Samaritan represents a class who are true helpers with Christ and who are imitating His example in doing good.

Those who have pity for the unfortunate, the blind, the lame, the afflicted, the widows, the orphans, and the needy, Christ represents as commandment keepers, who shall have eternal life. . . . Christ regards all acts of mercy, benevolence, and thoughtful consideration for the unfortunate, the blind, the lame, the sick, the widow, and the orphan as done to Himself; and these works are reserved in the heavenly records and will be rewarded. On the other hand, a record will be written in the book against those who manifest the indifference of the priest and the Levite to the unfortunate, and those who take any advantage of the misfortunes of others and increase their affliction in order to selfishly advantage themselves. God will surely repay every act of injustice and every manifestation of careless indifference to and neglect of the afflicted among us. Every one will finally be rewarded as his works have been. *Testimonies,* vol. 3, pp. 511-513.

# CHAPTER 18

# The Camp Meeting an Aid in Christian Service

### Importance

The camp meeting is one of the most important agencies in our work. It is one of the most effective methods of arresting the attention of the people. *Testimonies,* vol. 6, p. 31.

In our work we have been perplexed to know how to break through the barriers of worldliness and prejudice and bring before the people the precious truth which means so much to them. The Lord has instructed us that the camp meeting is one of the most important instrumentalities for the accomplishment of this work. *Testimonies,* vol. 6, pp. 31, 32.

### Object

What is the object of assembling together? Is it to inform God, to instruct Him by telling Him all we know in prayer? We meet together to edify one another by an interchange of thoughts and feelings, to gather strength, and light, and courage by becoming acquainted with one another's hopes and aspirations; by our earnest, heartfelt prayers, offered up in faith, we receive refreshment and vigor from the Source of our strength. *Testimonies,* vol. 2, p. 578.

Our camp meetings have another object. . . . They are to promote spiritual life among our own people. . . . God has committed to our hands a most sacred work, and we need to meet together to receive instruction, that we may be fitted to perform this work. We need to understand what part we shall individually be called upon to act in building up the cause of God in the earth, in vindicating God's holy law, and in lifting up the Saviour as "the Lamb of God, which taketh away the sin of the world." John 1:29. We need to meet together and receive the divine touch, that we may understand our work in the home. *Testimonies,* vol. 6, pp. 32, 33.

Properly conducted, the camp meeting is a school where pastors, elders, and deacons can learn to do more perfect work for the Master. It should be a school where the members of the church, old and young, are given opportunity to learn the way of the Lord more perfectly, a place where believers can receive an education that will help them to help others. *Testimonies,* vol. 6, p. 49.

In connection with our camp meetings in past years, God's servants have improved many precious opportunities for instructing our people in practical methods of presenting the saving truths of the third angel's message to their friends and acquaintances. Many have been taught how to labor as self-supporting missionaries in their home communities. Many have returned home from these annual gatherings to labor with greater zeal and intelligence than hitherto. It would be pleasing to God if far more of this practical instruction were given the church members who attend our camp meetings, than has usually been given in years past. Our general workers and our brethren and sisters in every conference should remember that one of the objects of our annual gatherings is that all may gain a knowledge of practical methods of personal missionary work. *Testimonies,* vol. 9, p. 81.

In some of our conferences the leaders have hesitated to introduce these practical methods of instruction. Some are naturally inclined to sermonize rather than to teach. But on such occasions as our annual camp meetings we must never lose sight of the opportunities afforded for teaching the believers how to do practical missionary work in the place where they may live. *Testimonies,* vol. 9, p. 82.

## *Practical Demonstration of Missionary Methods*

By engaging in work at the camp meeting, all may be learning how to work successfully in their home churches. *Testimonies,* vol. 6, p. 49.

At some of our camp meetings, strong companies of workers have been organized to go out into the city and its suburbs to distribute literature and invite people to the meetings. By this means hundreds of persons were secured as regular attendants during the last half of the meeting who otherwise might have thought little about it. *Testimonies,* vol. 6, p. 36.

We can go to the camp meeting, not merely to receive, but to impart. Everyone who is a partaker of Christ's pardoning love, everyone who has been enlightened by the Spirit of God and converted to the truth, will feel that for these precious blessings he owes a debt to every soul with whom he comes in contact. Those who are humble in heart the Lord will use to reach souls whom the ordained ministers cannot reach. They will be moved to speak words which reveal the saving grace of Christ. *Testimonies,* vol. 6, p. 43.

When we follow plans of the Lord's devising, "we are laborers together with God." Whatever our position—whether presidents of conferences, ministers, teachers, students, or lay members—we are held accountable by the Lord for making the most of our opportunities to enlighten those in need of present truth. And one of the principal agencies He has ordained for our use is the printed page. In our schools and sanitariums, in our home churches, and particularly in our annual camp meetings, we must learn to make a wise use of this precious agency. With patient diligence chosen workers must instruct our people how to approach unbelievers in a kindly, winning way and how to place in their hands literature in which the truth for this time is presented with clearness and power. *Testimonies,* vol. 9, pp. 86, 87.

The work at our camp meetings should be conducted, not according to man's devising, but after the manner of Christ's working. The church members should be drawn out to labor. *Testimonies,* vol. 9, p. 120.

## *Special Feature of Camp Meetings Near the End of Time*

It has been shown me that our camp meetings are to increase in interest and success. As we approach nearer the end, I have seen that in these meetings there will be less preaching and more Bible study. There will be little groups all over the ground with their Bibles in their hands, and different ones leading out in a free, conversational study of the Scriptures. *Testimonies,* vol. 6, p. 87.

## *Serious Loss in Remaining Away*

Our camp meetings are arranged and held at great expense. God's ministers who advocate unpopular truth, labor excessively at these large gatherings to bear the message of mercy from a crucified Redeemer to poor fallen sinners. To neglect or treat these messages with indifference is to slight the mercy of God and His voice of warning and entreaty. Your absence from these meetings has been very detrimental to your spiritual welfare. You have missed the strength that you might have gained there by listening to the preached word of God, and mingling with the believers of the truth. *Testimonies,* vol. 4, p. 115.

It is no small matter for a family to stand as representatives of Jesus, keeping God's law in an unbelieving community. We are required to be living epistles, known and read of all men. This position involves fearful responsibilities. In order to live in the light, you must come where the light shines. Brother K, at any sacrifice, should feel under solemn obligation to attend, with his family, at least the yearly gatherings of those who love the truth. It would strengthen him and them, and fit them for trial and duty. It is not well for them to lose the privilege of associating with those of like faith; for the truth loses its importance in their minds, their hearts cease to be enlightened and vivified by its sanctifying influence, and they lose spirituality. They are not strengthened by the words of the living preacher. Worldly thoughts and worldly enterprises are continually exercising their minds to the exclusion of spiritual subjects. *Testimonies,* vol. 4, p. 106.

Let all who possibly can, attend these yearly gatherings. All should feel that God requires this of them. If they do not avail themselves of the privileges which He has provided that they may become strong in Him and in the power of His grace, they will grow weaker and weaker, and have less and less desire to consecrate all to God.

Come, brethren and sisters, to these sacred convocation meetings, to find Jesus. He will come up to the feast. He will be present, and He will do for you that which you most need to have done. Your farms should not be considered of greater value than the higher interests of the soul. All the treasures which you possess, be they ever so valuable, would not be rich enough to buy you peace and hope, which would be infinite gain, if it cost you all you have and the toils and sufferings of a lifetime. A strong, clear sense of eternal things, and a heart willing to yield all to Christ, are blessings of more value than all the riches and pleasures and glories of this world. *Testimonies,* vol. 2, pp. 575, 576.

# CHAPTER 19

# The Home-Foreign Field

## *A Work Equal in Importance to That in Foreign Fields*

Wake up, wake up, my brethren and sisters, and enter the fields in America that have never been worked. After you have given something for foreign fields, do not think your duty done. There is a work to be done in foreign fields, but there is a work to be done in America that is just as important. In the cities of America there are people of almost every language. These need the light that God has given to His church. *Testimonies,* vol. 8, p. 36.

While plans are being carried out to warn the inhabitants of various nations in distant lands, much must be done in behalf of the foreigners who have come to the shores of our own land. The souls in China are no more precious than the souls within the shadow of our doors. God's people are to labor faithfully in distant lands, as His providence may open the way; and they are also to fulfill their duty toward the foreigners of various nationalities in the cities and villages and country districts close by. *Review and Herald,* Oct. 29, 1914.

In New York City, in Chicago, and in other great centers of population, there is a larger foreign element—multitudes of various nationalities, and all practically unwarned. Among Seventh-day Adventists there is a great zeal—and I am not saying there is any too much—to work in foreign countries; but it would be pleasing to God if a proportionate zeal were manifested to work the cities close by. His people need to move sensibly. They need to set about this work in the cities with serious earnestness. Men of consecration and talent are to be sent into these cities and set to work. Many classes of laborers are to unite in conducting these efforts to warn the people. *Review and Herald,* Oct. 29, 1914.

## A Heaven-sent Opportunity

In our own country there are thousands of all nations, and tongues, and peoples who are ignorant and superstitious, having no knowledge of the Bible or its sacred teachings. God's hand was in their coming to America, that they might be brought under the enlightening influence of the truth revealed in His Word and become partakers of His saving faith. *Review and Herald,* Mar. 1, 1887.

God in His providence has brought men to our very doors, and thrust them, as it were, into our arms, that they might learn the truth, and be qualified to do a work we could not do in getting the light to men of other tongues. *Review and Herald,* Oct. 29, 1914.

Many of these foreigners are here in the providence of God, that they may have opportunity to hear the truth for this time and receive a preparation that will fit them to return to their own lands as bearers of precious light shining direct from the throne of God. *Pacific Union Recorder,* Apr. 21, 1910.

Great benefits would come to the cause of God in the regions beyond, if faithful effort were put forth in behalf of the foreigners in the cities of our homeland. Among these men and women are some who, upon accepting the truth, could soon be fitted to labor for their own people in this country and in other countries. Many might return to the places from which they came, in the hope of winning their friends to the truth. They could search out their kinsfolk and neighbors and communicate to them a knowledge of the third angel's message. *Review and Herald,* Oct. 29, 1914.

## Slothful Neglect

There has been a slothful neglect and a criminal unbelief among us as a people, which has kept us back from doing the work God has left us to do in letting our light shine forth to those of other nations. *Life Sketches of Ellen G. White,* p. 213.

I have been shown that, as a people, we have been asleep as to our duty in regard to getting the light before those of other nations. *Life Sketches of Ellen G. White,* p. 212.

We are not keeping pace with the opening providence of God. Jesus and angels are at work. This cause is onward, while we are standing still and being left in the rear. If we would follow the opening providence of God, we should be quick to discern every opening, and make the most of every advantage within our reach, to let the light extend and spread to other nations. *Life Sketches of Ellen G. White,* p. 212, 213.

## *Strengthen the Hands of the Workers*

God would be pleased to see far more accomplished by His people in the presentation of the truth for this time to the foreigners of America, than has been done in the past. Let us strengthen the hands of Elder Olsen★ and his associates in labor. Let us not permit them to struggle on alone, with only a meager allowance for the prosecution of their great work. *Review and Herald,* Oct. 29, 1914.

Elder Olsen told us also of the encouraging beginnings among the Italians, Serbians, Rumanians, Russians, and several other nationalities. We rejoice with him in all that has been done, and yet our hearts were made sad by the knowledge that much that might have been done has been left undone because of lack of means. We hope that the special collection . . . taken in all our churches in America, will enable our brethren having this department in charge to do more aggressive work in the great cities of the land. Thus many may be won to our ranks, and from among these may be developed laborers who can proclaim the message to those of their own nationality in our own land and in the other nations of earth. *Review and Herald,* Oct. 29, 1914.

---

★Elder O. A. Olsen was then general secretary for the North American Foreign Department of the General Conference.

# CHAPTER 20

# Reaching the Wealthy and Influential

### *Not to Be Neglected*

There is a work to be done for the wealthy. They need to be awakened to their responsibility as those entrusted with the gifts of heaven. They need to be reminded that they must give an account to Him who shall judge the living and the dead. The wealthy man needs your labor in the love and fear of God. Too often he trusts in his riches and feels not his danger. The eyes of his mind need to be attracted to things of enduring value. *Christ's Object Lessons,* p. 230.

Those who stand high in the world for their education, wealth, or calling, are seldom addressed personally in regard to the interests of the soul. Many Christian workers hesitate to approach these classes. But this should not be. If a man were drowning, we would not stand by and see him perish because he was a lawyer, a merchant, or a judge. If we saw persons rushing over a precipice, we would not hesitate to urge them back, whatever might be their position or calling. Neither should we hesitate to warn men of the peril of the soul. None should be neglected because of their apparent devotion to worldly things. *Christ's Object Lessons,* p. 230, 231.

We are to have travail of soul for those who are in high places; we are to extend to them the gracious invitation to come to the marriage feast. *Southern Watchman,* Mar. 15, 1904.

The Lord desires that moneyed men shall be converted and act as His helping hand in reaching others. He desires that those who can help in the work of reform and restoration shall see the precious light of truth and be transformed in character and led to use their entrusted capital in His service. He would have them invest the means He has lent them, in doing good, in opening the way for the gospel to be preached to all classes nigh and afar off. *Testimonies,* vol. 9, p. 114.

Those who belong to the higher ranks of society are to be sought out with tender affection and brotherly regard. Men in business life, in high positions of trust, men with large inventive faculties and scientific insight, men of genius, teachers of the gospel whose minds have not been called to the special truths for this time—these should be the first to hear the call. To them the invitation must be given. *Christ's Object Lessons,* p. 230.

Mistakes have been made in not seeking to reach ministers and the higher classes with the truth. People not of our faith have been shunned altogether too much. While we should not associate with them to receive their mold, there are honest ones everywhere for whom we should labor cautiously, wisely, and intelligently, full of love for their souls. A fund should be raised to educate men and women to labor for these higher classes, both here and in other countries. *Testimonies,* vol. 5, pp. 580, 581.

## *Special Qualifications of Workers*

Some are especially fitted to work for the higher classes. These should seek wisdom from God to know how to reach these persons, to have not merely a casual acquaintance with them, but by personal effort and living faith to awaken them to the needs of the soul, to lead them to a knowledge of the truth as it is in Jesus. *The Ministry of Healing,* p. 213.

Let those who work for the higher classes bear themselves with true dignity, remembering that angels are their companions. Let them keep the treasure-house of mind and heart filled with "It is written." *The Ministry of Healing,* p. 215.

In every effort to reach the higher classes, the worker for God needs strong faith. Appearances may seem forbidding; but in the darkest hour there is light above. *The Acts of the Apostles,* p. 242.

God calls for earnest, humble workers, who will carry the gospel to the higher classes. *The Acts of the Apostles,* p. 140.

## Results Are Assured

There are miracles to be wrought in genuine conversions—miracles that are not now discerned. The greatest men of this earth are not beyond the power of a wonder-working God. If those who are workers together with Him will be men of opportunity, doing their duty bravely and faithfully, God will convert men who occupy responsible positions, men of intellect and influence. Through the power of the Holy Spirit many will accept the divine principles. Converted to the truth, they will become agencies in the hand of God to communicate the light. They will have a special burden for other souls of this neglected class. Time and money will be consecrated to the work of the Lord, and new efficiency and power will be added to the church. *The Acts of the Apostles,* p. 140.

Many in high social positions are heart-sore, and sick of vanity. They are longing for a peace which they have not. In the very highest ranks of society are those who are hungering and thirsting for salvation. Many would receive help if the Lord's workers would approach them personally, with a kind manner, a heart made tender by the love of Christ. *Christ's Object Lessons,* p. 231.

Many of the greatest scholars and statesmen, the world's most eminent men, will in these last days turn from the light, because the world by wisdom knows not God. Yet God's servants are to improve every opportunity to communicate the truth to these men. Some will acknowledge their ignorance of the things of God, and will take their place as humble learners at the feet of Jesus, the Master Teacher. *The Acts of the Apostles,* pp. 241-242.

## Wealthy Men of Bible Times

This Ethiopian was a man of good standing and of wide influence. God saw that when converted, he would give others the light he had received, and would exert a strong influence in favor of the gospel. Angels of God were attending this seeker for light, and he was being drawn to the Saviour. By the ministration of the Holy Spirit, the Lord brought him into touch with one who could lead him to the light. *The Acts of the Apostles,* p. 107.

When the Jews were trying to destroy the infant church, Nicodemus came forward in its defense. No longer cautious and questioning, he encouraged the faith of the disciples, and used his wealth in helping to sustain the church at Jerusalem and in advancing the work of the gospel. Those who in other days had paid him reverence, now scorned and persecuted him; and he became poor in this world's goods; yet he faltered not in the defense of his faith. *The Acts of the Apostles,* p. 105.

# CHAPTER 21

# The Home a Missionary Training Center

### *Of First Importance*

The home is the child's first school, and it is here that the foundation should be laid for a life of service. *The Ministry of Healing,* p. 400.

The first great business of your life is to be a missionary at home. *Testimonies,* vol. 4, p. 138.

The restoration and uplifting of humanity begins in the home. The work of parents underlies every other. . . . The well-being of society, the success of the church, the prosperity of the nation, depend upon home influences. *The Ministry of Healing,* p. 349.

The more fully the spirit of true ministry pervades the home the more fully it will be developed in the lives of the children. They will learn to find joy in service and sacrifice for the good of others. *The Ministry of Healing,* p. 401.

Let not parents forget the great mission field that lies before them in the home. In the children committed to her every mother has a sacred charge from God. "Take this son, this daughter," God says, "and train it for Me. Give it a character polished after the similitude of a palace, that it may shine in the courts of the Lord forever." The light and glory that shine from the throne of God rest upon the faithful mother as she tries to educate her children to resist the influence of evil. *Testimonies,* vol. 9, p. 37.

Our work for Christ is to begin with the family, in the home. . . . There is no missionary field more important than this. By precept and example parents are to teach their children to labor for the unconverted. The children should be so educated that they will sympathize with the aged and afflicted, and will seek to alleviate the sufferings of the poor and distressed. They should be taught to be diligent in missionary work; and from their earliest years self-denial and sacrifice for the good of others and the advancement of Christ's cause should be inculcated, that they may be laborers together with God. But if they ever learn to do genuine missionary work for others, they must first learn to labor for those at home, who have a natural right to their offices of love. *Testimonies,* vol. 6, p. 429.

Our households must be set in order, and earnest efforts must be made to interest every member of the family in missionary enterprises. We must seek to engage the sympathies of our children in earnest work for the unsaved, that they may do their best at all times and in all places to represent Christ. *Review and Herald,* July 4, 1893.

## *The Record of the Angel*

If married men go into the work, leaving their wives to care for the children at home, the wife and mother is doing fully as great and important a work as the husband and father. Although one is in the mission field, the other is a home missionary, whose cares and anxieties and burdens frequently far exceed those of the husband and father. Her work is a solemn and important one—to mold the minds and fashion the characters of her children, to train them for usefulness here and fit them for the future, immortal life. The husband in the open missionary field may receive the honors of men, while the home toiler may receive no earthly credit for her labor. But if she works for the best interest of her family, seeking to fashion their characters after the divine Model, the recording angel writes her name as one of the greatest missionaries in the world. God does not see things as man's finite vision views them. *Testimonies,* vol. 5, p. 594.

## *Children to Share Spiritual and Physical Burdens*

All can do something. In an effort to excuse themselves, some say: "My home duties, my children, claim my time and my means." Parents, your children should be your helping hand, increasing your power and ability to work for the Master. Children are the younger members of the Lord's family. They should be led to consecrate themselves to God, whose they are by creation and by redemption. They should be taught that all their powers of body, mind, and soul are His. They should be trained to help in various lines of unselfish service. Do not allow your children to be hindrances. With you the children should share spiritual as well as physical burdens. By helping others they increase their own happiness and usefulness. *Testimonies,* vol. 7, p. 63.

## *Far-reaching Influence of the Home*

A well-ordered Christian household is a powerful argument in favor of the reality of the Christian religion—an argument that the infidel cannot gainsay. All can see that there is an influence at work in the family that affects the children, and that the God of Abraham is with them. If the homes of professed Christians had a right religious mold, they would exert a mighty influence for good. They would indeed be the "light of the world." *Patriarchs and Prophets,* p. 144.

The mission of the home extends beyond its own members. The Christian home is to be an object lesson, illustrating the excellence of the true principles of life. Such an illustration will be a power for good in the world. Far more powerful than any sermon that can be preached is the influence of a true home upon human hearts and lives. As the youth go out from such a home, the lessons they have learned are imparted. Nobler principles of life are introduced into other households, and an uplifting influence works in the community. *The Ministry of Healing,* p. 352.

The greatest evidence of the power of Christianity that can be presented to the world is a well-ordered, well-disciplined family. This will recommend the truth as nothing else can, for it is a living witness of its practical power upon the heart. *Testimonies,* vol. 4, p. 304.

God designs that the families of earth shall be a symbol of the family in heaven. Christian homes, established and conducted in accordance with God's plan, are among His most effective agencies for the formation of Christian character and for the advancement of His work. *Testimonies,* vol. 6, p. 430.

Our sphere of influence may seem narrow, our ability small, our opportunities few, our acquirements limited; yet wonderful possibilities are ours through a faithful use of the opportunities of our own homes. If we will open our hearts and homes to the divine principles of life, we shall become channels for currents of life-giving power. From our homes will flow streams of healing, bringing life, and beauty, and fruitfulness where now are barrenness and dearth. *The Ministry of Healing,* p. 355.

## *Choosing the Household Banner*

I saw Satan planting his banner in the households of those who profess to be God's chosen ones, but those who are walking in the light should be able to discern the difference between the black banner of the adversary and the blood-stained standard of Christ. *Testimonies,* vol. 4, p. 200.

## *The Importance of the Family Altar*

You who profess to love God, take Jesus with you wherever you go; and, like the patriarchs of old, erect an altar to the Lord wherever you pitch your tent. A reformation in this respect is needed, a reformation that shall be deep and broad. *Testimonies,* vol. 5, pp. 320, 321.

Satan makes every effort to lead people away from God; and he is successful in his purpose when the religious life is drowned in business cares, when he can so absorb their minds in business that they will not take time to read their Bibles, to pray in secret, and to keep the offering of praise and thanksgiving burning on the altar of sacrifice morning and evening. *Testimonies,* vol. 5, p. 426.

Let the family worship be made pleasant and interesting. *Testimonies,* vol. 5, p. 335.

They [children] should be taught to respect the hour of prayer; they should be required to rise in the morning so as to be present at family worship. *Testimonies,* vol. 5, p. 424.

Children need to have religion made attractive, not repulsive. The hour of family worship should be made the happiest hour of the day. Let the reading of the Scriptures be well chosen and simple; let the children join in singing; and let the prayers be short, and right to the point. *Southern Watchman,* June 13, 1905.

At the family board and the family altar the guests are made welcome. The season of prayer makes its impression on those who receive entertainment, and even one visit may mean the saving of a soul from death. For this work the Lord makes a reckoning, saying: "I will repay." *Testimonies,* vol. 6, p. 347.

Children should be taught to respect and reverence the hour of prayer. Before leaving the house for labor, all the family should be called together, and the father, or the mother in the father's absence, should plead fervently with God to keep them through the day. Come in humility, with a heart full of tenderness and with a sense of the temptations and dangers before yourselves and your children; by faith bind them upon the altar, entreating for them the care of the Lord. Ministering angels will guard children who are thus dedicated to God. It is the duty of Christian parents, morning and evening, by earnest prayer and persevering faith, to make a hedge about their children. They should patiently instruct them, kindly and untiringly teach them how to live in order to please God. *Testimonies,* vol. 1, pp. 397-398.

Abraham, "the friend of God," set us a worthy example. His was a life of prayer. Wherever he pitched his tent, close beside it was set up his altar, calling all within his encampment to the morning and the evening sacrifice. When his tent was removed, the altar remained. In following years there were those among the roving Canaanites who received instruction from Abraham; and whenever one of these came to that altar, he knew who had been there before him; and when he had pitched his tent, he repaired the altar, and there worshiped the living God. *Patriarchs and Prophets,* p. 128.

# CHAPTER 22

# The Prayer and Missionary Meeting

### Secret of Effectual Prayer

The upbuilding of the kingdom of God is retarded or urged forward according to the unfaithfulness or fidelity of human agencies. The work is hindered by the failure of the human to cooperate with the divine. Men may pray, "Thy kingdom come. Thy will be done in earth, as it is in heaven"; but if they fail of acting out this prayer in their lives, their petitions will be fruitless. *Testimonies,* vol. 6, pp. 437, 438.

### Devotional Exercises in the Balance

All heaven is looking upon the inhabitants of the earth. The angels and the God of heaven are looking upon those who claim to be Christians, and weighing their devotional exercises. *Signs of the Times* (Australasian), June 22, 1903.

### Making the Meetings Interesting

Let the missionary meeting be turned to account in teaching the people how to do missionary work. *Appeal to Our Churches,* p. 11.

Our prayer and social meetings should be seasons of special help and encouragement. Each one has a work to do to make these gatherings as interesting and profitable as possible. This can best be done by having a fresh experience daily in the things of God, and by not hesitating to speak of His love in the assemblies of His people. If you allow no darkness or unbelief to enter your hearts, they will not be manifest in your meetings. *Southern Watchman,* Mar. 7, 1905.

Our meetings should be made intensely interesting. They should be pervaded with the very atmosphere of heaven. Let there be no long, dry speeches and formal prayers, merely for the sake of occupying the time. All should be ready to act their part with promptness, and when their duty is done, the meeting should be closed. Thus the interest will be kept up to the last. This is offering to God acceptable worship. His service should be made interesting and attractive, and not be allowed to degenerate into a dry form. We must live for Christ minute by minute, hour by hour, and day by day; then Christ will dwell in us, and when we meet together, His love will be in our hearts, welling up like a spring in the desert, refreshing all, and making those who are ready to perish, eager to drink of the waters of life. *Testimonies,* vol. 5, p. 609.

Do not imagine that you can arouse the interest of the young by going to the missionary meeting and preaching a long sermon. Plan ways whereby a live interest may be aroused. From week to week the young should bring in their reports, telling what they have tried to do for the Saviour, and what success has been theirs. If the missionary meeting were made an occasion for bringing in such reports, it would not be dull, tedious, and uninteresting. It would be full of interest, and there would be no lack of attendance. *Gospel Workers,* pp. 210, 211.

When faith lays hold upon Christ, the truth will bring delight to the soul, and the services of religion will not be dull and uninteresting. Your social meetings, now tame and spiritless, will be vitalized by the Holy Spirit; daily you will have a rich experience as you practice the Christianity you profess. *Testimonies,* vol. 6, p. 437.

## *Testimony of Personal Experience*

As followers of Christ we should make our words such as to be a help and an encouragement to one another in the Christian life. Far more than we do, we need to speak of the precious chapters in our experience. *Christ's Object Lessons,* p. 338.

The church needs the fresh, living experience of members who have habitual communion with God. Dry, stale testimonies and prayers, without the manifestation of Christ in them, are no help to the people. If everyone who claims to be a child of God were filled with faith and light and life, what a wonderful witness would be given to those who come to hear the truth! And how many souls might be won to Christ! *Testimonies,* vol. 6, p. 64.

Our confession of His faithfulness is Heaven's chosen agency for revealing Christ to the world. We are to acknowledge His grace as made known through the holy men of old; but that which will be most effectual is the testimony of our own experience. We are witnesses for God as we reveal in ourselves the working of a power that is divine. Every individual has a life distinct from all others, and an experience differing essentially from theirs. God desires that our praise shall ascend to Him, marked with our own individuality. These precious acknowledgments to the praise of the glory of His grace, when supported by a Christlike life, have an irresistible power that works for the salvation of souls. *The Ministry of Healing,* p. 100.

## *Praise and Thanksgiving*

To praise God in fullness and sincerity of heart is as much a duty as is prayer. We are to show to the world and to all the heavenly intelligences that we appreciate the wonderful love of God for fallen humanity, and that we are expecting larger and yet larger blessings from His infinite fullness. . . . After a special outpouring of the Holy Spirit, our joy in the Lord and our efficiency in His service would be greatly increased by recounting His goodness and His wonderful works in behalf of His children. These exercises drive back the power of Satan. They expel the spirit of murmuring and complaint, and the tempter loses ground. They cultivate those attributes of character which will fit the dwellers on earth for the heavenly mansions. Such a testimony will have an influence upon others. No more effective means can be employed for winning souls to Christ. *Christ's Object Lessons,* pp. 299, 300.

The Lord desires us to make mention of His goodness and tell of His power. He is honored by the expression of praise and thanksgiving. He says, "Whoso offereth praise glorifieth Me." The people of Israel, as they journeyed through the wilderness, praised God in sacred song. The commandments and promises of the Lord were set to music, and all along the journey these were sung by the pilgrim travelers. And in Canaan, as they met at their sacred feasts, God's wonderful works were to be recounted, and grateful thanksgiving offered to His name. God desired that the whole life of His people should be a life of praise. *Christ's Object Lessons,* pp. 298, 299.

## *A Dangerous Policy*

Some, fearing they will suffer loss of earthly treasure, neglect prayer and the assembling of themselves together for the worship of God, that they may have more time to devote to their farms or their business. They show by their works which world they place the highest estimate upon. They sacrifice religious privileges, which are essential to their spiritual advancement, for the things of this life and fail to obtain a knowledge of the divine will. They come short of perfecting Christian character and do not meet the measurement of God. They make their temporal, worldly interests first, and rob God of the time which they should devote to His service. Such persons God marks, and they will receive a curse, rather than a blessing. *Testimonies,* vol. 2, p. 654.

## *A Comforting Promise*

God will remember those who have met together and thought upon His name, and He will spare them from the great conflagration. They will be as precious jewels in His sight. *Testimonies,* vol. 4, p. 107.

# CHAPTER 23

# Miscellaneous Lines of Missionary Work

## *Consideration for the Blind*

Angels are sent to minister to the children of God who are physically blind. Angels guard their steps and save them from a thousand dangers, which, unknown to them, beset their path. *Testimonies,* vol. 3, p. 516.

He will not hearken to the prayer of His people while . . . the blind and the sick are neglected among them. *Testimonies,* vol. 3, p. 518.

If there are those in the church who would cause the blind to stumble, they should be brought to justice; for God has made us guardians of the blind, the afflicted, the widows, and the fatherless. The stumblingblock referred to in the Word of God does not mean a block of wood placed before the feet of the blind to cause him to stumble, but it means much more than this. It means any course that may be pursued to injure the influence of their blind brother, to work against his interest, or to hinder his prosperity. *Testimonies,* vol. 3, p. 519.

The blind man has disadvantages to meet on every side in the loss of his sight. That heart in which pity and sympathy are not excited at seeing a blind man groping his way in a world clothed to him in darkness, is hard indeed, and must be softened by the grace of God. *Testimonies,* vol. 3, p. 521.

## *Care for Orphans*

Until death shall be swallowed up in victory, there will be orphans to be cared for, who will suffer in more ways than one if the tender compassion and loving-kindness of our church members are not exercised in their behalf. The Lord bids us, "Bring the poor that are cast out to thy house." Christianity must supply fathers and mothers for these homeless ones. The compassion for the widow and the orphan manifested in prayers and deeds, will come up in remembrance before God, to be rewarded by and by. *Review and Herald,* June 27, 1893.

When you succor the poor, sympathize with the afflicted and oppressed, and befriend the orphan, you bring yourselves into a closer relationship to Jesus. *Testimonies,* vol. 2, p. 25.

There are orphans that can be cared for; but many will not venture to undertake such a work, for it involves more labor than they care to do, leaving them but little time to please themselves. But when the King shall make investigation, these do-nothing, illiberal, selfish souls will then learn that heaven is for those who have been workers, those who have denied themselves for Christ's sake. No provisions have been made for those who have ever taken such special care in loving and looking out for themselves. The terrible punishment the King threatened those on His left hand, in this case, is not because of their great crimes. They are not condemned for the things which they did do, but for that which they did not do. They did not those things Heaven assigned them to do. They pleased themselves and can take their portion with self-pleasers. *Review and Herald,* Aug. 16, 1881.

There are orphans whom Christ has bidden His followers receive as a trust from God. Too often these are passed by with neglect. They may be ragged, uncouth, and seemingly in every way unattractive; yet they are God's property. They have been bought with a price, and they are as precious in His sight as we are. They are members of God's great household, and Christians as His stewards are responsible for them. "Their souls," He says, "will I require at thine hand." *Christ's Object Lessons,* pp. 386, 387.

The Lord calls on every member of the church to do your duty to these orphans. Do not, however, work for them merely from the standpoint of duty, but because you love them, and Christ died to save them. Christ has purchased these souls that need your care, and He expects you to love them as He has loved you in your sins and waywardness. *Review and Herald,* June 27, 1893.

He will not hearken to the prayer of His people while the orphan, the fatherless, the lame, the blind, and the sick are neglected among them. *Testimonies,* vol. 3, p. 518.

There is a wide field before all who will work for the Master in caring for these friendless children and youth, placing them in a position favorable for the formation of a right character, that they may become children of God. There are unpromising children that need to be tenderly sought for; many that would otherwise grow up in ignorance and drift into associations that lead to vice and crime may be brought into favorable surroundings, and under Christlike, tender watchcare may be saved to Christ. . . . This work for others will require effort and self-denial and sacrifice; but what is the little sacrifice that we can make, in comparison with God's great gift of His only begotten Son? God has granted us the privilege of becoming laborers together with Him. *Review and Herald,* June 27, 1893.

## *The Colored Race*

There is in this country a great, unworked field. The colored race, numbering thousands upon thousands, appeals to the consideration and sympathy of every true, practical believer in Christ. These people do not live in a foreign country, and they do not bow down to idols of wood and stone. They live among us, and again and again, through the testimonies of His Spirit, God has called our attention to them, telling us that here are human beings neglected. This broad field lies before us unworked, calling for the light that God has given us in trust. *Testimonies,* vol. 8, p. 205.

Walls of separation have been built up between the whites and the blacks. These walls of prejudice will tumble down of themselves, as did the walls of Jericho, when Christians obey the Word of God, which enjoins on them supreme love to their Maker and impartial love to their neighbors. . . . Let every church whose members claim to believe the truth for this time look at this neglected, downtrodden race, that as a result of slavery have been deprived of the privilege of thinking and acting for themselves. *Review and Herald,* Dec. 17, 1895.

Let us set ourselves to do a work for the Southern people. Let us not be content with simply looking on, with simply making resolutions that are never acted upon; but let us do something heartily unto the Lord, to alleviate the distress of our colored brethren. *Review and Herald,* Feb. 4, 1896.

The black man's name is written in the book of life beside the white man's. All are one in Christ. Birth, station, nationality, or color cannot elevate or degrade men. The character makes the man. If a red man, a Chinaman, or an African gives his heart to God in obedience and faith, Jesus loves him none the less for his color. He calls him His well-beloved brother. *The Southern Work,* p. 8, Mar. 20, 1891.

The day is coming when the kings and the lordly men of the earth would be glad to exchange places with the humblest African who has laid hold on the hope of the gospel. *The Southern Work,* p. 8, Mar. 20, 1891.

God cares no less for the souls of the African race that may be won to serve Him, than He cared for Israel. He requires far more of His people than they have given Him in missionary work among the people of the South of all classes, and especially the colored race. Are we not under even greater obligation to labor for the colored people than for those who have been more highly favored? Who is it that held these people in servitude? Who kept them in ignorance? . . . If the race is degraded, if they are repulsive in habits and manners, who made them so? Is there not much due to them from the white people? After so great a wrong has been done them, should not an earnest effort be made to lift them up? The truth must be carried to them. They have souls to save as well as we. *The Southern Work,* pp. 11, 12, Mar. 20, 1891.

## *Temperance Reform*

Of all who claim to be numbered among the friends of temperance, Seventh-day Adventists should stand in the front ranks. *Gospel Workers,* p. 384.

On the temperance question, take your position without wavering. Be as firm as a rock. *Gospel Workers,* p. 394.

We have a work to do along temperance lines besides that of speaking in public. We must present our principles in pamphlets and in our papers. We must use every possible means of arousing our people to their duty to get into connection with those who know not the truth. The success we have had in missionary work has been fully proportionate to the self-denying, self-sacrificing efforts we have made. The Lord alone knows how much we might have accomplished if as a people we had humbled ourselves before Him and proclaimed the temperance truth in clear, straight lines. *Gospel Workers,* p. 385.

The temperance question is to receive decided support from God's people. Intemperance is striving for the mastery; self-indulgence is increasing, and the publications treating on health reform are greatly needed. Literature bearing on this point is the helping hand of the gospel, leading souls to search the Bible for a better understanding of the truth. The note of warning against the great evil of intemperance should be sounded; and that this may be done, every Sabbathkeeper should study and practice the instruction contained in our health periodicals and our health books. And they should do more than this: they should make earnest efforts to circulate these publications among their neighbors. *Southern Watchman,* Nov. 20, 1902.

Present the total abstinence pledge, asking that the money they would otherwise spend for liquor, tobacco, or like indulgences, be devoted to the relief of the sick, poor, or for the training of children and youth for usefulness in the world. *The Ministry of Healing,* p. 211.

## *Importance of Follow-up Effort*

As the result of the presentation of the truth in large congregations, a spirit of inquiry is awakened, and it is especially important that this interest be followed up by personal labor. Those who desire to investigate the truth need to be taught to study diligently the Word of God. Some one must help them to build on the sure foundation.

At this critical time in their religious experience, how important it is that wisely directed Bible workers come to their help and open to their understanding the treasure-house of God's Word. *Testimonies,* vol. 9, p. 111.

The golden moment is lost. The impressions made were not followed up. It would have been better had no interest been awakened; for when convictions have been once resisted and overcome, it is very difficult to impress the mind again with the truth. *Testimonies,* vol. 2, p. 118.

## *Stewardship of Means*

In all our expenditure of means we are to strive to fulfill the purpose of Him who is the alpha and omega of all Christian effort. *Testimonies,* vol. 9 p. 49.

Money has great value, because it can do great good. In the hands of God's children it is food for the hungry, drink for the thirsty, and clothing for the naked. It is a defense for the oppressed, and a means of help to the sick. But money is of no more value than sand, only as it is put to use in providing for the necessities of life, in blessing others, and advancing the cause of Christ. *Christ's Object Lessons,* p. 351.

God Himself originated plans for the advancement of His work, and He has provided His people with a surplus of means, that when He calls for help, they may respond, saying: "Lord, Thy pound hath gained other pounds." *Testimonies,* vol. 9 p. 58.

Money cannot be carried into the next life; it is not needed there; but the good deeds done in winning souls to Christ are carried to the heavenly courts. But those who selfishly spend the Lord's gifts on themselves, leaving their needy fellow creatures without aid, and doing nothing to advance God's work in the world, dishonor their Maker. Robbery of God is written opposite their names in the books of heaven. *Christ's Object Lessons,* p. 266.

What is the value of money at this time, in comparison with the value of souls? Every dollar of our means should be considered as the Lord's, not ours; and as a precious trust from God to us; not to be wasted for needless indulgences, but carefully used in the cause of God, in the work of saving men and women from ruin. *Life Sketches of Ellen G. White,* p. 214.

Is not the missionary work that is to be done in our world of sufficient importance to command our influence and support? Should we not deny ourselves of every extravagance, and put our gifts into the treasury of God, that the truth may be sent into other countries, and that home missions may be sustained? Will not this work meet the approval of Heaven? The work for these last days has not been supported by large legacies, or advanced by worldly influence. It has been sustained by gifts that were the result of self-denial, of the spirit of sacrifice. God has given us the privilege of becoming partakers with Christ in His sufferings here, and He has provided that we may have a title to an inheritance in the earth made new. *Review and Herald,* Dec. 2, 1890.

I was shown that the recording angel makes a faithful record of every offering dedicated to God and put into the treasury, and also of the final result of the means thus bestowed. The eye of God takes cognizance of every farthing devoted to His cause, and of the willingness or reluctance of the giver. The motive in giving is also chronicled. Those self-sacrificing, consecrated ones who render back to God the things that are His, as He requires of them, will be rewarded according to their works. Even though the means thus consecrated be misapplied, so that it does not accomplish the object which the donor had in view—the glory of God and the salvation of souls—those who made the sacrifice in sincerity of soul, with an eye single to the glory of God, will not lose their reward. *Testimonies,* vol. 2, pp. 518, 519.

Every opportunity to help a brother in need, or to aid the cause of God in the spread of the truth, is a pearl that you can send beforehand, and deposit in the bank of heaven for safekeeping. God is testing and proving you. He has been giving His blessings to you with a lavish hand, and is now watching to see what use you are making of them, to see if you will help those who need help and if you will feel the worth of souls and do what you can with the means that He has entrusted to you. Every such opportunity improved adds to your heavenly treasure. *Testimonies,* vol. 3, pp. 249, 250.

## *Heaven's Reporting System*

Angels keep a faithful record of every man's work. *Testimonies,* vol. 1, p. 198.

Every act of love, every word of kindness, every prayer in behalf of the suffering and oppressed, is reported before the eternal throne and placed on heaven's imperishable record. *Testimonies,* vol. 5, p. 133.

A report is borne to heaven of every successful effort on our part to dispel the darkness and to spread abroad the knowledge of Christ. As the deed is recounted before the Father, joy thrills through all the heavenly host. *The Acts of the Apostles,* p. 154.

Angels are commissioned to be our helpers. They are passing between earth and heaven, bearing upward the record of the doings of the children of men. *Southern Watchman,* April 2, 1903.

It were well . . . to remember the record kept on high—that book in which there are no omissions, no mistakes, and out of which they will be judged. There every neglected opportunity to do service for God is recorded; and there, too, every deed of faith and love is held in everlasting remembrance. *Prophets and Kings,* p. 639.

# CHAPTER 24

# Qualifications for Successful Christian Service

## Efficiency

Listlessness and inefficiency are not piety. When we realize that we are working for God, we shall have a higher sense than we have ever had before of the sacredness of spiritual service. This realization will put life and vigilance and persevering energy into the discharge of every duty. *Testimonies,* vol. 9, p. 150.

The time demands greater efficiency and deeper consecration. Oh, I am so full of this subject that I cry to God: "Raise up and send forth messengers filled with a sense of their responsibility, messengers in whose hearts self-idolatry, which lies at the foundation of all sin, has been crucified." *Testimonies,* vol. 9, p. 27.

The work committed to the disciples would require great efficiency, for the tide of evil ran deep and strong against them. *The Acts of the Apostles,* p. 31.

## Cultured Speech

The right culture and use of the power of speech has to do with every line of Christian work. . . . We should accustom ourselves to speak in pleasant tones, to use pure and correct language, and words that are kind and courteous. *Christ's Object Lessons,* p. 336.

Every minister and every teacher should bear in mind that he is giving to the people a message that involves eternal interests. The truth spoken will judge them in the great day of final reckoning. And with some souls the manner of the one delivering the message will determine its reception or rejection. Then let the word be so spoken that it will appeal to the understanding and impress the heart. Slowly, distinctly, and solemnly should it be spoken, yet with all the earnestness which its importance demands. *Christ's Object Lessons,* p. 336.

As you seek to draw others within the circle of His love, let the purity of your language, the unselfishness of your service, the joyfulness of your demeanor, bear witness to the power of His grace. *The Ministry of Healing,* p. 156.

Every Christian is called to make known to others the unsearchable riches of Christ; therefore he should seek for perfection in speech. He should present the word of God in a way that will commend it to the hearers. God does not design that His human channels shall be uncouth. It is not His will that man shall belittle or degrade the heavenly current that flows through him to the world. *Christ's Object Lessons,* p. 336.

They will be educated in patience, kindness, affability, and helpfulness. They will practice true Christian courtesy, bearing in mind that Christ, their companion, cannot approve of harsh, unkind words or feelings. Their words will be purified. The power of speech will be regarded as a precious talent, lent them to do a high and holy work. *Gospel Workers,* p. 97.

## *Mental Culture*

Mental culture is what we, as a people, need and what we must have in order to meet the demands of the time. *Testimonies,* vol. 4, p. 414.

We must not enter into the Lord's work haphazard and expect success. The Lord needs men of mind, men of thought. Jesus calls for coworkers, not blunderers. God wants right-thinking and intelligent men to do the great work necessary to the salvation of souls. *Testimonies,* vol. 4, p. 67.

Some need to discipline the mind by exercise. They should force it to think. While they depend upon some one to think for them, to solve their difficulties, and they refuse to tax the mind with thought, the inability to remember, to look ahead and discriminate, will continue. Efforts must be made by every individual to educate the mind. *Testimonies,* vol. 2, p. 188.

God does not want us to be content with lazy, undisciplined minds, dull thoughts, and loose memories. *Counsels to Parents, Teachers, and Students,* p. 506. .

Men of God must be diligent in study, earnest in the acquirement of knowledge, never wasting an hour. Through persevering exertion they may rise to almost any degree of eminence as Christians, as men of power and influence. *Testimonies,* vol. 4, p. 411.

Only let the moments be treasured. . . . The time spent in traveling; . . . the moments of waiting for meals, waiting for those who are tardy in keeping an appointment—if a book were kept at hand, and these fragments of time were improved in study, reading, or careful thought, what might not be accomplished! *Christ's Object Lessons,* pp. 343, 344.

A resolute purpose, persistent industry, and careful economy of time will enable men to acquire knowledge and mental discipline which will qualify them for almost any position of influence and usefulness. *Christ's Object Lessons,* p. 334.

Men in responsible positions should improve continually. They must not anchor upon an old experience and feel that it is not necessary to become scientific workers. Man, although the most helpless of God's creatures when he comes into the world, and the most perverse in his nature, is nevertheless capable of constant advancement. He may be enlightened by science, ennobled by virtue, and may progress in mental and moral dignity, until he reaches a perfection of intelligence and a purity of character but little lower than the perfection and purity of angels. *Testimonies,* vol. 4, p. 93.

Those who would be workers together with God must strive for perfection of every organ of the body and quality of the mind. True education is the preparation of the physical, mental, and moral powers for the performance of every duty; it is the training of body, mind, and soul for divine service. This is the education that will endure unto eternal life. *Christ's Object Lessons,* p. 330.

Mechanics, lawyers, merchants, men of all trades and professions, educate themselves that they may become masters of their business. Should the followers of Christ be less intelligent and, while professedly engaged in His service, be ignorant of the ways and means to be employed? The enterprise of gaining everlasting life is above every earthly consideration. In order to lead souls to Jesus there must be a knowledge of human nature and a study of the human mind. Much careful thought and fervent prayer are required to know how to approach men and women upon the great subject of truth. *Testimonies,* vol. 4, p. 67.

## *Christian Dignity and Politeness*

The lack of true dignity and Christian refinement in the ranks of Sabbathkeepers is against us as a people and makes the truth which we profess unsavory. The work of educating the mind and manners may be carried forward to perfection. If those who profess the truth do not now improve their privileges and opportunities to grow up to the full stature of men and women in Christ Jesus, they will be no honor to the cause of truth, no honor to Christ. *Testimonies,* vol. 4, pp. 358, 359.

Be sure to maintain the dignity of the work by a well-ordered life and godly conversation. Never be afraid of raising the standard too high. . . . All coarseness and roughness must be put away from us. Courtesy, refinement, Christian politeness, must be cherished. Guard against being abrupt and blunt. Do not regard such peculiarities as virtues; for God does not so regard them. Endeavor not to offend any unnecessarily. *Review and Herald,* Nov. 25, 1890.

There is the greatest necessity that men and women who have a knowledge of the will of God should learn to become successful workers in His cause. They should be persons of polish, of understanding, not having the deceptive outside gloss and simpering affectation of the worldling, but that refinement and true courteousness which savors of heaven, and which every Christian will have if he is a partaker of the divine nature. *Testimonies,* vol. 4, p. 358.

We have the greatest truth and hope that were ever given to our world, and the greatest faith; and we want to represent this in its exalted character to the world. We do not want to assume the attitude as though we were passing through the world begging pardon of the world because we venture to believe this precious, sacred truth; but we want to walk humbly with God, and conduct ourselves as though we were children of the most high God, and, although feeble instruments, as though we were handling most important and interesting subjects, higher and more exalted than any temporal, worldly themes. *Review and Herald,* July 26, 1887.

The laborer for souls needs consecration, integrity, intelligence, industry, energy, and tact. Possessing these qualifications, no man can be inferior; instead he will have a commanding influence for good. *Gospel Workers,* p. 111.

Men should be at work who are willing to be taught as to the best way of approaching individuals and families. Their dress should be neat, but not foppish, and their manners such as not to disgust the people. There is a great want of true politeness among us as a people. This should be cultivated by all who take hold of the missionary work. *Testimonies,* vol. 4, pp. 391, 392.

## *Genuineness*

There must be no pretense in the lives of those who have so sacred and solemn a message as we have been called to bear. The world is watching Seventh-day Adventists because it knows something of their profession of faith and of their high standard, and when it sees those who do not live up to their profession, it points at them with scorn. *Testimonies,* vol. 9, p. 23.

Men may have excellent gifts, good ability, splendid qualifications; but one defect, one secret sin indulged, will prove to the character what the worm-eaten plank does to the ship—utter disaster and ruin! *Testimonies,* vol. 4, p. 90.

Paul carried with him the atmosphere of heaven. All who associated with him felt the influence of his union with Christ. The fact that his own life exemplified the truth he proclaimed gave convincing power to his preaching. Here lies the power of the truth. The unstudied, unconscious influence of a holy life is the most convincing sermon that can be given in favor of Christianity. Argument, even when unanswerable, may provoke only opposition; but a godly example has a power that it is impossible wholly to resist. *Gospel Workers,* p. 59.

True character is not shaped from without, and put on; it radiates from within. If we wish to direct others in the path of righteousness, the principles of righteousness must be enshrined in our own hearts. Our profession of faith may proclaim the theory of religion, but it is our practical piety that holds for the word of truth. The consistent life, the holy conversation, the unswerving integrity, the active, benevolent spirit, the godly example—these are the mediums through which light is conveyed to the world. *The Desire of Ages.* p. 307.

Prayers, exhortation, and talk are cheap fruits, which are frequently tied on; but fruits that are manifested in good works, in caring for the needy, the fatherless, and widows, are genuine fruits, and grow naturally upon a good tree. *Testimonies,* vol. 2, p. 24.

## *Aggressiveness*

God does not generally work miracles to advance His truth. If the husbandman neglects to cultivate the soil, God works no miracle to counteract the sure results. He works according to great principles made known to us, and it is our part to mature wise plans, and set in operation the means whereby God shall bring about certain results. Those who make no decided effort, but simply wait for the Holy Spirit to compel them to action, will perish in darkness. You are not to sit still and do nothing in the work of God. *Southern Watchman,* Dec. 1, 1903.

Some who engage in missionary service are weak, nerveless, spiritless, easily discouraged. They lack push. They have not those positive traits of character that give power to do something—the spirit and energy that kindle enthusiasm. Those who would win success must be courageous and hopeful. They should cultivate not only the passive but the active virtues. *Gospel Workers,* p. 290.

The Lord is in need of workers who will push the triumphs of the cross of Christ. *Review and Herald,* May 6, 1890.

Not with tame, lifeless utterance is the message to be given, but with clear, decided, stirring utterances. *Testimonies,* vol. 8, p. 16.

It is not silver-tongued orators that are needed to give this message. The truth in all its pointed severity must be spoken. Men of action are needed—men who will labor with earnest, ceaseless energy for the purifying of the church and the warning of the world. *Testimonies,* vol. 5, p. 187.

God has no use for lazy men in His cause; He wants thoughtful, kind, affectionate, earnest workers. *Testimonies,* vol. 4, p. 411.

## *Determination*

Those in the service of God must show animation and determination in the work of winning souls. Remember that there are those who will perish unless we as God's instrumentalities work with a determination that will not fail nor become discouraged. *Testimonies,* vol. 6, p. 418.

He has given us a great work to do. Let us do it with accuracy and determination. Let us show in our lives what the truth has done for us. *Testimonies,* vol. 6, p. 418.

## *Zeal*

It is earnest Christian zeal that is wanted—a zeal that will be manifested by doing something. . . . No more could a soul who possesses Christ be hindered from confessing Him, than could the waters of Niagara be stopped from flowing over the falls. *Testimonies,* vol. 2, p. 233.

Everyone who accepts Christ as his personal Saviour will long for the privilege of serving God. Contemplating what heaven has done for him, his heart is moved with boundless love and adoring gratitude. He is eager to signalize his gratitude by devoting his abilities to God's service. He longs to show his love for Christ and for His purchased possession. He covets toil, hardship, sacrifice. *The Ministry of Healing,* p. 502.

There is a wide field for the Marthas, with their zeal in active religious work. But let them first sit with Mary at the feet of Jesus. Let diligence, promptness, and energy be sanctified by the grace of Christ; then the life will be an unconquerable power for good. *The Desire of Ages,* p. 525.

In the name of the Lord, with the untiring perseverance and unflagging zeal that Christ brought into His labors, we are to carry forward the work of the Lord. *Testimonies,* vol. 9, p. 25.

We need to break up the monotony of our religious labor. We are doing a work in the world, but we are not showing sufficient activity and zeal. If we were more in earnest, men would be convinced of the truth of our message. The tameness and monotony of our service for God repels many souls of a higher class, who need to see a deep, earnest, sanctified zeal. *Testimonies,* vol. 6, p. 417.

## *Patience*

To be a coworker with Jesus, you should have all patience with those for whom you labor, not scorning the simplicity of the work, but looking to the blessed result. When those for whom you labor do not exactly meet your mind, you often say in your heart: "Let them go; they are not worth saving." What if Christ had treated poor outcasts in a similar manner? He died to save miserable sinners, and if you work in the same spirit and in the same manner indicated by the example of Him whom you follow, leaving the results with God, you can never in this life measure the amount of good you have accomplished. *Testimonies,* vol. 4, p. 132.

Work disinterestedly, lovingly, patiently, for all with whom you are brought into contact. Show no impatience. Utter not one unkind word. Let the love of Christ be in your hearts, the law of kindness on your lips. *Testimonies,* vol. 9, p. 41.

## *Tact*

Those who surrender wholly to God will put thought and prayer and earnest, consecrated tact into their labors. *Signs of the Times,* May 29, 1893.

If a man has tact, industry, and enthusiasm, he will make a success in temporal business, and the same qualities, consecrated to the work of God, will prove even doubly efficient; for divine power will be combined with human effort. *Testimonies,* vol. 5, p. 276.

In the work of soul-winning, great tact and wisdom are needed. The Saviour never suppressed the truth, but He uttered it always in love. In His intercourse with others, He exercised the greatest tact, and He was always kind and thoughtful. He was never rude, never needlessly spoke a severe word, never gave unnecessary pain to a sensitive soul. He did not censure human weakness. He fearlessly denounced hypocrisy, unbelief, and iniquity, but tears were in His voice as He uttered His scathing rebukes. He never made truth cruel, but ever manifested a deep tenderness for humanity. Every soul was precious in His sight. He bore Himself with divine dignity; yet He bowed with the tenderest compassion and regard to every member of the family of God. He saw in all, souls whom it was His mission to save. *Gospel Workers,* p. 117.

Some rash, impulsive, yet honest souls, after a pointed discourse has been given, will accost those who are not with us in a very abrupt manner, and make the truth, which we desire them to receive, repulsive to them. "The children of this world are in their generation wiser than the children of light." Business men and politicians study courtesy. It is their policy to make themselves as attractive as possible. They study to render their address and manners such that they may have the greatest influence over the minds of those about them. They use their knowledge and abilities as skillfully as possible in order to gain this object. *Testimonies,* vol. 4, p. 68.

This message must be given; but while it must be given, we should be careful not to thrust and crowd and condemn those who have not the light that we have. We should not go out of our way to make hard thrusts at the Catholics. Among the Catholics there are many who are most conscientious Christians and who walk in all the light that shines upon them, and God will work in their behalf. *Testimonies,* vol. 9, p. 243.

## Constancy

The true Christian works for God, not from impulse, but from principle; not for a day or a month, but during the entire life. *Counsels to Parents, Teachers, and Students,* p. 518.

The Saviour was an untiring worker. He did not measure His work by hours. His time, His heart, His strength, were given to labor for the benefit of humanity. Entire days were devoted to labor, and entire nights were spent in prayer, that He might be braced to meet the wily foe in all his deceptive working, and fortified to do His work of uplifting and restoring humanity. The man who loves God does not measure his work by the eight-hour system. He works at all hours and is never off duty. As he has opportunity, he does good. Everywhere, at all times and in all places, he finds opportunity to work for God. He carries fragrance with him wherever he goes. *Testimonies,* vol. 9, p. 45.

He who by an unguarded act exposes the cause of God to reproach, or weakens the hands of his fellow workers, brings upon his own character a stain not easily removed, and places a serious obstacle in the way of his future usefulness. *Prophets and Kings,* p. 659.

"Take My yoke upon you," Jesus says. The yoke is an instrument of service. Cattle are yoked for labor, and the yoke is essential that they may labor effectually. By this illustration Christ teaches us that we are called to service as long as life shall last. We are to take upon us His yoke, that we may be coworkers with Him. *The Desire of Ages,* p. 329.

## Sympathy and Sociability

In every department of the cause of God, there is need of men and women who have sympathy for the woes of humanity; but such sympathy is rare. *Review and Herald,* May 6, 1890.

We need more of Christlike sympathy; not merely sympathy for those who appear to us to be faultless, but sympathy for poor, suffering, struggling souls, who are often overtaken in fault, sinning and repenting, tempted and discouraged. We are to go to our fellowmen, touched, like our merciful High Priest, with the feeling of their infirmities. *Gospel Workers,* p. 141.

As a people we lose much by lack of sympathy and sociability with one another. He who talks of independence and shuts himself up to himself is not filling the position that God designed he should. We are children of God, mutually dependent upon one another for happiness. The claims of God and of humanity are upon us. We must all act our part in this life. It is the proper cultivation of the social elements of our nature that brings us into sympathy with our brethren and affords us happiness in our efforts to bless others. *Testimonies,* vol. 4, p. 71.

The Saviour was a guest at the feast of a Pharisee. He accepted invitations from the rich as well as the poor, and, according to His custom, He linked the scene before Him with His lessons of truth. *Christ's Object Lessons,* p. 219.

## *Simplicity*

When Christ said to the disciples, Go forth in My name to gather into the church all who believe, He plainly set before them the necessity of maintaining simplicity. The less ostentation and show, the greater would be their influence for good. The disciples were to speak with the same simplicity with which Christ had spoken. *The Acts of the Apostles,* p. 28.

Thousands can be reached in the most simple and humble way. The most intellectual, those who are looked upon as the world's most gifted men and women, are often refreshed by the simple words of one who loves God, and who can speak of that love as naturally as the worldling speaks of the things that interest him most deeply. Often the words well prepared and studied have but little influence. But the true, honest expression of a son or daughter of God, spoken in natural simplicity, has power to unbolt the door to hearts that have long been closed against Christ and His love. *Christ's Object Lessons,* p. 232.

## *Faith*

God's workers need faith in God. He is not unmindful of their labors. He values their work. Divine agencies are appointed to cooperate with those who are laborers together with God. When we think that God will not do as He has said, and that He has no time to notice His workers, we dishonor our Maker. *Southern Watchman,* Aug. 2, 1904.

The worker for God needs strong faith. Appearances may seem forbidding; but in the darkest hour there is light beyond. The strength of those who, in faith, love and serve God, will be renewed day by day. *Gospel Workers,* p. 262.

There is in genuine faith a buoyancy, a steadfastness of principle, and a fixedness of purpose, that neither time nor toil can weaken. *Christ's Object Lessons,* p. 147.

Often the Christian life is beset by dangers, and duty seems hard to perform. The imagination pictures impending ruin before, and bondage or death behind. Yet the voice of God speaks clearly, "Go forward." We should obey this command, even though our eyes cannot penetrate the darkness, and we feel the cold waves about our feet. The obstacles that hinder our progress will never disappear before a halting, doubting spirit. Those who defer obedience till every shadow of uncertainty disappears, and there remains no risk of failure or defeat, will never obey at all. Unbelief whispers, "Let us wait till the obstructions are removed, and we can see our way clearly;" but faith courageously urges an advance, hoping all things, believing all things. *Patriarchs and Prophets,* p. 290.

## *Courage*

A great work is to be accomplished; broader plans must be laid; a voice must go forth to arouse the nations. Men whose faith is weak and wavering are not the ones to carry forward the work at this important crisis. We need the courage of heroes and the faith of martyrs. *Testimonies,* vol. 5, p. 187.

When in faith we take hold of His strength, He will change, wonderfully change, the most hopeless, discouraging outlook. He will do this for the glory of His name. God calls upon His faithful ones, who believe in Him, to talk courage to those who are unbelieving and hopeless.

May the Lord help us one another, and to prove Him by living faith. *Testimonies,* vol. 8, p. 12.

Hope and courage are essential to perfect service for God. These are the fruit of faith. Despondency is sinful and unreasonable. *Prophets and Kings,* p. 164.

Courage, energy, and perseverance they must possess. Though apparent impossibilities obstruct their way, by His grace they are to go forward. Instead of deploring difficulties, they are called upon to surmount them. They are to despair nothing, and to hope for everything. With the golden chain of His matchless love, Christ had bound them to the throne of God. It is His purpose that the highest influence in the universe, emanating from the Source of all power, shall be theirs. They are to have power to resist evil, power that neither earth, nor death, nor hell can master, power that will enable them to overcome as Christ overcame. *Gospel Workers,* p. 39.

## *Consecration*

True holiness is wholeness in the service of God. This is the condition of true Christian living. Christ asks for an unreserved consecration, for undivided service. He demands the heart, the mind, the soul, the strength. Self is not to be cherished. He who lives to himself is not a Christian. *Christ's Object Lessons,* pp. 48-49

The first thing to be learned by all who would become workers together with God, is the lesson of self-distrust; then they are prepared to have imparted to them the character of Christ. This is not to be gained through education in the most scientific schools. It is the fruit of wisdom that is obtained from the divine Teacher alone. *The Desire of Ages,* pp. 249, 250.

It is not a conclusive evidence that a man is a Christian because he manifests spiritual ecstasy under extraordinary circumstances. Holiness is not rapture: it is an entire surrender of the will to God; it is living by every word that proceeds from the mouth of God; it is doing the will of our heavenly Father; it is trusting God in trial, in darkness as well as in the light; it is walking by faith and not by sight; it is relying on God with unquestioning confidence, and resting in His love. *The Acts of the Apostles,* p. 51.

## *Wholeheartedness*

God's people are to be distinguished as a people who serve Him fully, wholeheartedly, taking no honor to themselves, and remembering that by a most solemn covenant they have bound themselves to serve the Lord and Him only. *Testimonies,* vol. 9, p. 17.

It is wholehearted, thoroughly decided men and women who will stand now. Christ sifted His followers again and again, until at one time there remained only eleven and a few faithful women, to lay the foundation of the Christian church. There are those who will stand back when burdens are to be borne; but when the church is all aglow, they catch the enthusiasm, sing and shout, and become rapturous; but watch them. When the fervor is gone, only a few faithful Calebs will come to the front and display unwavering principle. These are salt that retains the savor. It is when the work moves hard that the churches develop the true helpers. *Testimonies,* vol. 5, p. 130.

No man can succeed in the service of God unless his whole heart is in the work, and he counts all things but loss for the excellency of the knowledge of Christ. No man who makes any reserve can be the disciple of Christ, much less can he be His colaborer. *The Desire of Ages,* p. 273.

They are not to engage in speculation, neither are they to enter into business enterprises with unbelievers; for this would hinder them in their God-given work. *Testimonies,* vol. 9, p. 19.

The Redeemer will not accept divided service. Daily the worker for God must learn the meaning of self-surrender. *Gospel Workers,* p. 113.

## *Loyalty*

The Lord abhors indifference and disloyalty in a time of crisis in His work. The whole universe is watching with inexpressible interest the closing scenes of the great controversy between good and evil. The people of God are nearing the borders of the eternal world; what can be of more importance to them than that they be loyal to the God of heaven? All through the ages, God has had moral heroes; and He has them now—those who, like Joseph and Elijah and Daniel, are not ashamed to acknowledge themselves His peculiar people. His special blessing accompanies the labors of men of action; men who will not be swerved from the straight line of duty, but who with divine energy will inquire, "Who is on the Lord's side?" men who will not stop merely with the inquiry, but who will demand that those who choose to identify themselves with the people of God shall step forward and reveal unmistakably their allegiance to the King of kings and Lord of lords. Such men make their wills and plans subordinate to the law of God. For love of Him, they count not their lives dear unto themselves. Their work is to catch the light from the Word, and let it shine forth to the world in clear, steady rays. Fidelity to God is their motto. *Prophets and Kings,* p. 148.

## *Dexterity*

It is the duty of every Christian to acquire habits of order, thoroughness, and dispatch. There is no excuse for slow bungling at work of any character. When one is always at work, and the work is never done, it is because mind and heart are not put into the labor. The one who is slow, and who works at a disadvantage, should realize that these are faults to be corrected. He needs to exercise his mind in planning how to use the time so as to secure the best results. By tact and method, some will accomplish as much work in five hours as another does in ten. Some who are engaged in domestic labor are always at work, not because they have so much to do, but because they do not plan so as to save time. By their slow, dilatory ways, they make much work out of very little. But all who will may overcome these fussy, lingering habits. In their work let them have a definite aim. Decide how long a time is required for a given task, and then bend every effort toward accomplishing the work in a given time. The exercise of the will power will make the hands move deftly. *Christ's Object Lessons,* p. 344.

The service of Christ demands prompt obedience. *Southern Watchman,* Aug. 9, 1904.

The Lord demands that in His servants shall be found a spirit that is quick to feel the value of souls, quick to discern the duties to be done, quick to respond to the obligations that the Lord lays upon them. *Testimonies,* vol. 9, pp. 123, 124.

Industry in a God-appointed duty is an important part of true religion. Men should seize circumstances as God's instruments with which to work His will. Prompt and decisive action at the right time will gain glorious triumphs, while delay and neglect result in failure and dishonor to God. *Prophets and Kings,* p. 676.

## *Maintain High Standards*

Many who are qualified to do excellent work accomplish little because they attempt little. Thousands pass through life as if they had no great object for which to live, no high standard to reach. One reason of this is the low estimate which they place upon themselves. Christ paid an infinite price for us, and according to the price paid He desires us to value ourselves. *Gospel Workers,* p. 291.

Throughout His life on earth, Jesus was an earnest and constant worker. He expected much; therefore He attempted much. *The Desire of Ages,* p. 72.

Those who are engaged in service for the Master need an experience much higher, deeper, broader, than many have yet thought of having. Many who are already members of God's great family know little of what it means to behold His glory, and to be changed from glory to glory. Many have a twilight perception of Christ's excellence, and their hearts thrill with joy. They long for a fuller, deeper sense of the Saviour's love. Let these cherish every desire of the soul after God. *Gospel Workers,* p. 274.

To our ministers, physicians, teachers, and all others engaged in any line of service for the Master, I have a message to bear. The Lord bids you to come up higher, to reach a holier standard. You must have an experience much deeper than you have yet even thought of having. Many who are already members of God's great family know little of what it means to behold His glory and to be changed from glory to glory. Many of you have a twilight perception of Christ's excellence, and your souls thrill with joy. You long for a fuller, deeper sense of the Saviour's love. You are unsatisfied. But do not despair. Give to Jesus the heart's best and holiest affections. Treasure every ray of light. Cherish every desire of the soul after God. Give yourselves the culture of spiritual thoughts and holy communings. You have seen by the first rays of the early dawn of His glory. As you follow on to know the Lord, you will know that His going forth is prepared as the morning. "The path of the righteous is as the light of dawn, that shineth more and more unto the perfect day." Having repented of our sins, confessed them, and found pardon, we are to continue to learn of Christ, until we come into the full noontide of a perfect gospel faith. *Testimonies,* vol. 8, pp. 317, 318.

## *Prudence and Forethought*

While Nehemiah implored the help of God, he did not fold his own hands, feeling that he had no more care or responsibility in the bringing about of his purpose to restore Jerusalem. With admirable prudence and forethought he proceeded to make all the arrangements necessary to ensure the success of the enterprise. Every movement was marked with great caution. *Southern Watchman,* Mar. 15, 1904.

The example of this holy man [Nehemiah] should be a lesson to all the people of God, that they are not only to pray in faith, but to work with diligence and fidelity. How many difficulties we encounter, how often we hinder the working of Providence in our behalf, because prudence, forethought, and painstaking are regarded as having little to do with religion! This is a grave mistake. It is our duty to cultivate and to exercise every power that will render us more efficient workers for God. Careful consideration and well-matured plans are as essential to the success of sacred enterprises today as in the time of Nehemiah. *Southern Watchman,* Mar. 15, 1904.

## *How to Counteract Discouragement*

The servants of the Lord must expect every kind of discouragement. They will be tried, not only by the anger, contempt, and cruelty of enemies, but by the indolence, inconsistency, lukewarmness, and treachery of friends and helpers . . . Even some who seem to desire the work of God to prosper, will yet weaken the hands of His servants by hearing, reporting, and half believing the slanders, boasts, and menaces of their adversaries. . . . Amid great discouragements, Nehemiah made God his trust; and here is our defense. A remembrance of what the Lord has done for us will prove a support in every danger. "He that spared not His own Son, but delivered Him up for us all, how shall He not with Him also freely give us all things?" And "if God be for us, who can be against us?" However craftily the plots of Satan and his agents may be laid, God can detect them, and bring to naught all their counsels. *Southern Watchman,* Apr. 19, 1904.

Those who, standing in the forefront of the conflict, are impelled by the Holy Spirit to do a special work will frequently feel a reaction when the pressure is removed. Despondency may shake the most heroic faith, and weaken the most steadfast will. But God understands, and He still pities and loves. He reads the motives and the purposes of the heart. To wait patiently, to trust when everything looks dark, is the lesson that the leaders in God's work need to learn. Heaven will not fail them in their day of adversity. Nothing is apparently more helpless, yet really more invincible, than the soul that feels its nothingness, and relies wholly on God. *Prophets and Kings,* pp. 174, 175.

The Lord calls for soldiers who will not fail nor be discouraged; but who will accept the work with all its disagreeable features. He would have us all take Christ for our pattern. *Review and Herald,* July 17, 1894.

Those who today teach unpopular truths need not be discouraged if at times they meet with no more favorable reception, even from those who claim to be Christians, than did Paul and his fellow workers from the people among whom they labored. The messengers of the cross must arm themselves with watchfulness and prayers, and move forward with faith and courage, working always in the name of Jesus. *The Acts of the Apostles,* p. 230.

## Gentleness

The spirit that is kept gentle under provocation will speak more effectively in favor of the truth than will any argument, however forcible. *The Desire of Ages,* p. 353.

As the dew and the still showers fall upon the withering plants, so let words fall gently when seeking to win men from error. God's plan is first to reach the heart. We are to speak the truth in love, trusting in Him to give it power for the reforming of the life. The Holy Spirit will apply to the soul the word that is spoken in love. *The Ministry of Healing,* p. 157.

A tender spirit, a gentle, winning deportment, may save the erring, and hide a multitude of sins. The revelation of Christ in your own character will have a transforming power upon all with whom you come in contact. Let Christ be daily made manifest in you, and He will reveal through you the creative energy of His words—a gentle, persuasive, yet mighty influence to re-create other souls in the beauty of the Lord our God. *Thoughts From the Mount of Blessing,* p. 129.

## Impartiality

So long as he lived among men, our Saviour shared the lot of the poor. He knew by experience their cares and hardships, and He could comfort and encourage all humble workers. Those who have a true conception of the teaching of His life will never feel that a distinction must be made between classes, that the rich are to be honored above the worthy poor. *The Desire of Ages,* p. 73.

When you turn from those who seem unpromising and unattractive, do you realize that you are neglecting the souls for whom Christ is seeking? At the very time when you turn from them, they may be in the greatest need of your compassion. In every assembly for worship, there are souls longing for rest and peace. They may appear to be living careless lives, but they are not insensible to the influence of the Holy Spirit. Many among them might be won for Christ. *Christ's Object Lessons,* p. 191.

The gospel invitation is not to be narrowed down and presented only to a select few, who, we suppose, will do us honor if they accept it. The message is to be given to all. Wherever hearts are open to receive the truth, Christ is ready to instruct them. *The Desire of Ages,* p. 194.

## *Honesty-Faithfulness-Industry*

When responsibilities are to be entrusted to an individual, the question is not asked whether he is eloquent or wealthy, but whether he is honest, faithful, and industrious; for whatever may be his accomplishments, without these qualifications he is utterly unfit for any position of trust. *Testimonies,* vol. 4, p. 413.

## *Unselfishness*

Christ's work is to be our example. Constantly He went about doing good. In the temple and the synagogues, in the streets of the cities, in the marketplace and the workshop, by the seaside and among the hills, He preached the gospel and healed the sick. His life was one of unselfish service, and it is to be our lesson book. His tender, pitying love rebukes our selfishness and heartlessness. *Testimonies,* vol. 9, p. 31.

The motive that prompts us to work for Lord should have in it nothing akin to self-serving. Unselfish devotion and a spirit of sacrifice have always been and always will be the first requisite of acceptable service. Our Lord and Master designs that not one thread of selfishness shall be woven into His work. Into our efforts we are to bring the tact and skill, the exactitude and wisdom, that the God of perfection required of the builders of the earthly tabernacle; yet in all our labors we are to remember that the greatest talents or the most splendid services are acceptable only when self is laid upon the altar, a living, consuming sacrifice. *Prophets and Kings,* p. 65.

Of all the people in the world, reformers should be the most unselfish, the most kind, the most courteous. In their lives should be seen the true goodness of unselfish deeds. *The Ministry of Healing,* p. 157.

## Cease to Worry

Things will go wrong because of unconsecrated workers. You may shed tears over the result of this; but don't worry. The blessed Master has all His work from end to end under His masterly supervision. All He asks is that the workers shall come to Him for their orders, and obey His directions. Everything—our churches, our missions, our Sabbath schools, our institutions—is carried upon His divine heart. Why worry? The intense longing to see the church a living and shining light as God designs it shall be, must be tempered with entire trust in God. *Review and Herald,* Nov. 14, 1893.

Cultivate restfulness, and commit the keeping of your souls unto God as unto a faithful Creator. He will keep that which is committed to His trust. He is not pleased to have us cover His altar with our tears and complaints. You have enough to praise God for already, if you do not see another soul converted. But the good work will go on if you will only go forward and not be trying to adjust everything to your own ideas. Let the peace of God rule in your hearts, and be ye thankful. Let the Lord have room to work. Do not block His way. He can and will work if we will let Him. *Testimonies,* vol. 9, p. 136.

## Bear the Divine Credentials

God can use every person just in proportion as He can put His Spirit into the soul-temple. The work that He will accept is the work that reflects His image. His followers are to bear, as their credentials to the world, the ineffaceable characteristics of His immortal principles. *Testimonies,* vol. 7, p. 144.

Christ's name was to be their watchword, their badge of distinction, their bond of union, the authority of their course of action, and the source of their success. Nothing was to be recognized in His kingdom that did not bear His name and superscription. *The Acts of the Apostles,* p. 28.

## Minutemen

Be faithful minutemen, to show forth the praises of Him who hath called you out of darkness into His marvelous light. *Review and Herald,* Jan. 24, 1893.

God's servants should be minutemen, ever ready to move as fast as His providence opens the way. Any delay on their part gives time for Satan to work to defeat them. *Patriarchs and Prophets,* p. 423.

His commandment-keeping people are to stand constantly in readiness for service. *Testimonies,* vol. 8, p. 247.

Those who are really representatives of Christ are working for the good of others. They delight in advancing the cause of God both at home and abroad. They are seen and heard, and their influence is felt, at the prayer meeting. They will try to supply the place of the minister, whose labors they cannot have. They do not seek to exalt self, or to receive credit for doing a great work, but labor humbly, meekly, faithfully, doing small errands or doing a greater work, if necessary, because Christ has done so much for them. *Review and Herald,* Sept. 6, 1881.

## Brave and True

What the church needs in these days of peril, is an army of workers who, like Paul, have educated themselves for usefulness, who have a deep experience in the things of God, and who are filled with earnestness and zeal. Sanctified, self-sacrificing men are needed; men who will not shun trial and responsibility; men who are brave and true; men in whose hearts Christ is formed "the hope of glory," and who, with lips touched with holy fire, will "preach the word." For want of such workers the cause of God languishes, and fatal errors, like a deadly poison, taint the morals and blight the hopes of a large part of the human race. *The Acts of the Apostles,* p. 507.

By aggressive warfare, in the midst of opposition, peril, loss, and human suffering, the work of soul-saving is to be carried forward. At a certain battle, when one of the regiments of the attacking force was being beaten back by the hordes of the enemy, the ensign in front stood his ground as the troops retreated. The captain shouted to him to bring back the colors, but the reply of the ensign was: "Bring the men up to the colors!" This is the work that devolves upon every faithful standard-bearer—to bring the men up to the colors. The Lord calls for wholeheartedness. We all know that the sin of many professing Christians is that they lack the courage and energy to bring themselves and those connected with them up to the standard. *Testimonies,* vol. 9, pp. 45, 46.

God cannot use men who, in time of peril, when the strength, courage, and influence of all are needed, are afraid to take a firm stand for the right. He calls for men who will do faithful battle against wrong, warring against principalities and powers, against the rulers of the darkness of this world, against spiritual wickedness in high places. It is to such as these that He will speak the words: "Well done, good and faithful servant." *Prophets and Kings,* p. 142.

God calls for men like Elijah, Nathan, and John the Baptist—men who will bear His message with faithfulness, regardless of the consequences; men who will speak the truth bravely, though it call for the sacrifice of all they have. *Prophets and Kings,* p. 142.

## *Shepherdly Care*

The shepherd who discovers that one of his sheep is missing, does not look carelessly upon the flock that is safely housed, and say, "I have ninety and nine, and it will cost me too much trouble to go in search of the straying one. Let him come back, and I will open the door of the sheepfold, and let him in." No; no sooner does the sheep go astray than the shepherd is filled with grief and anxiety. He counts and recounts the flock. When he is sure that one sheep is lost, he slumbers not. He leaves the ninety and nine within the fold; and goes in search of the straying sheep. The darker and more tempestuous the night, and the more perilous the way, the greater is the shepherd's anxiety, and the more earnest his search. He makes every effort to find that one lost sheep.

With what relief he hears in the distance its first faint cry. Following the sound, he climbs the steepest heights, he goes to the very edge of the precipice, at the risk of his own life. Thus he searches, while the cry, growing fainter, tells him that his sheep is ready to die. At last his effort is rewarded; the lost is found. Then he does not scold it because it has caused him so much trouble. He does not drive it with a whip. He does not even try to lead it home. In his joy he takes the trembling creature upon his shoulders; if it is bruised and wounded, he gathers it in his arms, pressing it close to his bosom, that the warmth of his own heart may give it life. With gratitude that his search has not been in vain, he bears it back to the fold. *Christ's Object Lessons,* pp. 187, 188.

## *Humility*

In choosing men and women for His service, God does not ask whether they possess learning or eloquence or worldly wealth. He asks: "Do they walk in such humility that I can teach them My way? Can I put My words into their lips? Will they represent Me?" *Testimonies,* vol. 7, p. 144.

In trying to help the poor, the despised, the forsaken, do not work for them mounted on the stilts of your dignity and superiority, for in this way you will accomplish nothing. *Testimonies,* vol. 6, p. 277.

That which will make our churches vigorous and successful in their efforts is not bustle, but quiet, humble work; not parade and bombast, but patient, prayerful, persevering effort. *Testimonies,* vol. 5, p. 130.

The humiliation of defeat often proves a blessing by showing us our inability to do the will of God without His aid. *Patriarchs and Prophets,* p. 633.

The talents of the humble cottager are needed in the house-to-house labor and can accomplish more in this work than brilliant gifts. *Testimonies,* vol. 9, pp. 37, 38.

All heaven is interested in this work that God's messengers are carrying forward in the world, in the name of Jesus Christ of Nazareth. This is a great work, brethren and sisters, and we should humble ourselves daily before God and not feel that our wisdom is perfect. We should take hold of the work with earnestness. We should not pray for God to humble us; for when God takes hold of us, He will humble us in a way that we would not enjoy. But we must day by day humble ourselves under the mighty hand of God. We are to work out our own salvation with fear and with trembling. While it is God that works in us to will and to do of His own good pleasure, we are to cooperate with Him while He works through us. *Review and Herald,* July 12, 1887.

We are to strive to enter in at the strait gate. But this gate does not swing loosely on its hinges. It will not admit doubtful characters. We must now strive for eternal life with an intensity that is proportionate to the value of the prize before us. It is not money or lands or position, but the possession of a Christlike character, that will open to us the gates of Paradise. It is not dignity, it is not intellectual attainments, that will win for us the crown of immortality. Only the meek and lowly ones, who have made God their efficiency, will receive this gift. *Southern Watchman,* Apr. 16, 1903.

When you return from doing missionary work, do not praise yourself, but exalt Jesus; lift up the cross of Calvary. *Testimonies,* vol. 5, p. 596.

Before honor is humility. To fill a high place before men, Heaven chooses the worker who, like John the Baptist, takes a lowly place before God. The most childlike disciple is the most efficient in labor for God. The heavenly intelligences can cooperate with him who is seeking, not to exalt self, but to save souls. *The Desire of Ages,* p. 436.

## *Temperate*

Would that every child of God might be impressed with the necessity of being temperate in his eating, dressing, and working, that he may do the best work for the cause of God. When the laborer has been under a pressure of work and care, and is overworked in mind and body, he should turn aside and rest awhile, not for selfish gratification, but that he may be better prepared for future duties. We have a vigilant foe, who is ever upon our track, to take advantage of every weakness, that he may make his temptations effective for evil. When the mind is overstrained and the body enfeebled, he can take advantage, and press the soul with his fiercest temptations, that he may cause the downfall of the child of God. Let the laborer for God carefully husband his strength; and when wearied with toil that must come upon him, let him turn aside and rest and commune with Jesus. *Review and Herald,* Nov. 14, 1893.

The misuse of our physical powers shortens the period of time in which our lives can be used for the glory of God. And it unfits us to accomplish the work God has given us to do. By allowing ourselves to form wrong habits, by keeping late hours, by gratifying appetite at the expense of health, we lay the foundation for feebleness. By neglecting physical exercise, by overworking mind or body, we unbalance the nervous system. Those who thus shorten their lives unfit themselves for service by disregarding nature's laws, are guilty of robbery toward God. And they are robbing their fellowmen also. The opportunity of blessing others, the very work for which God sent them into the world, has by their own course of action been cut short. And they have unfitted themselves to do even that which in a briefer period of time they might have accomplished. The Lord holds us guilty when by our injurious habits we thus deprive the world of good. *Christ's Object Lessons,* pp. 346, 347.

Our God is ever merciful, full of compassion, and reasonable in all His requirements. He does not require that we shall pursue a course of action that will result in the loss of our health or the enfeeblement of our powers of mind. He would not have us work under a pressure and strain until exhaustion follows, and prostration of the nerves. The Lord has given us reason, and He expects that we shall exercise reason, and act in harmony with the laws of life implanted within us, obeying them that we may have a well-balanced organization. Day follows day, and each day brings its responsibilities and duties, but the work of tomorrow must not be crowded into today. The workers in the cause of God should feel how sacred is its character, and they should prepare themselves for tomorrow's work by a judicious employment of their powers today. *Review and Herald,* Nov. 7, 1893.

## *Rest and Reflection*

The disciples of Jesus needed to be educated as to how they should labor, and how they should rest. Today there is need that God's chosen workmen should listen to the command of Christ to go apart and rest awhile. Many valuable lives have been sacrificed, that need not have been, through ignorance of this command. . . . Though the harvest is great and the laborers are few, nothing is gained by sacrificing health and life. . . . There are many feeble, worn workmen who feel deeply distressed when they see how much there is to be done, and how little they can do. How they long for physical strength to accomplish more; but it is to this class that Jesus says, "Come ye yourselves apart into a desert place, and rest awhile." *Review and Herald,* Nov. 7, 1893.

The Christian life is not made up of unceasing activity, or of continual meditation. Christians must work earnestly for the salvation of the lost, and they must also take time for contemplation, for prayer, and the study of the Word of God. It will not do to be always under the strain of the work and excitement, for in this way personal piety is neglected, and the powers of mind and body are injured. *Review and Herald,* Nov. 7, 1893.

All who are under the training of God need the quiet hour for communion with their own hearts, with nature, and with God. In them is to be revealed a life that is not in harmony with the world, its customs, or its practices; and they need to have a personal experience in obtaining a knowledge of the will of God. We must individually hear Him speaking to the heart. When every other voice is hushed, and in quietness we wait before Him, the silence of the soul makes more distinct the voice of God. He bids us, "Be still, and know that I am God." This is the effectual preparation for all labor for God. Amidst the hurrying throng, and the strain of life's intense activities, he who is thus refreshed, will be surrounded with an atmosphere of light and peace. He will receive a new endowment of both physical and mental strength. His life will breathe out a fragrance, and will reveal a divine power that will reach men's hearts. *The Ministry of Healing,* p. 58.

# CHAPTER 25

# The Holy Spirit

### The Promise

To us today, as verily as to the first disciples, the promise of the Spirit belongs. God will today endow men and women with power from above, as He endowed those who on the day of Pentecost heard the word of salvation. At this very hour His Spirit and His grace are for all who need them and will take Him at His word. *Testimonies,* vol. 8, p. 20.

The promise of the Holy Spirit is not limited to any age or to any race. Christ declared that the divine influence of His Spirit was to be with His followers unto the end. From the day of Pentecost to the present time, the Comforter has been sent to all who have yielded themselves fully to the Lord and to His service. *The Acts of the Apostles,* p. 40.

God desires to refresh His people by the gift of the Holy Spirit, baptizing them anew in His love. There is no need for a dearth of the Holy Spirit in the church. After Christ's ascension, the Holy Spirit came upon the waiting, praying, believing disciples with a fullness and power that reached every heart. In the future the earth is to be lightened with the glory of God. A divine influence is to go forth to the world from those who are sanctified through the truth. The earth is to be encircled with an atmosphere of grace. The Holy Spirit is to work on human hearts, taking the things of God and showing them unto men. *Southern Watchman,* Sept. 5, 1905.

It is true that in the time of the end, when God's work in the earth is closing, the earnest efforts put forth by consecrated believers under the guidance of the Holy Spirit, are to be accompanied by special tokens of divine favor. Under the figure of the early and the latter rain that falls in Eastern lands at seedtime and harvest, the Hebrew prophets foretold the bestowal of spiritual grace in extraordinary measure upon God's church. The out-pouring of the Spirit in the days of the apostles was the beginning of the early, or former rain, and glorious was the result. To the end of time, the presence of the Spirit is to abide with the true church. *The Acts of the Apostles,* pp. 54, 55.

The outpouring of the Spirit in the days of the apostles was the "former rain," and glorious was the result. But the latter rain will be more abundant. What is the promise to those living in these days? "Turn you to the stronghold, ye prisoners of hope: even today do I declare that I will render double unto thee." "Ask ye of the Lord rain in the time of the latter rain; so the Lord shall make bright clouds, and give them showers of rain, to every one grass in the field." *Testimonies,* vol. 8, p. 21.

## *God's Willingness to Bestow*

The Lord is more willing to give the Holy Spirit to those who serve Him than parents are to give good gifts to their children. *The Acts of the Apostles,* p. 50.

At all times and in all places, in all sorrows and in all afflictions, when the outlook seems dark and the future perplexing, and we feel helpless and alone, the Comforter will be sent in answer to the prayer of faith. Circumstances may separate us from every earthly friend; but no circumstance, no distance, can separate us from the heavenly Comforter. Wherever we are, wherever we may go, He is always at our right hand to support, sustain, uphold, and cheer. *The Desire of Ages,* pp. 669, 670.

Morning by morning, as the heralds of the gospel kneel before the Lord and renew their vows of consecration to Him, He will grant them the presence of His Spirit, with its reviving, sanctifying power. As they go forth to the day's duties, they have the assurance that the unseen agency of the Holy Spirit enables them to be "laborers together with God." *The Acts of the Apostles,* p. 56.

We are living in the time of the Holy Spirit's power. It is seeking to diffuse itself through the agency of humanity, thus increasing its influence in the world. *Southern Watchman,* Nov. 3, 1903

## *Conditions of Receiving*

The Holy Spirit will come to all who are begging for the bread of life to give to their neighbors. *Testimonies,* vol. 6, p. 90.

When we bring our hearts into unity with Christ, and our lives into harmony with His work, the Spirit that fell on the disciples on the day of Pentecost will fall on us. *Testimonies,* vol. 8, p. 246.

It is not because of any restriction on the part of God that the riches of His grace do not flow earthward to men. *Christ's Object Lessons,* p. 419.

The Spirit awaits our demand and reception. *Christ's Object Lessons,* p. 121.

Since this is the means by which we are to receive power, why do we not hunger and thirst for the gift of the Spirit? Why do we not talk of it, pray for it, and preach concerning it? *The Acts of the Apostles,* p. 50.

If the fulfillment of the promise is not seen as it might be, it is because the promise is not appreciated as it should be. If all were willing, all would be filled with the Spirit. *The Acts of the Apostles,* p. 50.

For the daily baptism of the Spirit, every worker should offer his petition to God. Companies of Christian workers should gather to ask for special help, for heavenly wisdom, that they may know how to plan and execute wisely. Especially should they pray that God will baptize His chosen ambassadors in mission fields with a rich measure of His Spirit. *The Acts of the Apostles,* pp. 50, 51.

Let Christians put away all dissension and give themselves to God for the saving of the lost. Let them ask in faith for the promised blessing, and it will come. *Testimonies,* vol. 8, p. 21.

The disciples did not ask for a blessing for themselves. They were weighted with the burden of souls. The gospel was to be carried to the ends of the earth, and they claimed the endowment of power that Christ had promised. Then it was that the Holy Spirit was poured out, and thousands were converted in a day. *Southern Watchman,* Aug. 1, 1905.

# The Holy Spirit

Christ has promised the gift of the Holy Spirit to His church, and the promise belongs to us as much as to the first disciples. But like every other promise, it is given on conditions. There are many who believe and profess to claim the Lord's promise; they talk about Christ and about the Holy Spirit, yet receive no benefit. They do not surrender the soul to be guided and controlled by the divine agencies. We cannot use the Holy Spirit. The Spirit is to use us. Through the Spirit God works in His people "to will and to do of His good pleasure." But many will not submit to this. They want to manage themselves. This is why they do not receive the heavenly gift. Only to those who wait humbly upon God, who watch for His guidance and grace, is the Spirit given. The power of God awaits their demand and reception. This promised blessing, claimed by faith, brings all other blessings in its train. It is given according to the riches of the grace of Christ, and He is ready to supply every soul according to the capacity to receive. *The Desire of Ages,* p. 672.

The great outpouring of the Spirit of God, which lightens the whole earth with His glory, will not come until we have an enlightened people, that know by experience what it means to be laborers together with God. When we have entire, wholehearted consecration to the service of Christ, God will recognize the fact by an outpouring of His Spirit without measure; but this will not be while the largest portion of the church are not laborers together with God. *Review and Herald,* July 21, 1896.

## *Essential to Success*

The presence of the Spirit with God's workers, will give the proclamation of truth a power that not all the honor or glory of the world could give. *The Acts of the Apostles,* p. 51.

God does not ask us to do in our own strength the work before us. He has provided divine assistance for all the emergencies to which our human resources are unequal. He gives the Holy Spirit to help in every strait, to strengthen our hope and assurance, to illuminate our minds and purify our hearts. *Southern Watchman,* Aug. 1, 1905.

After the descent of the Holy Spirit, the disciples were so filled with love for Him [Christ] and for those for whom He died, that hearts were melted by the words they spoke and the prayers they offered. They spoke in the power of the Spirit; and under the influence of that power, thousands were converted. *The Acts of the Apostles,* p. 22.

There is no limit to the usefulness of the one who, putting self aside, makes room for the working of the Holy Spirit upon his heart, and lives a life wholly consecrated to God. *Southern Watchman,* Aug. 1, 1905.

What was the result of the outpouring of the Spirit upon the day of Pentecost?—The glad tidings of a risen Saviour were carried to the utmost bounds of the known world. . . . Under their labors there were added to the church chosen men, who, receiving the word of life, consecrated their lives to the work of giving to others the hope that had filled their hearts with peace and joy. Hundreds proclaimed the message, "The kingdom of God is at hand." They could not be restrained or intimidated by threatenings. The Lord spoke through them; and wherever they went, the sick were healed, and the poor had the gospel preached unto them. So mightily can God work when men give themselves up to the control of His Spirit. *Southern Watchman,* Aug. 1, 1905.

The Holy Spirit is the breath of spiritual life in the soul. The impartation of the Spirit is the impartation of the life of Christ. It imbues the receiver with the attributes of Christ. Only those who are thus taught of God, those who possess the inward working of the Spirit, and in whose life the Christ-life is manifested, are to stand as representative men, to minister in behalf of the church. *The Desire of Ages,* p. 805.

Peculiar and rapid changes will soon take place, and God's people are to be endowed with the Holy Spirit, so that with heavenly wisdom they may meet the emergencies of this age, and as far as possible counteract the demoralizing movements of the world. If the church is not asleep, if the followers of Christ watch and pray, they may have light to comprehend and appreciate the movements of the enemy. *Testimonies,* vol. 6, p. 436.

## *Promise Unappreciated*

Christ declared that the divine influence of the Spirit was to be with His followers unto the end. But the promise is not appreciated as it should be; and therefore its fulfillment is not seen as it might be. The promise of the Spirit is a matter little thought of; and the result is only what might be expected—spiritual drouth, spiritual darkness, spiritual declension and death. Minor matters occupy the attention, and the divine power which is necessary for the growth and prosperity of the church, and which would bring all other blessings in its train, is lacking, though offered in its infinite plenitude. *Testimonies,* vol. 8, p. 21.

## *Some Idly Waiting for Season of Refreshing*

There are some who, instead of wisely improving present opportunities, are idly waiting for some special season of spiritual refreshing by which their ability to enlighten others will be greatly increased. They neglect present duties and privileges, and allow their light to burn dim, while they look forward to a time when, without any effort on their part, they will be made the recipients of special blessing, by which they will be transformed and fitted for service. *The Acts of the Apostles,* p. 54.

## *Christ's Successor*

The Holy Spirit is Christ's representative, but divested of the personality of humanity, and independent thereof. Cumbered with humanity, Christ could not be in every place personally. Therefore it was for their interest that He should go to the Father, and send the Spirit to be His successor on earth. No one could then have any advantage because of his location or his personal contact with Christ. By the Spirit the Saviour would be accessible to all. In this sense He would be nearer to them than if He had not ascended on high. *The Desire of Ages,* p. 669.

## *Holy Spirit at Work From Beginning*

From the beginning God has been working by His Holy Spirit through human instrumentalities for the accomplishment of His purpose in behalf of the fallen race. This was manifest in the lives of the patriarchs. To the church in the wilderness also, in the time of Moses, God gave His "good Spirit to instruct them." And in the days of the apostles He wrought mightily for His church through the agency of the Holy Spirit. The same power that sustained the patriarchs, that gave Caleb and Joshua faith and courage, and that made the work of the apostolic church effective, has upheld God's faithful children in every succeeding age. It was through the power of the Holy Spirit that during the Dark Ages the Waldensian Christians helped to prepare the way for the Reformation. It was the same power that made successful the efforts of the noble men and women who pioneered the way for the establishment of modern missions, and for the translation of the Bible into the languages and dialects of all nations and peoples. *The Acts of the Apostles,* p. 53.

# CHAPTER 26

# Assurance of Success

### *The Divine Guaranty*
God will do the work if we will furnish Him the instruments. *Testimonies,* vol. 9, p. 107.

God will accept the wholehearted service, and will Himself make up the deficiencies. *The Ministry of Healing,* p. 150.

Every deed of righteousness will be immortalized, although the doer may not feel that he has done anything worthy of notice. *Testimonies,* vol. 2, p. 683.

If you are truly consecrated, God will, through your instrumentality, bring into the truth others whom He can use as channels to convey light to many that are groping in darkness. *Testimonies,* vol. 7, p. 63.

The truth is soon to triumph gloriously, and all who now choose to be laborers together with God will triumph with it. *Testimonies,* vol. 9, p. 135.

To every one who offers himself to the Lord for service, withholding nothing, is given power for the attainment of measureless results. *Testimonies,* vol. 7, p. 30.

When we labor diligently for the salvation of our fellowmen, God will prosper our very effort. *Testimonies,* vol. 9, p. 86.

The Lord has a place for everyone in His great plan. Talents that are not needed are not bestowed. Supposing that the talent is small, God has a place for it, and that one talent, if faithfully used, will do the very work God designs that it should do. *Testimonies,* vol. 9, p. 37.

The humblest workers, in cooperation with Christ, may touch chords whose vibrations shall ring to the ends of the earth, and make melody throughout eternal ages. *The Ministry of Healing,* p. 159.

True success in any line of work is not the result of chance or accident or destiny. It is the outworking of God's providences, the reward of faith and discretion, of virtue and perseverance. Fine mental qualities and a high moral tone are not the result of accident. God gives opportunities; success depends upon the use made of them. *Prophets and Kings,* p. 486.

Those who are impressed to enter the work, whether in the home field or in the regions beyond, are to go forward in the name of the Lord. If they depend on God for grace and strength, they will succeed. At the beginning their work may be small, but if they follow the Lord's plans, it will enlarge. God lives. He will work for the unselfish, self-sacrificing laborer, whoever and wherever he may be. *Southern Watchman,* Apr. 9, 1903.

## *Cooperation of Heavenly Agencies*

We need to understand better than we do the mission of the angels. It would be well to remember that every true child of God has the co-operation of heavenly beings. Invisible armies of light and power attend the meek and lowly ones who believe and claim the promises of God. Cherubim and seraphim, and angels that excel in strength, stand at God's right hand, "all ministering spirits, sent forth to minister for them who shall be heirs of salvation." *The Acts of the Apostles,* p. 154.

Remember that the Lord Jesus is the Master Worker. He waters the seed sown. He puts into your minds words that will reach hearts. *Testimonies,* vol. 9, p. 41.

Consecrate yourselves wholly to the work of God. He is your strength, and He will be at your right hand, helping you to carry on His merciful designs. *Testimonies,* vol. 9, p. 41.

The heavenly intelligences will work with the human agent who seeks with determined faith that perfection of character which will reach out to perfection in action. To every one engaged in this work Christ says, I am at your right hand to help you. *Christ's Object Lessons,* p. 332.

As the will of man cooperates with the will of God, it becomes omnipotent. Whatever is to be done at His command, may be accomplished in His strength. All His biddings are enablings. *Christ's Object Lessons,* p. 333.

In working for perishing souls, you have the companionship of angels. Thousands upon thousands, and ten thousand times ten thousand angels are waiting to cooperate with members of our churches in communicating the light that God has generously given, that a people may be prepared for the coming of Christ. *Testimonies,* vol. 9, p. 129.

In this work all the angels of heaven are ready to cooperate. All the resources of heaven are at the command of those who are seeking to save the lost. Angels will help you to reach the most careless and the most hardened. And when one is brought back to God, all heaven is made glad; seraphs and cherubs touch their golden harps, and sing praises to God and the Lamb for their mercy and loving-kindness to the children of men. *Christ's Object Lessons,* p. 197.

He who called the fishermen of Galilee is still calling men to His service. And He is just as willing to manifest His power through us as through the first disciples. However imperfect and sinful we may be, the Lord holds out to us the offer of partnership with Himself, of apprenticeship to Christ. He invites us to come under the divine instruction, that, uniting with Christ, we may work the works of God. *The Desire of Ages,* p. 297.

Think you not that Christ values those who live wholly for Him? Think you not that He visits those who, like the beloved John, are for His sake in hard and trying places? He finds His faithful ones, and holds communion with them, encouraging and strengthening them. And angels of God, that excel in strength, are sent forth by God to minister to His human workers who are speaking the truth to those who know it not. *Testimonies,* vol. 8, p. 17.

All heaven is in activity, and the angels of God are waiting to cooperate with all who will devise plans whereby souls for whom Christ died may hear the glad tidings of salvation. Angels who minister to those that shall be heirs of salvation, are saying to every true saint: "There is work for you to do." "Go, stand and speak . . . to the people all the words of this life." Acts 5:20. If those addressed would obey this injunction, the Lord would prepare the way before them, putting them in possession of means wherewith to go. *Testimonies,* vol. 6, pp. 433, 434.

In such a time as this, every child of God should be actively engaged in helping others. As those who have an understanding of Bible truth try to seek out the men and women who are longing for light, angels of God will attend them. And where angels go, none need fear to move forward. As a result of the faithful efforts of consecrated workers, many will be turned from idolatry to the worship of the living God. Many will cease to pay homage to manmade institutions, and will take their stand fearlessly on the side of God and His law. *Prophets and Kings,* p. 171.

The principalities and powers of heaven are watching the warfare which, under apparently discouraging circumstances, God's servants are carrying on. New conquests are being achieved, new honors won, as the Christians, rallying round the banner of their Redeemer, go forth to fight the good fight of faith. All the heavenly angels are at the service of the humble, believing people of God; and as the Lord's army of workers here below sing their songs of praise, the choir above join with them in ascribing praise to God and to His Son. *The Acts of the Apostles,* p. 154.

It is not the power that emanates from men that makes the work successful, it is the power of the heavenly intelligences working with the human agent that brings the work to perfection. A Paul may plant, and an Apollos may water, but it is God that giveth the increase. Man cannot do God's part of the work. As a human agent he may cooperate with the divine intelligences, and in simplicity and meekness do his best, realizing that God is the great Master Workman. Although the workmen may be buried, the work will not cease, but it will go on to completion. *Review and Herald,* Nov. 14, 1893.

The Christian always has a strong helper in the Lord. The way of the Lord's helping we may not know; but this we do know: He will never fail those who put their trust in Him. Could Christians realize how many times the Lord has ordered their way, that the purposes of the enemy concerning them might not be accomplished, they would not stumble along complainingly. Their faith would be stayed on God, and no trial would have power to move them. They would acknowledge Him as their wisdom and efficiency, and He would bring to pass that which He desires to work out through them. *Prophets and Kings,* p. 576.

All who engage in ministry are God's helping hand. They are coworkers with the angels; rather, they are the human agencies through whom the angels accomplish their mission. Angels speak through their voices, and work by their hands. And the human workers, cooperating with heavenly agencies, have the benefit of their education and experience. *Education,* p. 271.

Christ calls every man and woman to put on the armor of His righteousness and begin to work. "I am at your right hand to help you," He declares. Tell all your trials and perplexities to your God. He will never betray your confidence. There is nothing so precious to Christ as His purchased possession, His church, the workers who go forth to scatter the seeds of truth. . . . Think of Jesus. He is in His holy place, not in a state of solitude, but surrounded by ten thousand times ten thousand of heavenly angels who wait to do His bidding. And He bids them go and work for the weakest saint who puts his trust in God. High and low, rich and poor, have the same help provided. *Southern Watchman,* Nov. 7, 1905.

## *There Should Be No Thought of Failure*

Workers for Christ are never to think, much less to speak, of failure in their work. The Lord Jesus is our efficiency in all things; His Spirit is to be our inspiration; and as we place ourselves in His hands, to be channels of light, our means of doing good will never be exhausted. We may draw upon His fullness, and receive of that grace which has no limit. *Gospel Workers,* p. 19.

When we give ourselves wholly to God, and in our work follow His directions, He makes Himself responsible for its accomplishment. He would not have us conjecture as to the success of our honest endeavors. Not once should we even think of failure. We are to cooperate with One who knows no failure. *Christ's Object Lessons,* p. 363.

The Lord is disappointed when His people place a low estimate upon themselves. He desires His chosen heritage to value themselves according to the price He has placed upon them. God wanted them, else He would not have sent His Son on such an expensive errand to redeem them. He has a use for them, and He is well pleased when they make the very highest demands upon Him, that they may glorify His name. They may expect large things if they have faith in His promises. *The Desire of Ages,* p. 668.

## *Proportionate Success*

When God opens the way for the accomplishment of a certain work, and gives assurance of success, the chosen instrumentality must do all in his power to bring about the promised result. In proportion to the enthusiasm and perseverance with which the work is carried forward, will be the success given. *Prophets and Kings,* p. 263.

## *The Underlying Motive in Successful Service*

Whatsoever is done out of pure love, be it ever so little or contemptible in the sight of men, is wholly fruitful; for God regards more with how much love one worketh than the amount he doeth. *Testimonies,* vol. 2, p. 135.

Ten truly converted, willing-minded, unselfish workers can do more in the missionary field than one hundred who confine their efforts to set forms and preserve mechanical rules, working without deep love for souls. *Testimonies,* vol. 4, p. 602.

It is not the capabilities you now possess, or ever will have, that will give you success. It is that which the Lord can do for you. We need to have far less confidence in what man can do, and far more confidence in what God can do for every believing soul. He longs to have you reach after Him by faith. He longs to have you expect great things from Him. He longs to give you understanding in temporal as well as in spiritual matters. He can sharpen the intellect. He can give tact and skill. Put your talents into the work, ask God for wisdom, and it will be given to you. *Christ's Object Lessons,* p. 146.

The oil of grace gives to men the courage, and supplies to them the motives, for doing every day the work that God appoints to them. The five foolish virgins had lamps (this means a knowledge of Scripture truth), but they had not the grace of Christ. Day by day they went through a round of ceremonies and external duties, but their service was lifeless, devoid of the righteousness of Christ. The Sun of Righteousness did not shine in their hearts and minds, and they had not the love of the truth which conforms to the life and character, the image and superscription, of Christ. The oil of grace was not mingled with their endeavors. Their religion was a dry husk without the true kernel. They held fast to forms of doctrines, but they were deceived in their Christian life, full of self-righteousness, and failing to learn lessons in the school of Christ, which, if practiced, would have made them wise unto salvation. *Review and Herald,* Mar. 27, 1894.

The work of God is to be carried on to completion by the cooperation of divine and human agencies. Those who are self-sufficient may be apparently active in the work of God; but if they are prayerless, their activity is of no avail. Could they look into the censer of the angel that stands at the golden altar before the rainbow-circled throne, they would see that the merit of Jesus must be mingled with our prayers and efforts, or they are as worthless as was the offering of Cain. Could we see all the activity of human instrumentality, as it appears before God, we would see that only the work accomplished by much prayer, which is sanctified by the merit of Christ, will stand the test of the judgment. When the grand review shall take place, then shall ye return and discern between him that serveth God and him that serveth Him not. *Review and Herald,* July 4, 1893.

Legal religion will not answer for this age. We may perform all the outward acts of service and yet be as destitute of the quickening influence of the Holy Spirit as the hills of Gilboa were destitute of dew and rain. We all need spiritual moisture, and we need also the bright beams of the Sun of Righteousness to soften and subdue our hearts. We are always to be as firm as a rock to principle. Bible principles are to be taught, and then backed up by holy practice. *Testimonies,* vol. 6, pp. 417, 418.

Success depends not so much on talent as on energy and willingness. It is not the possession of splendid talents that enables us to render acceptable service; but the conscientious performance of daily duties, the contented spirit, the unaffected, sincere interest in the welfare of others. In the humblest lot true excellence may be found. The commonest tasks, wrought with loving faithfulness, are beautiful in God's sight. *Prophets and Kings,* p. 219.

The symmetrical structure of a strong, beautiful character is built up by individual acts of duty. And faithfulness should characterize our life in the least as well as in the greatest of its details. Integrity in little things, the performance of little acts of fidelity and little deeds of kindness, will gladden the path of life; and when our work on earth is ended, it will be found that every one of the little duties faithfully performed has exerted an influence for good—an influence that can never perish. *Patriarchs and Prophets,* p. 574.

## *Leave Results With God*

The good seed may for a time lie unnoticed in a cold, selfish, worldly heart, giving no evidence that it has taken root; but afterward, as the Spirit of God breathes on the soul, the hidden seed springs up, and at last bears fruit to the glory of God. In our lifework we know not which shall prosper, this or that. This is not a question for us to settle. We are to do our work, and leave the results with God. "In the morning sow thy seed, and in the evening withhold not thine hand." God's great covenant declares that "while the earth remaineth, seed-time and harvest . . . shall not cease." In the confidence of this promise the husbandman tills and sows. Not less confidently are we in the spiritual sowing to labor, trusting His assurance, "So shall

## *Assurance of Success*

My word be that goeth forth out of My mouth; it shall not return unto Me void, but it shall accomplish that which I please, and it shall prosper in the thing whereto I sent it." "He that goeth forth and weepeth, bearing precious seed, shall doubtless come again with rejoicing, bringing his sheaves with him." *Christ's Object Lessons,* p. 65.

# CHAPTER 27

# Reward of Service

### Priceless

It is not a vain thing to serve God. There is a priceless reward for those who devote their life to His service. *Testimonies,* vol. 4, p. 107.

Every sacrifice that is made in His ministry will be recompensed according to "the exceeding riches of His grace." *The Desire of Ages,* p. 249.

Our reward for working with Christ in this world is the greater power and wider privilege of working with Him in the world to come. *Christ's Object Lessons,* p. 361.

### Basis of Valuation

The value of service to God is measured by the spirit in which it is rendered, rather than by the length of time spent in labor. *Testimonies,* vol. 9, p. 74.

Their success in advancement in the divine life depends upon the improvement of the talents lent them. Their future reward will be proportioned to the integrity and earnestness with which they serve the Master. *Review and Herald,* Mar. 1, 1887.

The Lord has a great work to be done, and He will bequeath the most in the future life to those who do the most faithful, willing service in the present life. *Christ's Object Lessons,* p. 330.

Those who came into the vineyard at the eleventh hour were thankful for an opportunity to work. Their hearts were full of gratitude to the one who had accepted them; and when at the close of the day the householder paid them for a full day's work, they were greatly surprised. They knew they had not earned such wages. And the kindness expressed in the countenance of their employer filled them with joy. They never forgot the goodness of the householder, or the generous compensation they had received.

My word be that goeth forth out of My mouth; it shall not return unto Me void, but it shall accomplish that which I please, and it shall prosper in the thing whereto I sent it." "He that goeth forth and weepeth, bearing precious seed, shall doubtless come again with rejoicing, bringing his sheaves with him." *Christ's Object Lessons,* p. 65.

## CHAPTER 27

# Reward of Service

### Priceless

It is not a vain thing to serve God. There is a priceless reward for those who devote their life to His service. *Testimonies,* vol. 4, p. 107.

Every sacrifice that is made in His ministry will be recompensed according to "the exceeding riches of His grace." *The Desire of Ages,* p. 249.

Our reward for working with Christ in this world is the greater power and wider privilege of working with Him in the world to come. *Christ's Object Lessons,* p. 361.

### Basis of Valuation

The value of service to God is measured by the spirit in which it is rendered, rather than by the length of time spent in labor. *Testimonies,* vol. 9, p. 74.

Their success in advancement in the divine life depends upon the improvement of the talents lent them. Their future reward will be proportioned to the integrity and earnestness with which they serve the Master. *Review and Herald,* Mar. 1, 1887.

The Lord has a great work to be done, and He will bequeath the most in the future life to those who do the most faithful, willing service in the present life. *Christ's Object Lessons,* p. 330.

Those who came into the vineyard at the eleventh hour were thankful for an opportunity to work. Their hearts were full of gratitude to the one who had accepted them; and when at the close of the day the householder paid them for a full day's work, they were greatly surprised. They knew they had not earned such wages. And the kindness expressed in the countenance of their employer filled them with joy. They never forgot the goodness of the householder, or the generous compensation they had received.

Thus it is with the sinner, who, knowing his unworthiness, has entered the Master's vineyard at the eleventh hour. His time of service seems so short, he feels that he is undeserving of reward; but he is filled with joy that God has accepted him at all. He works with a humble, trusting spirit, thankful for the privilege of being a coworker with Christ. This spirit God delights to honor. *Christ's Object Lessons,* pp. 397, 398.

## *Sure Reward*

He who has appointed "to every man his work," according to his ability, will never let the faithful performance of duty go unrewarded. Every act of loyalty and faith will be crowned with special tokens of God's favor and approbation. To every worker is given the promise: "He that goeth forth and weepeth, bearing precious seed, shall doubtless come again with rejoicing, bringing his sheaves with him." *Testimonies,* vol. 5, p. 395.

However short our service or humble our work, if in simple faith we follow Christ, we shall not be disappointed of the reward. That which even the greatest and wisest cannot earn, the weakest and most humble may receive. Heaven's golden gate opens not to the self-exalted. It is not lifted up to the proud in spirit. But the everlasting portals will open wide to the trembling touch of a little child. Blessed will be the recompense of grace to those who have wrought for God in the simplicity of faith and love. *Christ's Object Lessons,* p. 404.

The brows of those who do this work will wear the crown of sacrifice. But they will receive their reward. *Testimonies,* vol. 6, p. 348.

To every worker for God this thought should be a stimulus and an encouragement. In this life our work for God often seems to be almost fruitless. Our efforts to do good may be earnest and persevering, yet we may not be permitted to witness their results. To us the effort may seem to be lost. But the Saviour assures us that our work is noted in heaven, and that the recompense cannot fail. *Testimonies,* vol. 6, p. 305.

Every act, every deed of justice and mercy and benevolence, makes music in heaven. The Father from His throne beholds and numbers the performer of them with His most precious treasures. "And they shall be Mine, saith the Lord of hosts, when I make up My jewels." Every merciful act to the needy or the suffering is as though done to Jesus. Whoever succors the poor, or sympathizes with the afflicted and oppressed, and befriends the orphan, brings himself into a more close relationship to Jesus. *Review and Herald,* Aug. 16, 1881.

Christ regards all acts of mercy, benevolence, and thoughtful consideration for the unfortunate, the blind, the lame, the sick, the widow, and the orphan as done to Himself; and these works are preserved in the heavenly records and will be rewarded. *Testimonies,* vol. 3, pp. 512, 513.

## *A Just Reward*

The Lord is good. He is merciful and tenderhearted. He is acquainted with every one of His children. He knows just what each one of us is doing. He knows just how much credit to give to each one. Will you not lay down your credit list and your condemnation list, and leave God to do His own work? You will be given the crown of glory if you will attend to the work that God has given you. *Southern Watchman,* May 14, 1903.

The Lord desires us to rest in Him without a question as to our measure of reward. When Christ abides in the soul, the thought of reward is not uppermost. This is not the motive that actuates our service. *Christ's Object Lessons,* p. 398.

From garrets, from hovels, from dungeons, from scaffolds, from mountains and deserts, from the caves of the earth and the caverns of the sea, Christ will gather His children to Himself. On earth they have been destitute, afflicted, and tormented. Millions have gone down to the grave loaded with infamy because they refused to yield to the deceptive claims of Satan. By human tribunals the children of God have been adjudged the vilest criminals. But the day is near when "God is judge Himself." Then the decisions of earth shall be reversed. "The rebuke of

His people shall He take away." White robes will be given to every one of them. And "they shall call them the holy people, the redeemed of the Lord." *Christ's Object Lessons,* pp. 179, 180.

## *Present Reward*

*Happiness.* Those who give their lives to Christlike ministry know the meaning of true happiness. Their interests and their prayers reach far beyond self. They themselves are growing as they try to help others. They become familiar with the largest plans, the most stirring enterprises, and how can they but grow when they place themselves in the divine channel of light and blessing? Such ones receive wisdom from heaven. They become more and more identified with Christ in all His plans. There is no opportunity for spiritual stagnation. *Testimonies,* vol. 9, p. 42.

The church that engages successfully in this work is a happy church. That man or that woman whose soul is drawn out in compassion and love for the erring, and who labors to bring them to the fold of the Great Shepherd, is engaged in a blessed work. And, oh, what a soul-enrapturing thought, that when one sinner is thus reclaimed, there is more joy in heaven than over ninety and nine just persons! *Testimonies,* vol. 2, p. 22.

Nothing is drudgery to the one who submits to the will of God. "Doing it unto the Lord" is a thought that throws a charm over whatever work God gives him to do. *Testimonies,* vol. 9, p. 150.

The Christian laborer knows no drudgery in his heaven-appointed work. He enters into the joy of His Lord in seeing souls emancipated from the slavery of sin; and this joy repays him for every self-denial. *Southern Watchman,* April 2, 1903.

To become a toiler, to continue patiently in well-doing which calls for self-denying labor, is a glorious work, which Heaven smiles upon. *Testimonies,* vol. 2, p. 24.

Christ delights to take apparently hopeless material, those whom Satan has debased and through whom he has worked, and make them the subjects of His grace. . . . He makes His children His agents in the accomplishment of this work, and in its success, even in this life, they find a precious reward. *Testimonies*, vol. 6, pp. 308, 309.

*Blessing.*—Every effort made for Christ will react in blessing upon ourselves. *Christ's Object Lessons*, p. 354.

Every duty performed, every sacrifice made in the name of Jesus, brings an exceeding great reward. In the very act of duty, God speaks and gives His blessing. *Testimonies*, vol. 4, p. 145.

We should live in this world to win souls to the Saviour. If we injure others, we injure ourselves also. If we bless others, we also bless ourselves; for the influence of every good deed is reflected upon our own hearts. *Testimonies*, vol. 4, p. 72.

Every ray of light shed upon others will be reflected upon our own hearts. Every kind and sympathizing word spoken to the sorrowful, every act to relieve the oppressed, and every gift to supply the necessities of our fellow beings, given or done with an eye to God's glory, will result in blessings to the giver. Those who are thus working are obeying a law of heaven and will receive the approval of God. *Testimonies*, vol. 4, p. 56.

While the great final reward is given at Christ's coming, true-hearted service for God brings a reward, even in this life. Obstacles, opposition, and bitter, heartbreaking discouragements the worker will have to meet. He may not see the fruit of his toil. But in face of all this he finds in his labor a blessed recompense. All who surrender themselves to God in unselfish service for humanity are in cooperation with the Lord of glory. This thought sweetens all toil, it braces the will, it nerves the spirit for whatever may befall. *Testimonies*, vol. 6, pp. 305, 306.

*Health.*—Doing good is an excellent remedy for disease. Those who engage in the work are invited to call upon God, and He has pledged Himself to answer them. Their soul shall be satisfied in drouth, and they shall be like a watered garden, whose waters fail not. *Testimonies*, vol. 2, p. 29.

In fellowship with God, with Christ, and with holy angels they are surrounded with a heavenly atmosphere, an atmosphere that brings health to the body, vigor to the intellect, and joy to the soul. *Testimonies,* vol. 6, p. 306.

The pleasure of doing good to others imparts a glow to the feelings which flashes through the nerves, quickens the circulation of the blood, and induces mental and physical health. *Testimonies,* vol. 4, p. 56.

*Strength.*—Let a strong man be shut away from labor, and he becomes feeble. That church or those persons who shut themselves away from bearing burdens for others, who shut themselves up to themselves, will soon suffer spiritual feebleness. It is labor that keeps the strong man strong. And spiritual labor, toil, and burden-bearing, is what will give strength to the church of Christ. *Testimonies,* vol. 2, p. 22.

*Peace.*—In doing for others, a sweet satisfaction will be experienced, an inward peace which will be a sufficient reward. When actuated by a high and noble desire to do others good, they will find true happiness in a faithful discharge of life's manifold duties. This will bring more than an earthly reward; for every faithful, unselfish performance of duty is noticed by the angels, and shines in the life record. *Testimonies,* vol. 2, p. 132.

## *Future Reward*

*Eternal Life.*—By earnest, thoughtful efforts to help where help is needed, the true Christian shows his love for God and for his fellow beings. He may lose his life in service; but when Christ comes to gather His jewels to Himself, he will find it again. *Testimonies,* vol. 9, p. 56.

*A Gracious Welcome Home.*—Stand on the threshold of eternity, and hear the gracious welcome given to those who in this life have cooperated with Christ, regarding it as a privilege and an honor to suffer for His sake. . . . There the redeemed ones greet those who directed them to the uplifted Saviour. They unite in praising Him who died that human beings might have the life that measures with the life of God. The conflict is over. All tribulation and strife are at an end. Songs of victory fill all heaven, as the redeemed stand around the throne of God. All take up the joyful strain, "Worthy, worthy is the Lamb that was slain," and hath redeemed us to God. *The Ministry of Healing,* pp. 506, 507.

If the record shows that this has been their life, that their characters have been marked with tenderness, self-denial, and benevolence, they will receive the blessed assurance and benediction from Christ: "Well done." "Come, ye blessed of My Father, inherit the kingdom prepared for you from the foundation of the world." *Testimonies,* vol. 3, p. 525.

*Heavenly Environment.*—Now the church is militant. Now we are confronted with a world in darkness, almost wholly given over to idolatry. But the day is coming when the battle will have been fought, the victory won. The will of God is to be done on earth as it is done in heaven. The nations of the saved will know no other law than the law of heaven. All will be a happy, united family, clothed with the garments of praise and thanksgiving—the robe of Christ's righteousness. All nature, in its surpassing loveliness, will offer to God a tribute of praise and adoration. The world will be bathed in the light of heaven. The light of the moon will be as the light of the sun, and the light of the sun will be sevenfold greater than it is now. The years will move on in gladness. Over the scene the morning stars will sing together, and the sons of God will shout for joy, while God and Christ will unite in proclaiming, "There shall be no more sin, neither shall there be any more death." *The Ministry of Healing,* p. 504.

*Joy.*—It is the reward of Christ's workers to enter into His joy. That joy, to which Christ Himself looks forward with eager desire, is presented in His request to His Father: "I will that they also, whom Thou hast given Me, be with Me where I am." *Testimonies,* vol. 6, p. 309.

In our life here, earthly, sin-restricted though it is, the greatest joy and the highest education are in service. And in the future state, untrammeled by the limitations of sinful humanity, it is in service that our greatest joy and our highest education will be found—witnessing, and ever as we witness learning anew "the riches of the glory of this mystery," "which is Christ in you, the hope of glory." *Education,* p. 309.

They share in the sufferings of Christ, and they will share also in the glory that shall be revealed. One with Him in His work, drinking with Him the cup of sorrow, they are partakers also of His joy. *Thoughts From the Mount of Blessing,* p. 12.

*Fruitage of Seed-Sowing.*—Every impulse of the Holy Spirit leading men to goodness and to God, is noted in the books of heaven, and in the day of God everyone who has given himself as an instrument for the Holy Spirit's working will be permitted to behold what his life has wrought. *Testimonies,* vol. 6, p. 310.

When the redeemed stand before God, precious souls will respond to their names who are there because of the faithful, patient efforts put forth in their behalf, the entreaties and earnest persuasions to flee to the Stronghold. Thus those who in this world have been laborers together with God will receive their reward. *Testimonies,* vol. 8, pp. 196, 197.

What rejoicing there will be as these redeemed ones meet and greet those who have had a burden in their behalf! And those who have lived, not to please themselves, but to be a blessing to the unfortunate who have so few blessings—how their hearts will thrill with satisfaction! They will realize the promise, "Thou shalt be blessed; for they cannot recompense thee: for thou shalt be recompensed at the resurrection of the just." *Gospel Workers,* p. 519.

In heaven we shall see the youth whom we helped, those whom we invited to our homes, whom we led from temptation. We shall see their faces reflecting the radiance of the glory of God. *Testimonies,* vol. 6, p. 348.

To be a coworker with Christ and the heavenly angels in the great plan of salvation! What work can bear any comparison with this! From every soul saved there comes to God a revenue of glory, to be reflected upon the one saved and also upon the one instrumental in his salvation. *Testimonies,* vol. 2, p. 232.

The redeemed will meet and recognize those whose attention they have directed to the uplifted Saviour. What blessed converse they will have with these souls! "I was a sinner," it will be said, "without God and without hope in the world; and you came to me, and drew my attention to the precious Saviour as my only hope. And I believed in Him. I repented of my sins, and was made to sit together with His saints in heavenly places in Christ Jesus." Others will say: "I was a heathen in heathen lands. You left your friends and comfortable home, and came to teach me how to find Jesus, and believe in Him as the only true God. I demolished my idols, and worshiped God, and now I see Him face to face. I am saved, eternally saved, ever to behold Him whom I love. I then saw Him only with the eye of faith, but now I see Him as He is. I can now express my gratitude for His redeeming mercy to Him who loved me, and washed me from my sins in His own blood." *Gospel Workers,* p. 518.

Others will express their gratitude to those who fed the hungry and clothed the naked. "When despair bound my soul in unbelief, the Lord sent you to me," they say, "to speak words of hope and comfort. You brought me food for my physical necessities, and you opened to me the Word of God, awakening me to my spiritual needs. You treated me as a brother. You sympathized with me in my sorrows, and restored my bruised and wounded soul, so that I could grasp the hand of Christ that was reached out to save me. In my ignorance you taught me patiently that I had a Father in heaven who cared for me. You read to me the precious promises of God's Word. You inspired in me faith that He would save me. My heart was softened, subdued, broken, as I contemplated the sacrifice which Christ had made for me. I became hungry for the bread of life, and the truth was precious to my soul. I am here, saved, eternally saved, ever to live in His presence, and to praise Him who gave His life for me." *Gospel Workers,* pp. 518, 519.

## *Patiently Wait for the Reward*

If the time seems long to wait for our Deliverer to come; if, bowed by affliction and worn with toil, we feel impatient

The redeemed will meet and recognize those whose attention they have directed to the uplifted Saviour. What blessed converse they will have with these souls! "I was a sinner," it will be said, "without God and without hope in the world; and you came to me, and drew my attention to the precious Saviour as my only hope. And I believed in Him. I repented of my sins, and was made to sit together with His saints in heavenly places in Christ Jesus." Others will say: "I was a heathen in heathen lands. You left your friends and comfortable home, and came to teach me how to find Jesus, and believe in Him as the only true God. I demolished my idols, and worshiped God, and now I see Him face to face. I am saved, eternally saved, ever to behold Him whom I love. I then saw Him only with the eye of faith, but now I see Him as He is. I can now express my gratitude for His redeeming mercy to Him who loved me, and washed me from my sins in His own blood." *Gospel Workers,* p. 518.

Others will express their gratitude to those who fed the hungry and clothed the naked. "When despair bound my soul in unbelief, the Lord sent you to me," they say, "to speak words of hope and comfort. You brought me food for my physical necessities, and you opened to me the Word of God, awakening me to my spiritual needs. You treated me as a brother. You sympathized with me in my sorrows, and restored my bruised and wounded soul, so that I could grasp the hand of Christ that was reached out to save me. In my ignorance you taught me patiently that I had a Father in heaven who cared for me. You read to me the precious promises of God's Word. You inspired in me faith that He would save me. My heart was softened, subdued, broken, as I contemplated the sacrifice which Christ had made for me. I became hungry for the bread of life, and the truth was precious to my soul. I am here, saved, eternally saved, ever to live in His presence, and to praise Him who gave His life for me." *Gospel Workers,* pp. 518, 519.

## *Patiently Wait for the Reward*

If the time seems long to wait for our Deliverer to come; if, bowed by affliction and worn with toil, we feel impatient for our commission to close, and to receive an honorable release from the warfare, let us remember—and let the remembrance check every murmur—that God leaves us on earth to encounter storms and conflicts, to perfect Christian character, to become better acquainted with God our Father and Christ our Elder Brother, and to do work for the Master in winning many souls to Christ, that with glad heart we may hear the words, "Well done, good and faithful servant; enter thou into the joy of thy Lord." *Review and Herald,* Oct. 25, 1881.

Be patient, Christian soldier. Yet a little while, and He that shall come, will come. The night of weary waiting, and watching, and mourning is nearly over. The reward will soon be given; the eternal day will dawn. There is no time to sleep now—no time to indulge in useless regrets. He who ventures to slumber now will miss precious opportunities of doing good. We are granted the blessed privilege of gathering sheaves in the great harvest; and every soul saved will be an additional star in the crown of Jesus, our adorable Redeemer. Who is eager to lay off the armor, when by pushing the battle a little longer, he will achieve new victories and gather new trophies for eternity? *Review and Herald,* Oct. 25, 1881.

# INDEX

## A

Abraham, rest of 181
Action called for 82
Admonition to workers 169
Affirmative, hold to the 126
Aggressiveness 228
Angel record of wife's efforts 207
Angels, cooperation of 258
  prepare the way 154
  waiting for human agents 89
Appeal to slothful church 88
Archdeceiver at work 54
Audience, the one-soul 116

## B

Bible study, invite people to your home for 122
Bible workers, work of 142
Blind, consideration for 215
Blinded eyes 161
Books, selling 151
Bravery 244
Burden-bearers wearing out 45

## C

Call, a definite 141
  to awake 80
Camp meeting, loss in not attending 197
  object and importance of 194
Camp meetings, special feature of near end 196
Channels of light and blessing 18
Children to share burdens in home 207
Christ the great medical missionary 133
Christian, families, call to 182
  help work 186
  life in landscape 105
Christian's watchwords 106
Church, a training center 58
  conditions in 35
  expansion movement, divine plan for 178
  members, place for each 74
    to educate selves 62
  organization, model 73
  slothful, appeal to 88
  work of 13, 135
  work, youth in 30
Cities, work in 152

Colored race, work for 217
Coming events 155
Common walks of life, called from 24
Cooking schools 139
Cooperation, divine 135
Consecration 235
Constancy 232
Convincing combination 67
Courage 234
Covetousness 40
Credentials, divine 243
Crime, epidemic of 53
Crisis of the ages 51
Crown, heavy, aim for a 108
Culture, mental 224

## D

Dead in trespasses 44
Death, not one in twenty prepared for 41
Death stupor, satanic 37
Delay, fatal 43
  no time for 78
Depositories, establish 154
Determination 229
Devotional exercises, angels weighing 211
Dexterity 237
Dignity 226
Discouragement, how to counteract 239
Discrimination, circulate without 153
Disciples sent forth two by two 127
Divine, appointment 30
  commission, the 22
  guaranty 257
  measurement 85
  protection 166
  standard 62
Drama, last act in 160
Dream, an impressive 46
  of web of cloth 63
Duties of God's people 161

## E

Education, industrial 129
Efficiency 223
Elijah, lessons from experience of 57
Encouragement to beginners 99

Evangelism, Bible, a heaven-born idea 141
Excuses, unwarranted 108
Experience, cite personal 124
Eyesalve, heavenly, need of 39

**F**

Failure, to be no thought of 261
Faith 233
Faith, prayer, work 107
Faithfulness 242
Family altar, importance of 209
Families, call to 182
Fanaticism 40
Fire, vision of ball of 111
Follow-up effort, importance of 219
Footprints, tracing the divine 186
Forethought 239
Formalism, cold 40
Fragments, treasure the 153
Franklin, Sir John 93
Fundamentals, deal with 126

**G**

Gentleness 241
Genuineness 227
Good Samaritan, parable applied 192
Go forward 110
Gospel medical missionaries 128
Gospel meetings, invite to 130

**H**

Harvest Ingathering 167
Health literature 152
Heaven's register 86
Heaven-sent opportunities 200
Holy Spirit, at work from beginning 256
  being withdrawn 52
  Christ's successor 255
  conditions of receiving 252
  essential to success 253
  God's willingness to bestow 251
  promise of 250
Home, a missionary training center 206
  children to share burdens in 207
  far-reaching influence of 208
  invite people to your 122
  vs. foreign missions 170
Home-foreign work, importance of 199
Honesty 242
Hospitality a Christian duty 191
Household banner, choosing a 209

House-to-house labor 113
Human agents, depending on 7
Humanity 246

**I**

Illustrations effective 125
Impartiality 241
Individual, call to 9
Indorsement, the 186
Industrial education 129
Industry 242
Influential, reaching the 202
Institutional work 138
Instruction, adapt
Interest on capital, Christ will demand 109
Interest, sympathetic 123
Israel, lesson from failure of 184

**J**

Joyous work 144
Judgment, vision of 87

**L**

Learning by doing 64
Ledger of heaven 87
Lethargy, danger in 91
Liberty, religious 155
Life that wins, the 26
Light in darkness 165
Light, responsibility for 88
Literature, free distribution of 150
Loyalty 236

**M**

Man perishing in snow 92
Marching orders 77
Medical, and gospel missionary work 133
  evangelistic tours 128
  extension plan 137
  missionaries, gospel 128
  missionary, Christ the great 133
    work of first importance 132
Message, a timely 139
  right arm of 134
Minister's duty 69
Ministers and laymen, cooperation of 67
Ministry of, printed page 145
  song 66
Minutemen 243
Missionary, activity, danger accompanying 98
  curriculum of church 59
  methods, practical demonstration of 195

spirit, encourage a 65
    lacking 35
    work, students to do 64
Mistake, fatal 68
Moralists, human 45

## N

Need of the hour 58
Needy to be remembered 189
Neglect, of souls 92
    slothful 200
Negroes, work for 217
Nehemiah, lessons from life of 171
Nehemiahs, modern, call for 177

## O

Officers, qualified to train 61
One-soul audience 116
Organization, essential 72
    lessons in 73
    of church, first step in 73
Organizing for service 34
Orphans, care for 215
Others, doing for 69

## P

Parable of good Samaritan applied 192
Paralytic, a spiritual 106
Patience 230
Paul, example of 71
Pen and voice, by 130
People, go to the 121
Persecuting union, threefold 160
Persecution, essential 159
    why it slumbers 159
Personal, experience, testimony of 212
    touch, close 117
    work and spiritual revival 121
Pesthouse, the world a 53
Pioneers, young men to be 32
Plan, a successful 167
Policy, a dangerous 214
Politeness 226
Praise and thanksgiving 213
Prayer, an appropriate 155
    and missionary meeting, interest of 211
    secret of effectual 211
Preparation for the work 143
Printed page, ministry of 145
Problem, the perplexing 167
Producers and consumers 43

Profession vs. expression 94
Promise, a comforting 214
Prophetic roll, tracing down 46
Prudence 239
Publishing, extension 148
    houses effective agencies 147

## Q

Qualifications for service 233
Questions, important 80

## R

Reason for faith, unable to give 45
Record, a spotted 45
Reflection 249
Refreshing, idly waiting for 255
Remedy, a sure 107
Reporting system, heaven's 222
Reserves to fill ranks 32
Responsibilities of God's people 161
Rest 249
Results, assurance of 184, 204
    leave with God 264
Revival, and reformation needed 41
    combined with personal work 121
Reward, a just 268
    future 271
    patiently wait for 274
    present 269
    sure 267
Right arm of the message 134

## S

Sabbath school, gather into 130
Satan at work 54
Satanic death stupor 37
School, close of 65
Self-complacency 36
Selfishness, narrowed by 40
Separating wheat from tares 56
Service, motive in 262
    organizing for 34
    redeemed for 109
    reward of 266
Shepherdly care 245
Simplicity 233
Sin, commandment keeping a cloak for 44
Sociability 122, 232
Song, ministry of 66
Soul-winning not dependent alone on ministry 68

Speech, cultured 223
Spiritual, darkness 55
    discernment dimmed 38
    revival and personal work 121
    weakness, church in state of 39
Standards, high 238
Stewardship of means 220
Students to do missionary work 64
Subscriptions, securing 151
Success, assurance of 257
    essentials to 169
    Holy Spirit essential to 153
    proportionate 262
    secret of 33, 75, 144
Summons, the 77
Sunday laws, not to defy 163
Sympathy 232

## T

Tact 230
Temperance reform 218
Temperate 247
Test to be met 49
Testing process, the 191
Thoroughfares of travel, Jesus frequented 126
Timothy, a youth when chosen 31
Training, for service 70
    responsibility for providing 60
    special 59
Transplanting 183
Truth, triumph of 164
Truthful 244

## U

Unselfishness 242

## V

Valuation, basis of 266
Vision of ball of fire 111

## W

Warning, timely 75
War, world stirred by spirit of 54
Watchwords, the Christian's 106
Wealthy, men of Bible times 204
    not to be neglected 202
Well, caved in, man saved 94
What doest thou here? 182
What might have been 86
Wheat, separating from tares 56
Wholeheartedness 236
Widow, the poor 171
Witnesses 15
Wives of ministers, reward of 207
Women as missionaries 27
Workers, admonition to 169
    foreign, strengthen hands of 201
    special qualifications of 203
Work for church members 69
World drama 50
Worry, cease to 243

## Y

Young men to be pioneers 32
Young people, call to 30
Youth, future before 31
    in church work 30

## Z

Zeal 229